Defending the Defenseless

Defending the Defenseless

A Guide to Protecting and Advocating for Pets

Allie Phillips

ROWMAN & LITTLEFIELD PUBLISHERS, INC.
Lanham • Boulder • New York • Toronto • Plymouth, UK

Published by Rowman & Littlefield Publishers, Inc.
A wholly owned subsidiary of The Rowman & Littlefield Publishing Group, Inc.
4501 Forbes Boulevard, Suite 200, Lanham, Maryland 20706
www.rowmanlittlefield.com

Estover Road, Plymouth PL6 7PY, United Kingdom

British Library Cataloguing in Publication Information Available

Library of Congress Cataloging-in-Publication Data
Phillips, Allie, 1966–
  Defending the defenseless : a guide to protecting and advocating for pets / Allie
Phillips.
      p. cm.
  ISBN 978-1-4422-0214-6 (alk. paper) — ISBN 978-1-4422-0216-0 (electronic)
  1. Animal rights—United States. 2. Animal rights activists—United States.
3. Animal welfare—Law and legislation—United States. I. Title.
  HV4764.P45 2011
  179'.3—dc22   2011007582

∞™ The paper used in this publication meets the minimum requirements of
American National Standard for Information Sciences—Permanence of Paper for
Printed Library Materials, ANSI/NISO Z39.48-1992.

Printed in the United States of America

This book is dedicated to every person who has ever adopted an animal, helped an animal get to safety, or supported those that do the work every day to care for homeless, abused, and neglected animals. It is dedicated to those organizations and facilities that do better each day to nurture the animals in their care, knowing that sharing their heart, a hug, and a comfy blanket may make all the difference in the life of that animal. This book is in honor of the volunteers who re-home pets in overcrowded shelters, open their homes to provide foster care, and remove animals from inhumane environments. Without your compassionate hearts, we as humans would have no hope of evolving to possess the unconditional love and nonjudgmental hearts of our animal companions.

This book is also dedicated to my parents, who raised me to love animals of all kinds, to help those in need, and to be charitable toward animals. This book is also for all the cats I have saved and re-homed over the years, as well as those I could not save in time. Looking into the accepting eyes of my cats Oscar, Lucy, and Sammy gives me the strength and desire to help just one more.

Contents

Foreword

By Mark Goldstein, DVM, CAWA
President, San Diego Humane Society and SPCA

We live in a world where the body of knowledge is expanding exponentially, and social causes are being increasingly evaluated by the impact they have. Appropriately, the value that decision makers, philanthropists, and members of our community will look to in determining their level of support or rejection of social causes will be determined by that cause's impact, not its output. Thus, the ability to identify and communicate that impact may very well determine the opportunity for success or failure.

Understanding the importance of clear communications, along with a lifelong love of animals and my respect for the incredible work so many people contribute in strengthening the human-animal bond, led me to realize it was a great honor when Allie Phillips asked me to write the foreword for this book. As a veterinarian and animal welfare advocate of more than thirty years, I am constantly looking to increase the impact I have in supporting that bond—a bond with animals that provides us with unconditional love on a daily basis and asks for nothing in return.

As I sat down to write this foreword, fate intervened and I ran into a young man by the name of Kele. Before he became aware of what I was writing, he shared with me that he had recently "purchased an orange cat for his wife." He went on to explain how important the cat had become in both of their lives. I asked him why he chose to purchase a cat from a pet store rather than adopt one from any number of animal welfare organizations in the area. He noted that he had called a few of these organizations to inquire about the possibility of adopting an orange cat. He explained to them that the color was a really important attribute for his wife. He shared with me that the responses he received from the organizations he had called were less than helpful or supportive. He said they could not assure him that an orange cat would be available when he came for a visit, and they even went so far as to trivialize him and his family's desire to select an orange cat. He intimated that the customer service he received from the pet store was much more supportive of his and his wife's needs. In contemplating Kele's encounter, it occurred to me to ask him to describe what he thought a visit to a local humane society or animal services organization would be like. To my disappointment but not to my surprise, he provided an image of "a place with stale air, with a caring staff that struggle and often fail in their work to save animals that are there because it is their last chance to escape death and find a home." It was left unsaid but implied that the place he was describing was not one that he wished to visit and certainly not one where he thought he would find a new family member. Ironically, in sharing his experience, painful as it was for me to hear, it validated my thoughts and the words I am choosing for this foreword.

In our desire to advocate for and advance society's understanding and value of animals, I firmly believe there are two critical goals that must be achieved: The first is respecting, supporting, and celebrating the hard work of the people who work tirelessly day after day to strengthen the human-animal bond, and in doing so make animals' lives and our communities much better. The second is maintaining a high level of trust and respect from the communities we serve so that they value and support the work being done.

As I stated at the beginning of this foreword, our world is becoming much more complex, and social causes are being increasingly evaluated by the impact they have. As animal welfare advocates, adapting the language we use to clearly identify the successes we've had and our ability to overcome the challenges we face allows us to be even more successful on behalf of strengthening the human-animal bond. However, to accept language that at best does not clearly speak to what we are capable of, or at worst disparages the work we do, jeopardizes our ability to be successful in dealing with today and tomorrow's challenges.

So why does Kele have this image of animal welfare organizations? I would advocate that it is partially due to the language we use every day that falsely and negatively identifies the investment made by people on behalf of the animals.

To illustrate this point, the following example incorporates many of the words and/or statements that are commonly used to describe or criticize an animal welfare organization:

"The local animal shelter is called the **pound**, and we must **rescue** animals from these **pounds** since they employ people who **don't care**. The recent program offered by this **pound** is a **misappropriation** of public funds and a **violation** of the public trust. These **pounds** use **low-cost methods** to do surgery and **kill** animals."

Based on this description and choice of words, why would a person choose to visit, rely on, or support an institution such as this?

Typically, you would not expect to see all these words used in one statement, but it illustrates how these words can be very damaging. Since Kele had never visited any of these organizations, the perception he had was based on the words used to describe them. Unfortunately, this is a terrible injustice since Kele lives in a county where no healthy animal that came into any of the recognized public or nonprofit animal shelters has had to be euthanized in over three years. He is a member of a community that has provided the resources for the San Diego Humane Society and SPCA to not have to euthanize a healthy or treatable animal in over ten years, and where annually more than five hundred children come to Animal Adventure Camp to learn that life is to be treasured and revered. And instead of the expected stale air that Kele describes, a campus has been constructed using modern engineering whereby the entire campus has an air exchange system that circulates 100 percent of the air eleven times per hour. The San Diego Campus for Animal Care has been developed so that a visitor leaves feeling better than when they came, no matter what the reason for their visit. A culture has been created that respects, embraces, and celebrates the investment of the staff, volunteers, and donors. A communication plan has been initiated that includes identifying the misleading words and replacing them with words that properly characterize the work being done and instills a belief that we can overcome tomorrow's challenges. Here is a sample of the evolution of words that we have purposely chosen:

- The Pound => Shelter => **Campus** (*Campus* communicates the variety of programs offered with an emphasis on humane education and does not suggest jail or an organization that speaks only to one aspect of our work.)
- Low-Cost Spay and Neuter => **Affordable** (*Affordable* addresses the importance of making spay and neuter programs accessible without implying that it is done cheaply at the expense of the animal; I have not found anyone that would take low-cost parachute lessons!)
- Animal Control => **Animal Services** (*Animal Services* speaks to the importance of serving animals and people in our work, not controlling them.)

- Rescue => **Adopt** (If an animal needs to be rescued from the shelter, this denigrates the people working there and the organization as a whole.)
- Kill => **Euthanize** (*Kill* implies intent to do harm with malice. *Euthanize* is assuring a humane death and recognizes the concern of the person performing the act.)

I am aware that some people would argue passionately that when we take an animal's life, we should use the term *kill* to emphasize rather than minimize the loss of life. I am in agreement that the loss of life, especially when it is due to limited resources, including space, is tragic, but I do not believe that we will resolve the issues leading to the loss of life by disrespecting those who are called upon to do it and who do so with compassion. A key aspect of understanding this issue relies on the public's awareness of the state of animal welfare in their community, including those communities where some animal organizations, despite their best efforts, are called upon to euthanize animals due to reasons we can correct. I would advocate, on the other hand, that at the end of the day it's to do the most we can to help the animals we care about. We must respect the people who try their best and maintain the trust and confidence of the community. It is an abomination to suggest that individuals who passionately work, volunteer, or donate to animal welfare organizations are doing so with the intent to cause harm. We do a great disservice when we mischaracterize the painful process of a caring person having to take the life of an animal. This is the clearest example I can make to illustrate the point that to further advance the well-being of animals in our communities we must reject language that continues to denigrate and misrepresent the hard work, care, and love that people offer when helping animals. In addressing the work various organizations do, we must respect that just like individuals, organizations may elect different paths to a common destination, and because someone or some group may choose to take a different path does not make them wrong. Instead, we must speak to the enormous positive impact our collective work has had and continues to have on behalf of the animals.

By supporting one another through our words and our actions, despite the divergent paths we may choose, we can overcome future challenges, continue to advance animal welfare, and ultimately save the lives of countless healthy or treatable companion animals.

Acknowledgments

I extend my deepest gratitude to the following individuals and organizations for their wisdom, experiences, and advice during the creation of this book:

- Claire Gerus (my literary agent)
- Maya Alcala (youth volunteer, Virginia)
- Peggy Atkerson (Barn Cats, Inc., Texas)
- Diane Balkin (Denver District Attorney's Office, Colorado)
- Laurel Barrick (Rolling Rescue, Michigan)
- Kristen Brock (cat rescuer, Nantucket Island)
- Donna Cascarelli (Pets from Paradise and Love Is in the Air Programs, St. Croix)
- Jenny Coffey (Mayor's Alliance for New York City Animals)
- Tracy Coppola (animal advocate, Virginia)
- Steve Dale (Steve Dale Pet World, Illinois)
- Jane Greco Deming (humane educator, Rhode Island)
- Julie Fershtman (animal law attorney, Michigan)
- Kris Fields (Barncat Rescue, Colorado)
- Kristen Flory (cat rescuer, Michigan)
- Mark Goldstein and Michael Baehr (San Diego Humane Society and SPCA, California)
- Melissa Henchen (Going to the Dogs, New York)
- Dr. Stacia Jung (The Sunshine Foundation, St. Croix, Virgin Islands)
- Randy Lockwood (American Society for the Prevention of Cruelty to Animals, New York)
- Maria Lott, Marie Green, Gretchen Harrison, and Doug Deitlein (Help Furry Friends, Michigan)

- Carol Manos (Carol's Ferals, Michigan)
- Terry MacKillop (Roscommon County Animal Center, Michigan)
- Christina Montana (animal whisperer, Virginia)
- Mandy Moore (Harrisburg Cat Examiner, Pennsylvania)
- Sheryl Pipe (humane educator, New Jersey)
- Kathleen Prasad (Shelter Animal Reiki Association)
- Dusty Rainbolt (Cat Writer's Association, Texas)
- Tracy Reis (American Humane Association, Colorado)
- Diane Roadcap (animal communicator, Virginia)
- Diane Robinson (American Humane Association, Colorado)
- Professor Joan Schaffner (George Washington School of Law, Washington, D.C.)
- Lauren Silverman Simon (The Humane Society of the United States, Washington, D.C.)
- Steve Smith (Rolling Dog Ranch Sanctuary, New Hampshire)
- Kathleen Summers (The Humane Society of the United States, Washington, D.C.)
- Dr. Andrea Tasi (Just Cats Naturally, Virginia)
- Holly Thoms (Voiceless-MI, Michigan)
- Neil Wackerle (The Humane Society of Midland County, Michigan)
- Stacey Zeitland (San Diego Humane Society and SPCA, California)

I would like to thank Kristen Brock for opening her home on the island of Nantucket in October 2010 so that I could focus on writing this book. I have always found my creative energies in New England and appreciate those quiet moments to write.

> "Never doubt that a small group of thoughtfully committed citizens can change the world; indeed, it's the only thing that ever has."
>
> —Margaret Mead

Introduction

Success is the key to happiness
Happiness is the key to success
If you love what you are doing
You will be successful.

—Buddha

It is estimated that as of 2010 there are as many as 411 million companion pet animals in the United States (including 93 million cats and 77 million dogs).[1] Daily news reports of violence plague our televisions and newspapers, and animals are not immune. Human victims of violence have one advantage that animals do not . . . they can speak out, yell no, call the police, file a complaint, seek therapy, and testify against their abuser. Animals cannot do this. Humans harm animals, yet animals rely on humans for protection.

Every state in America has laws that protect animals from harm, and those laws primarily protect companion animals. But many of these laws are weak, poorly written, and enforced sporadically, if at all. Much of this lack of enforcement is due to overworked professionals attempting to prioritize their cases. But sometimes it is simply a lack of care, or understanding, about animals and why we have laws to protect them. Too often we hear "it's just an animal" in response to learning that an animal has been harmed by a human. I have never understood the meaning behind that statement and often retort back, "and you are just a human, so what's the point?" The blank stares I receive equally match my blank stare toward their statement.

It is the duty of all mankind to speak up against harm to animals. Why is it a duty? Cruelty erodes communities and jeopardizes everyone's safety. Violence is violence no matter who is the victim. Cruelty to an animal can negatively impact a community as much as harm to a human. When I speak of cruelty, I am not referring to legalized sport hunting or situations involving animals in entertainment (circuses, rodeos, etc.). These are certainly controversial issues, and animal advocates often receive interference from the industries protecting these endeavors and opposition thwarting efforts to recognize animals as sentient beings.

What I am referring to are acts of neglect toward an animal, as well as intentional cruelty with the intention to harm an animal. Acts of setting a cat on fire to see what happens; hacking a dog to death with a machete because of a vendetta; setting out poison because you are angry that a stray cat keeps coming into your property; tying a dog outside perpetually without sufficient food, water, or shelter to the point of death; killing a pet fish in order to get back at an estranged lover; or collecting so many animals (whether for breeding profit or out of an initially kind heart) to where there is not enough food or veterinary care and one by one they languish and often die in squalid conditions. And then in addition to those horrors, we have the epidemic of homeless animals seeking a chance at life in a loving home with approximately half being euthanized in America's shelters.

These animals have rights under the law. Who is speaking for these animals? Who is defending their right to be protected under the law? Is it you? Or are you hoping that "someone else" will take action? Maybe you think your local animal shelter and its investigators are the only ones that can and should speak for these animals? Or that your prosecutor's office will take on the task of representing the interest of the animal while prosecuting the offender? Maybe you hope that the media will raise awareness regarding one particular act of heinous cruelty toward an animal? Or that a veterinarian will step in and save the animal from certain death? It is easy to look the other way and hope that someone else will take care of the problem. As a society, we cannot afford to wait for "someone else" to stand up for what's right.

Abuse of animals is largely ignored, given low priority, not investigated or prosecuted, and simply not given the attention that the law provides. Most often, it is one person or a small group of concerned people who decide enough is enough. They push for public exposure of these crimes and demand enforcement of the law, and they work to rally communities to protect animals. Effectuating change for how we house and protect homeless animals is also a widespread concern for people who call themselves "animal people." It is often one person or a small group that provides the tipping point for change.

This book is for anyone who wants to join a growing crusade to bring animal protection to its rightful place in a civilized society; to protect animals from harm inflicted by humans and allow them to live happily in an environment that appreciates their unique qualities. Regardless of your chosen career or how you choose to spend your nonwork time, you can become one in a growing movement to defend the defenseless. There is a place, and a need, for everyone.

I have been asked, "Why is this book needed?" The answer is plainly simple. Those who want to help animals often do not know where to go for answers and do not know how to get started. Resources on the Internet, social media sites, magazines, and e-mail groups are so voluminous on how to become an animal advocate that it causes people to move on and not become involved. This book breaks down the issues and ways to get involved by focusing only on protecting companion animals (those domesticated pets that bless our homes), and then focusing on specific ways to help. Throughout the book I will use the words *animals* and *pets* interchangeably while speaking about companion animals. This book will show you how to get involved, from the simplest of tasks to dedicating your career to help animals. Most people believe that unless you can obtain employment to help animals, nothing much can be done. That is untrue, and there are countless ways, from small to in-depth, that people like you can get involved to help animals. For me, I spent years stumbling through the process and at times seemed divinely guided to end up where I am.

I was asked to write this book for several reasons: (1) I have lived through the baby steps of getting entrenched in animal protection, particularly the legal and advocacy pieces, and the ugliness that humans inflict on animals; (2) I am frequently asked how to find work as an animal protection attorney or animal advocate and have found few resources or mentors available; and (3) there is a little information available on how to find employment or volunteer to help animals. Now is the time for this book. Now is the time for us to do more for animals.

Throughout this book, I discuss some of my experiences in animal protection; some involve outrageous joy, and others involve life-altering devastation. I also feature amazing people and organizations that are making a difference in the lives of companion animals in a variety of different ways. As you delve into this world, you will see the vast array of areas in which to get involved. This book will cover some of the most interesting and needed areas in which to help companion animals; to write about all animals and all issues would take many volumes.

I suspect that anyone reading this book already has a love of animals and wants to protect them from harm. However, this book is also intended for those who are undecided and have not consciously made choices to help animals, adopt an animal, or provide assistance to a cause to benefit animals. My hope is that you will share this book with others who we need to get involved in the movement to create a more humane world for everyone. By getting involved, it is important to understand that you will bear witness to inexcusable system failures and the current inability to save them all. Together, I truly believe we can change that sentence to soon read, "You will bear witness to outrageous joy and contentment as you participate in the transformation of how we think about and treat animals in our society to where animals are safe from harm." Some may say that thinking is naive; however, all difficult social movements start with an idealistic vision and steady steps to reach success. It is easy to give up and go back to an ignorant state of mind where you look the other way and hope that the proverbial "someone else" will take care of the problem.

If you feel the pull toward helping animals, if you feel your life's purpose is to make a difference, once you get started you will never stop. So let me tell you a little about me so that the rest of the book is put in context.

FIRST, YOU BECOME AWARE

I am often asked what pivotal moment thrust me into animal protection. I wish I had a gripping story or newsworthy event that opened my eyes. Instead, it has been a path for my soul that took years to uncover and realize. I grew up in the small town of Owosso, Michigan, with about 15,000 residents. It was a safe place and still remains that way today. I had a traditional upbringing with two parents who have been married more than fifty years, an older sister, and grandparents who lived just down the street.

I was surrounded by animals since my first day. Michelle, our brown tabby cat, would frequently join me while I read my Nancy Drew books. We had several bunnies, all named Bugsy, a sickly cat named Tramp that I brought home one day, and we frequently nursed stray animals back to health, including a baby bird that fell from my grandparents' tree during a

Michigan ice storm. My grandparents always seemed to have cats for me to play with and a backyard duck named Duck, and my childhood best friends had a Dachshund named Tobey and a black Labrador named Onyx.

For as long as I can remember, my mother said I was "sensitive." I would cry to melancholy music, which made ballet classes unbearable for me and anyone else who had to witness the spectacle. I could never watch a television show or movie involving animals if anything remotely terrible was to happen to the animal. I am still that way today, which is ironic given that I can handle the horrors of animal cruelty that are conveyed to me in my work. This sensitivity made me a kindred spirit to animals.

I have always had a way of relating to animals that others could not understand. Many of my childhood memories involve animals rather than significant events or people. When I was about eight years old, I remember a white poodle lying in the road on Christmas Eve when my parents drove my sister and me around to look at Christmas lights. The family surrounded the poodle, and I remember wondering whether all their future Christmases would involve memories of losing their dog. I will never understand why memories like that remain clear in my mind, yet significant conversations and events have faded, much to the chagrin of my longtime friends.

While attending college at Michigan State University, I had no conscious plans to get involved in animal protection or even the law. Like many students, I switched majors a few times, but ended up seriously studying political science and Chinese history and culture. My first awareness of animal shelters occurred in college when I adopted a brown tabby kitty named Tabitha for my then-boyfriend Ted. Walking around the shelter and seeing the overcrowded and less-than-sanitary conditions left me questioning the quality of life for shelter animals. When I was halfway through my senior year at Michigan State, I adopted the first pet I could call my own: an all-white cat that I named Chyna. Again, being exposed to the deplorable shelter conditions and wondering what happens to all those wonderful cats and dogs left a mark on my subconscious.

I then attended University of Detroit School of Law in the evenings for four years while working full-time during the day as a legal secretary and then later as a law clerk. Life existed solely of working, going to class, studying, and Chyna keeping my sanity in check. I attended law school because I had always had a bent toward criminal justice. I think it goes back to my Nancy Drew days. So the law chose me.

I went to law school with an open mind and the goal to stubbornly prove that I could academically excel while working full time. I wanted to use my law degree to help others, but I had no real plan for how to do that. In the early 1990s, there were no animal law classes, no Student Animal Legal Defense Fund Programs, and no Animal Law Moot Court competitions. Animal law was undefined and not a career path requiring education. In what little free time I had, I found myself writing letters to research laboratories and legislators regarding the treatment of animals. Yet I was still lost in how to utilize my quickly approaching law degree.

In addition to my full-time employment during law school, I interned in a variety of different legal offices to get a feel for what type of law was best suited to me. My paid jobs were as a legal secretary with a large law firm in Detroit, and then as a law clerk with a midsize insurance defense firm in the Detroit suburbs. The money was nice, but the work was not my style. After sitting as a juror on a high-profile criminal case after my first year of law school, I instinctively knew that I would be a prosecutor. Watching the prosecutor control the courtroom as his own, I knew I had found my calling. I then received a coveted summer internship through the Prosecuting Attorneys Association of Michigan and was handling cases like a licensed attorney while still a student. I also interned for the United States Attorney's Office. I finally felt like my education was forming a purpose; a purpose to defend the defenseless.

After graduating and passing the bar in both Michigan and Maryland, I was hired as an associate attorney with the law firm I had clerked at for two years. However, the billable hours of insurance defense, and working to reduce injured people's claims against insurance companies, went against my calling to help others. After a few short months, I became an assistant prosecuting attorney and held that position for almost eight years. In that position, I found my calling as my internal "righteous indignation" grew to such strength that I felt empowered to speak for those who were terrified, victimized, and voiceless.

I spent most of my career handling a felony trial docket with a large number of human violence cases, including homicide, rape, robbery, child abuse, and the first case prosecuted under Michigan's racketeering law. I even took on the 1999 Michigan State University riot that resulted in 15,000 participants descending on East Lansing after MSU's loss to Duke in the Final Four basketball game, resulting in over $750,000 in damage. I was tenacious in being the prosecutor heading the Riot Task Force and identifying rioters for prosecution. I obtained a 96 percent conviction rate for almost one hundred rioters and created a novel Riot Restitution Fund for each convicted rioter to contribute $5,000 to restore the community. I then began to question the nonexistent number of animal cruelty cases in the office. I certainly did not wish for cases involving animal cruelty, and I was not volunteering to handle them, but I thought it was odd that so few cases were brought to the office for review. Instinctively, I knew that if people were hurtful to people, they would also be hurtful to animals.

The atrocities that people committed toward each other were unbearable most days, so I stopped looking for animal cruelty cases and prayed that none would come in for warrant screening. I found it bizarre that I had no problem working on a homicide case and going to crime scenes with dead bodies lying on the street. I could more easily keep violence toward humans in perspective, but never violence toward animals.

Halfway through my career as a prosecutor, I became enmeshed in volunteering at the local animal shelter; the same shelter where Chyna had been adopted during college. Chyna had passed away suddenly from an undetected heart disease while I was a prosecutor, leaving my heart shattered. One afternoon, free from my court docket, I made a trip back to that same shelter so that I could find another cat or two to bless my home. After adopting Oscar and Lucy, an employee at my veterinary clinic convinced me to join a volunteer group at the shelter. Little did I know that in September 2000, approximately nine months after volunteering, I would band together with six other volunteers to form Friends of Ingham County Animal Shelter (FICAS), a 501(c)(3) nonprofit.

In my initial days as a shelter volunteer, my eyes were opened to abused and neglected animals and how some of those pets were owned by defendants on my felony criminal docket. I was also exposed to the underbelly of animal sheltering that is often kept quiet . . . high euthanasia rates and selling shelter animals for research (called pound seizure). I learned of animals being sold to research when I adopted my third and final cat, Sammy, from the shelter. Sammy, a beautiful flame point Siamese, had sat at the shelter for six weeks, and it was unbearable to watch him in a small cage week after week. While processing his adoption paperwork, a staff person told me Sammy was being "eyed" by the dealer. The comment did not register with me until many months later when I learned that the dealer was a USDA Class B dealer who brokered and resold shelter cats and dogs for experimentation.

Although holding down a busy felony court docket as a prosecutor and handling several special prosecution assignments, including the aftermath of the 1999 Michigan State University riots, I became entrenched in volunteering at the shelter. I instinctively knew that this was where I would do the most good, and my legal training might come in handy. I was on the board of directors of FICAS and was in charge of overseeing cats at the shelter. I would take their photos, post each cat on our website, locate rescue organizations to help get the cats and dogs safely out of the shelter, recruit volunteers to provide foster homes for the pets, run advertisements in the local newspaper, raise money, and eventually ended up running the business side of FICAS. I even opened my home to provide foster care to shelter cats and kittens that had run out of time. All of this was done to reduce the euthanasia rate and to dwindle the supply of cats and dogs to the dealer.

Our group raised the adoption rate from about forty animals per month to almost two hundred per month in just two years. Although the high euthanasia rate was disturbing to me, what drove me to volunteer long hours was the practice of pound seizure, or selling shelter animals for research. I attended and spoke at county commissioner meetings to stop the practice and raised awareness throughout the community. This is where I truly became an outspoken animal advocate. As detailed in chapter 5, I worked with others to successfully ban pound seizure from the shelter in June 2003, but at great personal and professional costs.

The stress of being a prosecutor and a shelter volunteer resulted in nightmares and restless sleep. Most nights I could only sleep if I ingested Tylenol PM. The sleepless nights occurred not solely as a result of volunteering at an animal shelter but also because the shelter director and most of the staff were not welcoming our efforts as volunteers and frequently went out of their way to make our volunteer work difficult. Their actions against the volunteers and animals were downright cruel.

As I became more involved in my shelter volunteer work, word quickly spread regarding my involvement, and that is when the animal cruelty prosecutions started arriving on my desk. One notable case involved four young adults who were charged with a four-year felony animal cruelty for torturing and killing wildlife and convicting themselves in the process by photographing their crimes. All four teens pled guilty and through my advocacy at sentencing received a significant sentence that was fitting for their crimes. After that case in early 2003, I was asked to give a speech to the Thomas Cooley Law School Young Republican chapter on animal cruelty and how prosecutors need to take the cases seriously. To prepare, I reviewed all our office animal cruelty cases and found a disturbing trend of plea bargaining the felony cases to misdemeanors, failure to issue criminal charges in cases with sufficient facts, or even ordering an animal abuser to community service at the local animal shelter. My speech at the law school was powerful and straight to the point that prosecutors are charged with upholding the laws, regardless of who was victimized. Unbeknownst to me, all of these baby steps were unconsciously moving me toward a new career.

Shortly after that, I was forced by my employer in March 2003 to choose between ignoring what I had uncovered at the shelter regarding pound seizure or losing my position. As an advocate for the truth, I kept my honor and chose not to retract what I had learned. It was difficult to choose integrity and courage, but instinctively I knew that was the right choice for me. I then moved to the Washington, D.C., area and became a senior attorney for the American Prosecutors Research Institute (APRI), the research and training division of the National District Attorneys Association (NDAA). I was hired to work and train on child abuse issues. Something clicked as soon as I started working at APRI/NDAA. Maybe it was training prosecutors and law enforcement all over the country that allowed me to have a global perspective. Maybe it was being out of the courtroom trenches that allowed the fog to clear. It was then that I finally recognized that most prosecutors did not understand animal law and did not fully appreciate or understand the connection between animal cruelty and human violence. I also discovered that APRI/NDAA did not have a training program on animal cruelty or its connection to human violence. I quickly changed that and spent considerable time reviewing the research and preparing articles and presentations to help educate others.

After three-and-a-half years at APRI/NDAA traveling the country and conducting trainings, I was sought to be the director of public policy for the American Humane Association in February 2007 and was later promoted to vice president of public policy in 2009 and then vice president of human-animal strategic initiatives in 2010. I was hired to oversee the legislative agenda for the only national organization that works to protect children and animals from harm. American Humane Association is *not* "the humane society," as I frequently said.

As a lobbyist and advocate for American Humane Association, I delved into the technical issues of animal protection so that I could effectively draft and advocate for better animal welfare laws. One issue that I immediately started working on was legislation to end pound seizure, particularly in my home state of Michigan. In 2009, a legislative bill that I drafted was filed in the Michigan House of Representatives to finally end this practice.[2] While the bill passed the House of Representatives on July 28, 2010, it languished and died in the Senate Agriculture Committee when the session ended in December 2010. I testified in support of the bill before House and Senate committees and have joined forces with others to form a coalition called Michiganders for Shelter Pets for reintroduction of the bill in 2011. At times I sit back and am amazed how the tragedy of having to choose to do the right thing, rather than keep quiet to maintain my career as a prosecutor, also ended up being a positive move for me; a move that thrust me into the professional world of training prosecutors and advocating for animals, where I am now making a great impact nationally for animals.

While at American Humane Association, I also continued to train human and animal welfare professionals on the connection between violence to animals and humans. I created the Pets and Women's Shelters (PAWS)® Program that guides domestic violence shelters in allowing families to bring pets with them to the shelter. I had thought of this concept in the mid-1990s when I was a prosecutor and finally was able to bring the program to life. I also cocreated Therapy Animals Supporting Kids (TASK)™, which sets forth guidelines and procedures for effectively and legally incorporating therapy animals with abused children throughout the court process. In May 2010 I became the vice president of human-animal strategic initiatives for American Humane Association due to my innate ability to create national initiatives and guidelines to promote the human-animal bond and keep people and pets together, even during times of crisis. Again, my career path took another twist and turn that seemed divinely guided.

Then in August 2010, my first book was published on a practice that I had dedicated ten years of my life to eradicating from shelters in the United States: pound seizure. *How Shelter Pets Are Brokered for Experimentation: Understanding Pound Seizure* was the first book of its kind to focus on the hidden practice of shelters selling or giving cats and dogs to research or training laboratories for experimentation. Again, another divine twist in my life and career to help animals. And in 2011, I returned to the National District Attorneys Association to delve more into training and education of prosecutors and allied professionals on animal abuse and its connection to human violence.

My evolution into animal welfare and protection law has been driven by a higher power. Opportunities appear, and my action has always seemed right, even though not necessarily popular. As a certified Law of Attraction Counselor, I now know that my true inner purpose was guiding me and attracting these opportunities into my life.

To this day, I mix my professional work with volunteer work to help animals. Since moving to the East Coast in 2003, I have been a volunteer for King Street Cat Rescue in Alexandria, Virginia, a limited-admission free-roaming cat orphanage. From October 2008 to July 2009, I served as president to help the organization transition to a new location and weave through the legal and permit process. I have also been in charge of the website and photographs of the cats since March 2004. I have seen many abused and neglected cats come to the shelter and have grown my awareness of how emotional cats can be when they are harmed or lose their homes. I have learned that many people mislabel cats as "aloof," which is incredibly inaccurate.

I also distantly volunteer to help the St. Croix Animal Welfare Center. I was invited to speak at an animal cruelty conference in January 2009 and made the fortuitous step of visiting the island animal shelter. I was saddened to learn that the shelter was receiving about 4,000 animals a year, and having to euthanize well over 90 percent due to lack of homes on the island. It had been several years since I'd been in a shelter of that nature, and it broke my heart when I sat with a group of cats in a large walk-in cage. The cats were beautiful, a unique combination of breeds that gave them an Oriental-shaped face. The cats climbed all over me, and I kept thinking, "Will you make it out alive?" I said hello and petted every single cat in the shelter, about forty of them. In particular, Whisper, Lioness, Kiki, and Starburst all worked to get my attention. And then there was the little black cat who was losing her hair. In the middle of paradise, I was grief stricken. I remember holding each cat, saying goodbye, and telling them not to be afraid.

I spent the evening sitting on my hotel walk-out patio, watching the crystal blue ocean, and listening to the rhythm of the crashing waves, distraught at the plight of the shelter animals. The shelter workers were wonderful and cared so much about the animals; they just had few resources and little hope except for a program called Pets from Paradise. When a traveler leaving St. Croix and heading to the mainland is willing to take a cat or dog with them, most often as a carry-on item under the seat in front of them, the shelter will prepare the cat or dog with the appropriate veterinary work for the flight. There's also a fee to pay for the pet's travel. So when I arrived at the conference the next day, I asked to bring back a cat. After all, I volunteered for a cat orphanage, and that was the least I could do. I needed to take action; it would have haunted me if I had left the island empty-handed.

The next morning, I arrived at the airport at 7 o'clock in the morning for a long day of travel back to D.C. I asked the shelter staff to pick the cat they wanted most to travel. I was met by Whisper, a gray tabby who'd spent much time working to get my attention when I visited the shelter. I was so happy for Whisper and felt that she had been working her magic on me two days before, yet I was sad about the fate of her friends left behind. Traveling with Whisper was an adventure, and it was the first time I had flown with a pet. She broke out of her carrier within the first five minutes, but the shelter staff brought me another sturdier carrier. She was a good girl on the flights to St. Thomas, Philadelphia, and then D.C. She was in that carrier for fourteen hours and traveled with a look of contentment on her face. She knew that all was well.

Whisper is now in a wonderful home, adopted with a King Street Cat kitty named Bonkers who instantly adored Whisper when they met. I have visited her several times. But helping just one cat was not enough. So I created a program whereby King Street Cats will accept cats from St. Croix when a traveler is coming to D.C. or Baltimore. In the first two years we took in twenty-three cats that were quickly adopted to wonderful homes. I enjoy sending updates on the cats back to the shelter staff; they need the happy stories to keep them going. I also help the shelter with supplies, especially the pet travel carriers that they desperately need in order to save a life. Although there are some shelters and organizations on the mainland who accept transported pets from St. Croix, only three hundred animals are saved a year. The St. Croix transport program will be featured in chapter 7.

To further help animals (and people), I became a certified Reiki Master Practitioner and an Advanced Integrated Energy Therapy practitioner in 2008 and provide healing energy to abused and frightened shelter cats, provide healing to pets with health issues, counsel pet owners who have lost a pet, and educate on homeopathic and holistic care for animals. In 2010 I became a Practitioner Member with the Sara Reiki Animal Association, which is featured in chapter 14. I have also watched animal communicators in action to unlock the thoughts of animals and help them heal. These techniques may seem foreign to you, but I am amazed at the well-being these animals achieve with these treatments. For anyone who says animals are not sentient beings capable of feelings such as love, jealousy, fear, and understanding of pain, I could write a separate book solely on that subject. This amazing work will be featured in chapter 14.

Looking back over the years, the path where I stand now has been joyful, tragic, and bizarre and has certainly had a life of its own. I could not have predicted I would be where I am today. And I certainly could have never predicted that I would have the joy and honor of writing this book (my second). I would not change a thing, and each day I look forward to my next adventure as an animal advocate.

CHANGING THE CONVERSATION

As eloquently outlined by Dr. Mark Goldstein in the foreword, we are at the threshold where we need to change the conversation about the world of homeless companion animals and how we relate to animals in general. Throughout this book, I have aimed to change how I speak about companion animals, particularly those in shelters. Specifically, I use the term *animal protection organization* instead of *animal rescue organization*. Although these organizations are benefiting shelters and the animals by "rescuing" the animals, the term *rescue* leaves the shelter in a wake of negativity that subsequently causes others to not want to support that shelter through donations, volunteer work, or adoption. In reality it may be a rescue for the animal, but it may harm the next animal if assistance is not available.

I hope to inspire you to become involved, even small steps at a time, and to also be a part of the change in how we speak about animals and view the care and treatment of companion animals. As stated by humanitarian Albert Schweitzer, "Anyone who has accustomed himself to regard the life of any living creature as worthless is in danger of arriving also at the idea of worthless human lives."

All my best,
Allie Phillips

CHAPTER 1

Animal Rights and Animal Welfare: Where Do You Stand?

People sacrifice their lives to save their cats and dogs, as we saw during Hurricane Katrina; yet they may engage in the sports of hunting or fishing on the weekend. There is a movement to pass laws to include family pets in domestic violence protection orders, yet more cities and states are pushing to pass breed-specific legislation that would ban certain dog breeds. There is growing opposition to using animals in research laboratories, yet people still buy and use products that are tested on animals. Americans have growing concern regarding the housing and treatment of farm animals, yet many people eat meat or animal products without checking to see if the animal was raised humanely. I am not passing judgment on any of these practices. However, it is interesting to point out the ironies in the business, beliefs, and habitual human behaviors involving animals.

Issues involving the protection of animals are emotional and controversial. It is a complex field where gaining consensus from society on how to protect animals is difficult due to widely differing opinions. Animal welfare laws date back to the 1860s, when the first animal cruelty law was passed in Massachusetts. Laws have been passed because most people abhor cruelty in any form to any living creature and want to see animals humanely cared for or allowed to live free and naturally in the wild. Yet it is humans that inflict torture and pain on animals. These acts of torture and pain have resulted in a plethora of animal welfare laws.

Americans have come a long way when we look at animal protection. In 1993, only seven states had felony animal cruelty law, yet today all states but three have felony laws.[1] When I entered law school in 1990, the concept of a Student Animal Legal Defense Fund chapter was nonexistent, but today there are chapters at more than 125 law schools in the

United States. No animal law courses were taught at law schools in the 1990s; however, today just over one hundred law schools educate on the complexities of animal law. The first state bar animal law section was created in 1995 within the State Bar of Michigan (of which I am a council member), and now there are thirty animal law sections nationwide.

Protecting animals through the law and advocacy is gaining in popularity. We now have Animal Planet, an entire cable television network dedicated to animal issues, and we see animal stories played out in mainstream media every day. Why? Are we growing more compassionate and empathetic as a society? Are animals catching up with the laws that protect humans? Do we now desire to treat all living creatures better? What we are seeing in the United States is an overall change in perception regarding animal protection, and the influence of that perception is pushing animal welfare and the law into the light.

What is ironic is that animal protection laws preexisted child protection laws and domestic protection laws. In fact, in 1874, the American Society for the Prevention of Cruelty to Animals was the organization that helped to save Mary Ellen Wilson from an abusive foster home, the first case of child protection. In the late 1800s, a few states had animal protection laws, but laws protecting women and children from abuse did not exist. Today the laws have shifted, and prosecutions for child abuse and domestic violence are commonplace, whereas an animal cruelty prosecution is so rare that it frequently gets significant media attention due to community outcry.

So again we have these hypocrisies about protecting animals, and many question where to draw the line. Is it okay to pass laws that protect cats and dogs (primary companion animals in American homes) from being killed, tortured, or poisoned? Yet many states allow an animal shelter to gas (poison) a cat or dog to death in a chamber filled with carbon monoxide or dioxide as the pet howls and scratches to get out. Should we permit legal protection of an animal in one context but not another? A rabbit may have protection from cruelty (killing, torture, neglect) as a companion animal, yet if found in the wild the rabbit can be shot and killed, or if found in a research lab it is not given the same protections as rabbits in a home. And while companion animals are protected under the law from intentional and negligent acts of harm by humans, farm animals and wildlife are systematically excluded. Is one species more important or socially acceptable than another?

As a society, Americans are attempting, but struggling, to decide how we want to treat animals. We witness clashes among the humane animal welfare organizations, farm bureaus, veterinary associations, and even animal care organizations over the appropriate laws to protect animals. The law is usually quite clear and gives us absolutes that we must abide by. Overall, the law tends to be black or white, with just enough gray area to allow for creative arguing. Consistency in the law is required to maintain a humane and law-abiding society. The growing area of animal law may be the movement that helps to define how Americans will treat animals and to eliminate some of the hypocrisy. However, the humane treatment of animals goes far beyond the law and treads on how we view animals.

U.S. ADULTS' FEELINGS ABOUT ANIMAL PROTECTION

The Humane Research Council (HRC) is a team of professionals that formed in 2000 to conduct research so that animal advocates would have accurate and helpful information. HRC is conducting a longitudinal study that currently encompasses three annual reports on Americans' feelings about animals with the conclusion that "the importance of animal welfare may be strengthening over time."[2] The first report from 2008 was created as a baseline for the study and found:

- 72% of U.S. adults have a "favorable" opinion of the animal protection movement.
- 32% give animal protection groups "significant" credibility regarding information about animal welfare.
- Many people "strongly support" using anti-cruelty investigations (47%), the media (37%), and speaking in schools (33%) to advocate for animals.
- 44% think the animal protection movement has had a "moderate" or "significant" impact.
- 35% "strongly support" the specific goal to "minimize and eventually eliminate all forms of animal cruelty and suffering."[3]

The second report was issued in 2009 and repeated six of the sixteen questions from the previous report. The third report found that "seven in ten people say they personally support the animal protection movement's goals to 'minimize and eventually eliminate all forms of animal cruelty and suffering.' Despite the fact that these types of questions often yield positive responses, it is significant to think about what this support would mean for animals if taken to its logical conclusion. The challenge for advocates is to determine how to translate this sentiment into tangible gains for animals."[4] The third report also claimed:[5]

- 28% strongly support and 41% somewhat support the specific goal to minimize and eventually eliminate all forms of animal cruelty and suffering.[6]
- When asked how much of an impact the animal protection movement has had on our nation's policies (i.e., federal and state laws and regulations, corporate policies), responses were[7] very little impact (36% in second wave, 32% in third wave), moderate impact (35%), to significant impact (10%).
- When asked how important is the protection of animals when it comes to making the following personal choices on these issues, listed is the percentage of responders indicating "very" or "somewhat" important[8]:
  ○ Getting a new pet (83%)
  ○ Buying food (i.e., meat, eggs, dairy) (70%)
  ○ Going hunting or fishing (62%)
  ○ Buying consumer products (61%)
  ○ Buying clothing (55%)
  ○ Attending circuses or rodeos (54%)
  ○ Voting for a political candidate (51%)
  ○ Going to dog or horse races (49%)
- When asked if farm animals deserve the same protection as pets and other animals, only 53% of people agreed. And only 56% of people agreed that people have an obligation to avoid harming all animals.[9]

Seventy-seven percent of those surveyed agreed that animals are capable of thinking and feeling emotions, and the animal protection movement ranked within the top three causes (with workers' rights and tax reform/relief ranking ahead).[10] Advocacy tactics, such as investigations, media reports, school education, lawsuits, ballot initiatives, lobbying, and product boycotts, were supported by more than half of those surveyed, except for demonstrating and protesting.[11] And when asked if their concern for animals caused action, the top answers included spaying-neutering their pet (58%), buying products not tested on animals (40%), adopting an animal from a shelter (35%), and signing a petition (31%).[12] Lastly, the protection of companion animals ranked higher than all other animals (with 62% citing "very important").[13]

It is easy, as an animal advocate, to believe that all humans share the belief that animals, regardless of species, deserve protection. The studies from the HRC are important in that they provide a compass for how Americans overall view the welfare and protection of animals. This is important to keep in mind as you advocate for animals.

THE CONTINUUM OF ANIMAL RIGHTS AND ANIMAL WELFARE

When it comes to animal rights and animal welfare, where do you stand on the continuum? What really is the difference between the two? In the most basic terms, those supporting animal rights believe that all animals should be free from human exploitation. This includes not using animals for food or clothing as well as not having animals as actors in movies. Some animal rights activists go as far to say that cats and dog should not be "adopted" or "owned" by humans and should not be confined in animal shelters. On the other hand, animal welfare stands for providing the strongest protection and humane treatment of animals based on the situation of the animal. For example, if a cow is on a farm destined to be used as food, animal welfare proponents will work toward the humane raising, treatment, and slaughter of that cow. Moreover, understanding that euthanasia is a tragic reality in many animal shelters, animal welfare advocates work toward banning inhumane practices such as gassing or drowning. So let's delve into these two philosophies more.

Animal Rights: "The philosophy of animal rights rejects the idea that one can evaluate the appropriateness of some action, such as, killing an animal, by weighing the benefits of this action, such as, finding a cure to a disease, against its cost (animal death or suffering). In other words, the ends do not justify the means, especially when the means, that is, animal use, are wrong. If one were considering behavior only as it applies to humans, most would agree with this philosophy. Some people concur that we shouldn't kill another individual even if we could save many in so doing (capital punishment notwithstanding)."[14]

According to People for the Ethical Treatment of Animals (PETA), an animal rights organization, "supporters of animal rights believe that animals have an inherent worth—a value completely separate from their usefulness to humans. We believe that every creature with a will to live has a right to live free from pain and suffering. Animal rights is not just a philosophy—it is a social movement that challenges society's traditional view that all nonhuman animals exist solely for human use. As PETA founder Ingrid Newkirk has said, 'When it comes to pain, love, joy, loneliness, and fear, a rat is a pig is a dog is a boy. Each one values his or her life and fights the knife. Only prejudice allows us to deny others the rights that we expect to have for ourselves. Whether it's based on race, gender, sexual orientation, or species, prejudice is morally unacceptable. If you wouldn't eat a dog, why eat a pig? Dogs and pigs have the same capacity to feel pain, but it is prejudice based on species that allows us to think of one animal as a companion and the other as dinner.'"[15]

As I have advocated against pound seizure (shelters providing cats and dogs for experimentation) for a decade, the primary argument from the opposition has been concern over the demise of vital medical research without the use of animals. Hence, the collision of animal rights versus animal welfare. I doubt anyone would find it appropriate to take a healthy family member and subject them to numerous experimentations resulting in their death. Yet many people do not think twice when this is done to millions of animals in American laboratories. Animal rights believes that animals should not be used, period, even if it benefits humans, because there is no difference between animals and humans. Animals and humans feel pain, have an instinct to survive, and should not exploit each other. Humans do have more rights, currently, than animals; however, animal rights advocates believe animals have similar and equal rights to protection from harm and exploitation.

Toward that end, the Animal Legal Defense Fund has created an Animal Bill of Rights[16] promoting a petition to Congress that says:

I, the undersigned American citizen, believe that animals, like all sentient beings, are entitled to basic legal rights in our society. Deprived of legal protection, animals are defenseless against exploitation and abuse by humans. As no such rights now exist, I urge you to pass legislation in support of the following basic rights for animals:

The Right of animals to be free from exploitation, cruelty, neglect, and abuse.

The Right of laboratory animals not to be used in cruel or unnecessary experiments.

The Right of farm animals to an environment that satisfies their basic physical and psychological needs.

The Right of companion animals to a healthy diet, protective shelter, and adequate medical care.

The Right of wildlife to a natural habitat, ecologically sufficient to a normal existence and self-sustaining species population.

The Right of animals to have their interests represented in court and safeguarded by the law of the land.

The Bill of Rights is an effort to recognize the voiceless and those that need humans to defend them from harm. As written, however, the Bill of Rights is a combination of both animal rights and animal welfare philosophies.

Opponents of animal rights argue that animals are incapable of making moral judgments like humans and, therefore, are not entitled to the same rights as humans. Moreover, humans behave differently toward varying species. For example, we may treat a cat or chimpanzee with the kindness that we want, but we have no problem killing a cockroach that invades our home.

Animal Welfare: Animal welfare advocates understand that animals should have rights and protections from harm but are not equal to humans. The rationale and approach to protection is quite different from animal rights beliefs. According to Larry Katz, professor at Rutgers University, "because we recognize that some animals are capable of having interests or suffering, we have evolved culturally to respect those interests. One might argue that we don't strive to save endangered species, wilderness preserves, old growth forests or the coral reefs because they have rights. Rather, we place value in these rare or complex systems because our moral laws teach us to preserve and protect our environment, whether it is the physical or biological environment."[17]

Animal welfare has typically been promoted through the passage of laws that recognize that animals are "used" in some capacity by humans but deserve humane treatment. I have always been intrigued by the phrase *humane treatment* and what it really means. Again, the definition depends on whether you sit on the side of animal rights or animal welfare. For example, humane treatment of shelter animals means no death at the hands of humans for animal rights advocates; on the contrary, it means a painless death (euthanasia by injection rather than gassing, drowning, or other "inhumane" methods) for animal welfare advocates. Some animal welfare advocates believe that assessing the behavior of the animal helps to achieve humane treatment for that same animal. For example, Temple Grandin has dedicated her life and career to understanding the feelings and natural behaviors of farm animals so that humane housing and slaughter facilities can be created. She is promoting humane treatment through the lens of animal welfare, whereas the No Kill Advocacy Center is promoting guidelines for creating "no-kill" animal shelters. It is approaching humane treatment through the lens of animal rights.

So where do you stand? Like many animal advocates I know, we blend between the two areas depending on the topic. Is it hypocritical to pick and choose when to believe in animal rights and when to promote animal welfare? I don't think so. Critics may say that it is hypocrisy to dabble in animal rights and animal welfare alike; however, I believe, as do many others, that to take an all-or-nothing stance and force people to choose will turn away many animal advocates. As with any situation in life, you should assess each issue independently and determine your position on that issue. Maybe you will be across-the-board animal rights, or maybe you will be a blend. Or maybe you will simply fall under the category of "animal protection," which encompasses differing scenarios for safeguarding animals. There is no right or wrong answer. Just know where you stand.

CHAPTER 2

Becoming an Animal Advocate: Where to Start

Do you love animals and want to help them, but you don't know where to start? Does the plight of animals or a certain issue about animals bother you or keep you awake at night? When you see media stories about animal cruelty or animals in need of help, does your heart call out for you to do something? If you answer yes to any of these questions, you are ready to become an animal advocate or may already be one. Becoming an animal advocate does not mean that you need to quit your job and dedicate twelve hours a day in the trenches helping animals, unless you want to. As outlined throughout this book, you will find tasks that you can do from the most simple to the most in-depth. But before delving into the world of animal protection, you should decide where you stand on the issues.

ADVOCATE OR ACTIVIST?

Are you an advocate or an activist? In many ways, these two terms are similar. But in the arena of public perception, especially with governmental officials and legislators, the distinction can be important.

Every time I am called an activist, I correct the person to use the term *advocate* instead. People may have different reasons for wanting to be called an activist or an advocate. My personal choice is advocate. In general, the term *activist* conjures up an image of someone who cares to speak out for those who cannot. However, when you use the phrase *animal activist*, it conjures up an entirely different image, one that may not be favorable. There really is no justifiable reason for this; however, it is what it is. The phrase *animal activist* brings to mind people who protest or demonstrate, maybe even tying themselves to a tree or fence, or extremists who engage in threatening or illegal conduct. I have found that it is the image of this extremist conduct that comes to mind with decision makers. On the other hand, *animal advocate* does not conjure up the same charged images. *Animal advocate* appears less contentious to decision makers and, therefore, may open doors to you and your message. An animal advocate is often perceived as someone who is passionate about the treatment of animals yet may be viewed as more reasonable, rational, and knowledge-able.

Throughout this book, the term *advocate* is intended to cover a wide range of actions and is not solely related to advocating before politicians. There is no right or wrong answer for what you want to call yourself when you speak up for animals. Regardless of the terminology, the way you conduct yourself will shape how you are perceived. We often hear that perception is reality; in the world of animal advocacy, those words are true. How others perceive you will relate to your level of success.

ADVOCACY TECHNIQUES

A variety of advocacy tactics can be implemented to help animals. The advocacy topic, your location, and the beliefs of the decision makers will impact your strategy choice. Although some animal advocates and animal lobbyists may believe there is only one way (their way) to influence deci-sion makers, there is no one right way to advocate, since every situation and community is different. Having the wherewithal to be resilient is one of the most successful advocacy strategies you can have.

To get the thought process started, listed below are some strategies to consider when advocating on behalf of animals:

- *First step.* Please visit my website at www.alliephillips.com or "You Can Do More for Animals" Facebook page. In these venues, we discuss ways to get involved and positive actions to take for animals.
- *Learn your advocacy topic.* It is easy to learn about a variety of animal advocacy topics simply through the Internet. National animal welfare organizations have an abundance of educational and advocacy infor-mation on their websites for people to download, print, and distribute. Advocates featured in this book will also offer advice on how to get involved. Attend meetings and conferences on your topic of interest to

learn what is being done and what needs to be done for animals. Some national conferences include:

- Taking Action for Animals,[1] sponsored by The Humane Society of the United States and held each summer in Washington, D.C. It includes a Lobby Day on Capitol Hill. This conference is for advocates interested in a variety of animal rights issues.
- The Humane Society of the United States Expo,[2] a conference aimed at those involved in animal shelter and rescue work.
- Animal Rights National Conference, primarily sponsored by In Defense of Animals and the Farm Animal Rights Movement. The conference website states, "It brings our movement together under the banner of animal liberation from all forms of human oppression. All viewpoints that support this goal are welcome (except for advocacy of injury)."[3]
- No-Kill Conference,[4] sponsored by the No-Kill Advocacy Center, which involves a movement to end euthanasia in animal shelters due to overcrowding.
- No More Homeless Pets Conference,[5] sponsored by Best Friends Animal Sanctuary, which promotes learning about the latest innovative ideas and proven practices to help save animals in your community.
- Association of Professional Humane Educators Conference[6] for those interested in educating others, especially children, about humane and compassionate treatment of animals.

It is essential that you learn as much as you can about your animal topic of interest before starting any advocacy. It can harm your credibility if you are unprepared to answer questions, especially questions posed by opponents or decision makers who do not support your position. You will also want to obtain targeted information on your topic. For example, if you are working to reduce the euthanasia rate at your local animal shelter, you will want to ask the shelter for their annual records (if they exist) or submit a written request for documents that show the number of animals they take in each year, how many animals are adopted, and how many are euthanized. Having specific data on your issue will help in your persuasion and also help you to create a solution, such as advocating for a volunteer organization that assists the shelter.

- *Connect with other advocates.* If you can locate other advocates in your community, or advocates that specialize in an animal topic, it will be helpful to gain insights from them based on their past experiences.

These advocates can provide you with information regarding potential arguments from the opposition, pitfalls, and techniques that worked for them. They may also have resources that can be shared so that you do not have to re-create information or materials. They can also share successful and unsuccessful strategies from past efforts. In any animal advocacy work it is important to connect with others, since going forward alone can be challenging and exhausting. Working with others can provide strength in numbers and recognition for your message.

- *Get alerted.* All national animal welfare organizations, and even many state and local organizations, give you the option to sign up for action alerts through their website. For example, American Humane Association, American Society for the Prevention of Cruelty to Animals, Animal Legal Defense Fund, and The Humane Society of the United States will alert you on animal welfare legislation, primarily related to companion animals, occurring in your state or at the federal level. The alert will give you a brief overview of the issue and then provide you with a form letter to e-mail to legislators, with an option to insert your own words. The alerts also have your legislator selected so that you do not have to look up that information. This is an easy way to get involved without having to do any work. It can take just a minute to review the materials and take action. Since not all animal welfare organizations work on every animal issue, it is wise to sign up for alerts from multiple organizations so that you receive a cross-section of news on what is occurring legislatively in your state and in Congress.

- *Get your hands dirty.* Depending on what specific issue interests you in the protection of companion animals, it is beneficial to your knowledge base and credibility to get directly involved at the ground level. For example, if you want to help shelter animals, your advocacy will be best served if you understand the workings of the animal shelter in your community. Therefore, volunteering at the shelter, or visiting the shelter so that you can advocate for the creation of a volunteer group, will be essential to your success. If you are interested in healing animals, you will need to take classes to become certified in various healing techniques that can benefit animals. If you are interested in lobbying for animals, you will need to understand the systems that you are lobbying to change. I have consulted with advocates who wanted to achieve change in their local animal shelter, yet they had never been to the animal shelter. It was difficult to provide guidance to these advocates, since they were missing key pieces of information regarding the actual structure and operation of the shelter. It also impacted their credibility because they were deemed outsiders to the shelter, and the shelter was not inclined to listen to their concerns. I hear from many people that they love animals, "but I could never go into an animal shelter" or "I could never rescue dogs from a puppy mill." It is certainly heartbreaking to walk away knowing you cannot save them all. However, it can also be the most rewarding work that you do when you help an animal leave the shelter and go to its adoptive home or into foster care, where it will be safe until it is adopted. The feeling that you have saved a life cannot be compared to anything else and generates momentum to then go forward and help the next animal. I, too, am very sensitive around animals and found it difficult to volunteer in shelters where euthanasia rates were high and the animals were being sold off for experimentation. However, knowing that was occurring in the shelter pushed me even more to help the animals. Without my work and advocacy, and that of the other volunteers, thousands of animals we saved would have certainly died (either at the shelter or in a laboratory). However, there are other options in "getting your hands dirty" without going into shelters, puppy mills, or other locations that are too difficult to handle. You can join an animal rescue organization that limits its intake of animals so that all animals are adopted and none are euthanized due to lack of space. Organizations like this may have a shelter or work through a foster care system, and you can help the animals in that way. No matter how you choose to get involved, it is important to understand the system that you are advocating to change before you begin your advocacy.

- **Seek the volunteer services of an animal law attorney.** You may find it beneficial to seek out the volunteer services of an attorney that specializes in, or is interested in, animal law and advocacy. An attorney can help you to frame your advocacy materials in a reasonable and organized manner and assist in reviewing materials to ensure accuracy and compliance with laws (especially to avoid disseminating defamatory information). Moreover, oftentimes a legislator or local politician may be willing to listen to an attorney who is professional and highly regarded. An attorney's assistance may provide the initial credibility to get in the door and discuss the issue. As an attorney myself, I found that to be the case. Eighteen states have a state bar association animal law section that may have attorney members willing to provide pro bono assistance. For example, the Michigan State Bar Animal Law Section is composed of attorneys knowledgeable in numerous aspects of animal law, and they are available to provide consultation and assistance, often at no cost. For additional resources, contact the American Bar Association's Animal Law Committee.

- *Be credible and trustworthy.* You will only be as successful as your level of credibility and trustworthiness. If you engage in advocacy based on rumors and undocumented facts, you will quickly earn a reputation as someone who cannot be trusted. Since advocacy involves the use of your words to convey information in an effort to persuade, you will lose your power of persuasion if you disseminate inaccurate or false information. I have seen well-intentioned advocates become overly emotional during a campaign and resort to arguing unproven rumors to make their point. Those advocates ensured that the decision makers stopped listening to them. And once you lose your credibility, it is very difficult to recover and be taken seriously.

- *Balance facts and emotion.* Animal protection can be emotional for advocates, and you can lose your audience if you rely solely on emotion to make your point. Legislators, local politicians, and even shelter directors may relate better to well-reasoned and balanced factual arguments for why change is needed. Although there is a time and a place for parading banners and posters depicting photos of animals that have been tortured or killed, oftentimes those tactics fall on deaf ears. Instead, decision makers are interested in facts and evidence-based solutions. So although it can be effective to show the innocent faces of shelter animals being sold to research laboratories, it may be more persuasive to also back up your arguments with facts on how the shelter will benefit, in terms of donations, adoptions, and overall community support, by ceasing the practice. Although some decision makers may internally be moved by the emotional arguments, they may want to project an outward appearance that they are making decisions based only on fact rather than emotion. Gather facts and use them to your advantage.

- *Collaborate with others.* In many advocacy situations, it may be helpful to establish a group of other concerned citizens who are willing to advocate collectively on the issue. For example, it is not advisable to advocate alone to dismantle a puppy mill in your community. You will need a support system of people covering different aspects of the advocacy and providing each other much-needed breaks to rejuvenate. Your

group may want to form a nonprofit organization, particularly a 501(c)
(3) charitable organization, to provide some protection from personal
liability during your advocacy and allow all donations to be tax deductible. Be sure to list in your organizational bylaws that liability on behalf
of organization members falls to the organization and not to the individuals personally. If you are concerned about a lawsuit to thwart your
advocacy, consider purchasing insurance for your nonprofit organization directors and volunteers. When working in a group, be sure to have
all volunteers sign an agreement that they will work collaboratively,
will publicize only factual information approved by the organization,
and will not engage in conduct that could result in legal liability for the
organization. Such an agreement can be important if a rogue volunteer
enters the organization and engages in conduct not condoned by the
organization. Not all advocacy necessitates joining forces with others;
for example, getting involved in humane education, performing healing
for animals, or volunteering can be done individually.

- *Create advocacy materials, a strategy, and a solution.* Your advocacy
materials (both written and verbal) must be based on fact. Period.
Discussing unfounded rumors, gossip, or even making up information
could land you in the middle of a defamation lawsuit as well as destroy
your credibility as an advocate. Your advocacy materials need a common and powerful message. Spending time framing your message and
preparing your materials will open more doors to success and save you
from having to redraft your materials down the road due to message
confusion. Always have a detailed solution prepared. Advocating for
change without a solution will get you nowhere.

- *Network!* Create a website and consider putting your message out on
social media (Facebook, Twitter). You can reach more interested people
through the Internet and social media, and it takes little time to update
your website or social media pages and garner more action. I have a
Facebook page called "You Can Do More for Animals" that received
more than five hundred friends within the first two weeks. It showed me
the power of social media when it comes to protecting animals.

- *Create relationships.* One of the initial tactics should be to speak
directly to the person who is in charge of making the change you are
seeking. Your approach can determine the nature of your relationship.
If you approach the decision maker to point out all the problems that
need to be corrected, that person will likely become defensive and may

not want to work with someone who is perceived to be an outsider sticking their nose into the situation. However, if you approach the decision maker with a genuine desire to be a resource or volunteer to help effect the change, your offer might be accepted. If you know a friend or professional colleague of this decision maker, consider taking this person along for your initial meeting. The goal is to create a positive and collaborative relationship so that the change can happen. If that tactic is unsuccessful, begin to work your way up the decision-making ladder and create positive relationships with those that can help you achieve change. For example, if you want to promote spaying and neutering of animals adopted from your local animal shelter, first start with the shelter director and ask what you can do to help to get such a program started. If the shelter director is not interested in this program, attempt to find out why. The reason may involve lack of financial support or staff to oversee the program. Knowing this information can then help you to create a solution to address the concerns, such as finding funding or locating a veterinarian who will donate these services. If the shelter director is still uninterested in this program and you feel you have exhausted all your efforts, then consider going to the local governmental unit that oversees the shelter (it may be the county government or the police department). Always start at the ground level when advocating and work to create positive relationships. But if you feel that your efforts are not successful, do not hesitate to climb the ladder until you find someone who can help to implement change.

- *Talk with the opponents.* Although it may be difficult to get an opponent to open up and discuss their business, it will help to learn as much as possible about the opponent's position so that you can research and prepare responses based on evidence and fact. Having your facts in order and promoting your advocacy with professionalism may give a positive impression to the opposition that may hinder their status quo techniques to discredit animal advocates.

- *Garner support from other animal shelters or animal organizations.* Your advocacy issue may benefit from the support of others, such as animal shelters or animal organizations. For example, if you are working with a legislator to change state law to provide more penalties for those who are cruel to animals, the issue will have more credibility if supported by those in the animal protection field. Reaching out to animal shelters and animal cruelty investigators will not only educate them that efforts are being made, but will also allow them to support these efforts. If you are advocating at the local level for your schools to have classes on humane education, reach out to humane educators within your community or throughout the state and ask for their support.

- *Involve your community.* If you have not been successful in garnering the support of the legislator, local politician, or other decision maker, consider a public campaign to raise awareness in your community and garner support. When dealing with an issue that is before local, state, or federal politicians, it can be very powerful to have voters express their opinion. For example, if you are waging a campaign to end gas chambers at your local shelter, you could garner community support through a petition or method for citizens to contact their local politician. Or you could have a state legislative bill filed to ban gas chambers in your state. This is a much larger campaign; however, engaging your community of voters can result in measurable change. Methods for engaging the community could involve creating an online or paper petition for people to support the effort; posting information around your community regarding the issue (including ads in the local newspaper and fliers at veterinary clinics or pet stores); providing preprinted postcards on the issue for people to mail in to their legislators; and starting an e-mail distribution list with e-mail action alerts, where people can submit prewritten letters in support of an effort. You could even set up an online survey through SurveyMonkey. com and gauge the beliefs of your community on a certain issue. Then the results of the survey could be used in your advocacy. Also consider attending community events and asking to speak on the issue.

- *Befriend the media.* When efforts to work directly with the decision maker have failed, yet others in your community are supportive of change to benefit animals, consider locating someone within the media who could write or air a story on the situation showing why change is needed. But be careful and make sure you provide sufficient facts and details to the reporter regarding your position; otherwise the article or story could end up publicizing your opponent's position. Such a campaign was successful in Montcalm County, Michigan, in 2009 when advocates pushed for a ban on pound seizure, gas chambers, and an overall reform to the shelter. The local media took great interest in county meetings where issues were publicly discussed. The media stories engaged more citizens to attend meetings and speak up for the shelter animals.

- *Be patient.* An advocacy campaign can take years before you see results. Do not give up, even in the face of strong opposition. Some campaigns take two to four years, and some longer. Yet all the successes for animals have been due to perseverance.
- *Keep emotions in check.* Do not let your emotions override reasonableness and common sense. Emotions can run high when you work to help animals. Everyone must work together to keep tempers in check so that unsupported beliefs are not spoken publicly.
- *Trust your intuition.* When you are in the heat of the advocacy, it can be difficult to remain focused and centered due to the flurry of activity. It is important to take a little time each day, even just ten minutes, to sit quietly and attempt to clear your mind. Although the thought of meditating can be intimidating to many people, it actually is a simple concept that involves sitting quietly and focusing on your breath to calm your mind. If you can do this every day, you will be amazed at the insights that you receive on how to best proceed with your advocacy. Some of my best ideas and techniques have come from simply doing nothing and thinking nothing, allowing intuitive ideas come to me.
- *Creativity: Think outside the cage.* Sometimes the old and tired methods of persuasion are no longer successful. Do you have a creative idea on how to effect change in your community? If so, create your plan and implement it. As was mentioned earlier, there is not one way to engage in advocacy. Due to the numerous issues before legislators and significant financial constraints in state and local agencies, now is the time for creative thinking.
- *Take action.* Once you decide that you need to get involved, take action!

WHERE DO YOU START?

Many people may not know where to start in animal advocacy. You know that you love animals but do not know of the vast array of opportunities. There are numerous topics, even in the limited field of protecting companion animals. The chapters throughout this book will detail some areas that you should consider if you are serious about helping companion animals. And within each chapter are "You Can Do More" tips that range from the simple task of making a donation, to writing a letter, to the more in-depth tasks of volunteering with animals or working on a legislative campaign.

No action is too small; every action from every person adds up and creates change that is needed to speak for those animals that do not have a voice or a vote.

Employment

You may wonder if there are employment opportunities available to work on behalf of animals. The answer is yes. There are numerous opportunities to work with and on behalf of animals. Some jobs include humane investigator; animal control officer; lobbyist (either in a private lobbying firm retained on behalf of an animal protection agency, or working directly for a state or national animal protection organization); working with an animal protection organization (shelter or kennel worker, clerical, administrative, managerial, fund-raising, marketing, public relations, accounting, interactive media, web design); writer (writing books or articles for publication); humane educator; safety representative for animals in film and television; opening and running an animal shelter; creating an animal organization that offers foster care and adoption for animals; disaster and emergency responder for animals; civil attorney handling lawsuits to protect animals; prosecuting attorney handling animal cruelty cases; veterinarian; veterinary technician; teacher (training at conferences or in classrooms); engineer (to create new comfortable housing systems for animals); energy healer; animal communicator; and even politician (local, state, or national level), where you introduce and promote legislation to protect animals.

No matter what your education, background, or experience may be, there are opportunities for employment where you can work toward the protection of animals. If you are in a job right now that does not appear to relate to protecting animals, look to unique skills or talents you have and see if they apply to helping animals. For example, you may currently be an engineer for the automotive industry, but you could put your engineering skills to work by creating animal cages that are beneficial to the lifestyles and needs of particular species and breeds. Or if you are a dentist who has a hobby of web design, you could create a business to build and host websites for animal organizations. Furry Friends Web Design in Mammoth, Pennsylvania, is one company dedicated to web services for animal organizations. Or consider making your current work environment pet-friendly by designating one day per week when the staff is allowed to bring their pets to work. I have worked in an office that allowed pets, and it increased morale and productivity for everyone. If your office engages in "casual Fridays," consider making it an event where people donate a few dollars to dress casually and the money goes to animal causes. In the workplace, there are many ways to help animals.

Volunteer

There are endless opportunities to volunteer to benefit companion animals. Much of this book is dedicated toward volunteer opportunities to advocate for companion animals. You are limited only by your creativity in how to help. Some opportunities involve very little thought or effort, and others can become a full-time endeavor. There is something for everyone. Keep reading to learn how you can do more!

Start a Nonprofit to Help Animals

Regardless of the area of interest, if you are determined to make a difference for animals, consider formalizing your efforts in a nonprofit organization. There are two ways to go about creating a nonprofit. You can create a nonprofit at the state level.[7] A state nonprofit organization generally costs less than a federal one when filing paperwork to be designated as a nonprofit, and it has less paperwork annually to file; but it does not allow for donors to claim a tax deduction on donations. You will need to prepare articles of incorporation and bylaws that set forth the purpose and mission of the organization.

On the other hand, a 501(c)(3) nonprofit, filed through the Internal Revenue Service,[8] is more complicated but worth the effort and cost in the long run because donations are tax deductible. Numerous books and websites provide detailed instructions on how to file for 501(c)(3) status. In general, you will first need a certificate from your state showing that your nonprofit has been registered. You will then fill out IRS Form 1023 and pay either $300 (for raising under $10,000 per year for four years) or $750 (for raising over $10,000 per year for four years) when filing the paperwork.[9] You will need at least three officers for the nonprofit and will be required to file annual tax returns. However, donors can claim a tax deduction on donations, which is a significant benefit when working to raise money through a nonprofit. "The exempt purposes set forth in section 501(c)(3) are charitable, religious, educational, scientific, literary, testing for public safety, fostering national or international amateur sports competition, and preventing cruelty to children or animals."[10] The IRS website provides the guidelines for applying for 501(c)(3) status, including appropriate language for the application[11] and limitations on advocacy and influencing legislation. A 501(c)(3) organization cannot engage in political activities such as donating to political campaigns or endorsing political candidates.[12] However, a 501(c)(3) organization can engage in advocacy activities to influence legislation or public policy so long as the activities are not a "substantial part" of the organization.[13] It is always wise to seek out the services of an attorney who can assist you with the 501(c)(3) filing paperwork.

Lifestyle

You can go about living in ways that also protect and benefit animals. One of the most obvious choices involves dietary and food selection, including vegetarianism or veganism. However, becoming vegetarian or vegan is not for everyone, and not doing so does not mean that you are not an advocate for animals. Again, strict positions on what you can and cannot do as an animal advocate can drive many people away from getting involved. So just do what you can to protect animals in your daily living.

You can advocate in other lifestyle choices, particularly when you shop and spend money. Ask your local grocery store or restaurants to provide humanely raised food, including food from these humane certification labels: American Humane Certified,[14] Animal Welfare Approved,[15] and Certified Humane.[16] The World Society for the Protection of Animals has an Eat Humane website, where you can search for restaurants providing humanely raised food.

When purchasing cosmetics and household cleaning supplies, check out the Leaping Bunny[17] and Caring Consumer[18] websites to locate products and companies that do not perform animal testing. Check labels to ensure you are purchasing fur-free items. When purchasing toys for your pets, the Healthy Stuff[19] website has nontoxic toys. If you are looking for a gift for an animal lover, many animal protection organizations sell items through their websites. For example, Born Free USA[20] has a website of animal-friendly, eco-friendly gifts; calendars or other gift items can often be purchased through your local animal protection shelters or organizations, as well as national organizations. Purchase books about animals to support authors, like me, who are passionate about animal protection. Make a gift donation in the name of the gift recipient to an animal protection shelter or organization, or sponsor an animal at a shelter or sanctuary in the name of the gift recipient. Best Friends Animal Sanctuary offers sponsorship opportunities for as little as $25, and there are even opportunities to sponsor farm animals at sanctuaries. Simply being conscious and aware of purchases that you make to ensure that no animal is harmed in the process can make a big difference to protect animals. And speaking of "No Animals Were Harmed®,"[21] you can even support the protection of animals who appear in films by patronizing only movies that receive the coveted "No Animals Were Harmed" end credit.

As detailed throughout this book, you can help companion animals in countless ways, from the smallest of efforts to larger-scale involvement. If everyone who loves cats, dogs, rabbits, and other companion animals simply did one thing per day to benefit an animal, we would witness a significant shift in the well-being and protection of animals. Performing one act daily to help an animal is a small thing to ask for companions who provide so much to benefit humans.

CHAPTER 3

Staying Strong and Resilient: Overcoming Conflict and Compassion Fatigue

If you are new to animal advocacy, you will quickly learn that not everyone in a position of power will treat you with respect or understanding. You may want to believe that those in elected positions or hired into positions of authority are open-minded and can be influenced by well-thought-out and supported arguments from an advocate. What you will learn is that some decision makers have personal beliefs that may not align with your advocacy or even the latest documented research, and that they are unwilling to listen to any argument that challenges their belief. This can be frustrating, and I have encountered it on many occasions. One thing that I kept in mind is how I would react if someone approached me with an opposing viewpoint and was attempting to change one of my beliefs. For example, I am an ardent opponent to pound seizure, a topic on which I published a book. So I have very strong, educated beliefs on the topic. If someone approached me with the intent of persuading me to change my opinion to support pound seizure, I would not be open to that discussion. Although I might politely listen to this advocate in order to learn the arguments of the supporters of pound seizure, I would not be persuaded due to my firm and knowledgeable commitment against the issue. That is the attitude you may receive from federal and state legislators, local politicians, animal shelter directors, and others in authority over the animals that you are advocating to protect. Although it may be difficult to respect an opposing belief, hopefully those words will at least help you understand and put opposing beliefs in perspective.

CONFLICT WITH DECISION MAKERS

When advocating to decision makers, you may quickly be labeled "an animal activist" and compared to organizations that engage in extreme tactics or illegal conduct. The label "activist" is noble in many other areas of advocacy yet is sometimes perceived negatively in the world of animal protection. You may find that officials, legislators, and those in charge of animal issues (such as an animal shelter director) may ignore your phone calls and e-mails and even publicly dismiss you once this label is thrown out against you. They may even be the people labeling you to discredit your advocacy. And this will be done without your accuser knowing you, your level of credibility and trustworthiness, or the depth of knowledge you may have in your chosen field of advocacy. It is often done out of fear that the status quo is changing and you are driving that change. You will be negatively labeled in hopes that others will be persuaded to ignore or disrespect you; it may even be done to raise your level of frustration so that you quit your advocacy.

Regardless of how you are labeled, your goal should be to work for the decision makers' time so that you can convey your message. Your goal should be to seek like-minded politicians or decision makers that agree with your advocacy and will join in the efforts to move toward change. You should strive to always be professional and always be sure to convey facts and the latest research that supports your advocacy.

CONFLICT WITH OPPONENTS

In any scenario involving animals, you will undoubtedly encounter opposition from people, organizations, and businesses who will advocate to maintain a practice that you want to change. What you may not realize is that people and organizations you believed to be "animal friendly" may actually hold opposing viewpoints and may actively lobby against your efforts. For example, the American Veterinary Medical Association, and many of the state veterinary associations, have position statements supporting the practice of pound seizure (taking shelter cats and dogs for experimentation) and have developed euthanasia guidelines that indicate when it is appropriate to use gas chambers. Yet a large majority of shelters, including the National Animal Control

Association, condemn both of these practices. As a result of these position statements issued by a national organization, I have experienced opposition from state veterinary associations in efforts to ban pound seizure and gas chambers. Many people are confused as to why that would happen, since most view veterinarians as animal protectors. Although many individual veterinarians do not support the positions of these associations, the associations have paid lobbyists who will work full time to thwart your efforts.

Depending on the advocacy topic, you may also find opponents you did not anticipate. Regardless of who the opponent is, it is advisable to initially speak with them regarding their concerns and the evidence to support their position and to have a professional conversation to find common ground. Do not ever underestimate the opposition. You may believe that your opponents do not wield any power or that they have a publicly unpopular position, yet you may discover that they have a relationship with legislators, local politicians, or other decision makers and they will systematically work to undercut your credibility and success.

CONFLICT WITH YOUR OWN SUPPORTERS

It may sound incredible that you could encounter conflict among a group of people you work with in animal advocacy. However, I have witnessed these breakdowns far too often, from advocating for legislation to helping homeless animals. The nastiness and outrageous behavior I have witnessed has anchored me even more firmly in the "camp of sanity" so that I maintain a strong, rational, and effective voice for the animals. But sometimes that requires walking away from those individuals and ending all interactions with them.

I have been, and continue to be, an advocate to protect children, victims of domestic violence, and elders, and I am a voice for crime victims. In animal advocacy, I have found that those on the same side can turn on each other without notice and without rational cause, and I have not encountered this in other advocacy areas. Why does this happen? My best guess is that although other areas of advocacy are sensitive, the animal welfare issues are supercharged with emotions but also with people who likely work better with animals than with people. So when dealing with conflict or differing opinions, some people in animal advocacy do not possess the social or conflict-resolution skills to work through the situation. Sadly, it is only the animals that end up suffering when this occurs.

I would like to give an example of how conflict can unfold in these situations. In 2009–2010, I headed a legislative advocacy campaign for American Humane Association to ban pound seizure (the taking of shelter cats and dogs for experimentation) and ban gas chambers in shelters in a particular state. One year into the campaign, with both bills showing signs of progress and having received committee hearings, I was shocked to find that a handful of local supportive advocates had begun to turn on those of us doing the daily work of running the advocacy campaigns. With each update we sent out to keep the advocates informed, we would see public e-mails disseminated by these advocates criticizing the strategy and literally picking apart every sentence in the update. We had gone to great extremes to keep the local advocates updated every step of the way. While I was initially shocked at this behavior, I had seen these same advocates turn on others in their local animal advocacy campaigns. It comes back to the old saying "If your friend talks badly about others to you, your friend likely talks badly about you to others." And that is what I saw. I saw once friendly and good-intentioned advocates believing that their aggressive, unplanned, take-no-prisoners strategy was the best strategy, that anyone not following in their path (or heaven forbid having success with a different and more rational tactic) would be publicly criticized and cut down to size, and that their possessiveness, jealousy, and ego-driven methods were prevailing over common sense and working together toward our common goal. And these tactics were coming from less than a handful of people who had done little to contribute to the state campaign and had no strategic plan for success. It was yet another example of how when success is occurring, some people will attempt to throw the focus off the success and onto themselves.

Many times advocates will disagree on strategy and tactics and may have strong opinions. That should be expected, because differing opinions are a part of everyday life. When dealing with advocacy, there is no one way to success, and all people and opinions must be respected. Every state, county, city, and situation is different. Sometimes the best solution is to allow people to vent and express their opinions without ramifications. However, when differing opinions result in divisiveness within your advocacy group, the situation must be addressed head-on. In the scenario just mentioned, efforts to reason with the disgruntled advocates resulted in more distribution of public and nasty e-mails and began to negatively affect the efforts to help the animals. It became best to simply uninvolve those particular advocates in the strategy and planning so that the rest of us could stay focused on the true goal.

When behavior in advocates turns destructive and treating them with respect does not work, often the only solution is to cease communication and move forward toward the goal. But if the divisiveness continues and/ or becomes more publicly widespread through e-mails or social media sites, then bold steps need to be taken to bring everyone back to center. Those steps may include (1) a private conversation with the instigator to find out the reason behind the behavior; (2) speaking with friends of the instigator to find out if anything stressful or upsetting has happened in his/her life to cause the sudden change in behavior; (3) asking an objective mediator to get involved; or (4) if a peaceful resolution cannot be achieved, removing the instigator from the campaign or group to protect the overall integrity of the message.

San Diego Humane Society's president, Dr. Mark Goldstein, published an editorial in the *San Diego Union-Tribune* newspaper in 2010 addressing the problem of critics within the animal protection community. When people who work in the animal protection community begin to publicly criticize others working to protect animals, he likes to look at the underlying intentions that bring out this behavior. "The solution lies in turning to the lessons that animals teach us. Animal welfare has long recognized the value of positive reinforcement as one of the most effective tools for training animals. Positive reinforcement teaches us that we embrace the positive and ignore the negative. As such, we as animal lovers and professionals need to avoid behaviors that hurt each other, putting our collective energies toward reinforcing the positive actions of those . . . whom I am honored to work with and who work tirelessly on behalf of animals. We need positive dialogue and challenge to improve. At the end of the day it's about respect."[1]

I have learned that opponents to animal advocacy often rely on divisiveness to occur within the ranks of animal advocates. And sadly, it often does. Many days I am amazed that any progress for animals has been made based on the amount of havoc that I have witnessed. Some days, it seems as if no one gets along. And I think to myself, "If we could only set our egos and agendas aside and work together, we would have made significantly more achievements on behalf of animals than has been done." But each day, I continue to watch the egos puffing and the personal agendas interfering with real effectiveness for animals. What I see are individual people or organizations clamoring to take 100 percent of the credit for a successful result when it was a group effort of many organizations and people that earned it. No one person or group succeeds alone when it comes to advocacy campaigns. However, the public officials and legislators most surely will learn of the divisiveness and that, in the end, will harm any advocacy campaign and ruin your credibility. The opposition will also exploit the dissension for their benefit. It then becomes a self-fulfilling prophecy for the phrase "crazy animal activist."

Discouraging? I hope not. I hope this empowers you to join in the protection of companion animals as a rational voice. But it is something that you should be aware of as you enter the world of animal advocacy. Then if it happens, you can quickly move around it. I frequently remind people that any advocacy for animals is not about us; it is about the animals. They cannot speak for themselves. And because humans have taken it upon themselves to treat animals as their own personal property to harm and dispose of, we need strong, rational, and effective voices speaking up for these wondrous, voiceless creatures. So when conflict arises, and it surely will, keep these words in mind so you can forge ahead and defend the defenseless.

DEALING WITH COMPASSION FATIGUE AND STAYING STRONG

Advocacy campaigns to improve the lives of animals are generally run by people with incredible depths of emotion and empathy. "Animal people" are among the most caring and compassionate individuals I have met. Those who volunteer or work to help animals are even more passionate about helping and giving a voice to the voiceless. However, it is these same benevolent traits that can contribute to unrealistic expectations of humans who are "not animal people," as well as strife within the advocacy group itself. In any animal advocacy situation, you will encounter those who are not "animal people" and believe that humans have the right to treat animals in whatever way is deemed easy or beneficial for humans. Or they just simply do not care about the animals. It is important to accept that not everyone feels about animals the way that you and I may.

As mentioned before, in all my years of advocating for animals, I have witnessed scenes of caring advocates turning against each other when the stress of the situation becomes overwhelming. Advocates that once worked well together are now bickering and distracting themselves and others from the primary goal of victory. The opposition thrives when the animal advocates have inner strife, because this weakens the advocates individually and collectively.

A few simple methods can ensure that you and/or your advocacy group stay strong. *First,* manage expectations from the start by establishing a written mission for the group and a specific set of goals. These can often be incorporated into the bylaws for your organization. *Second*, write out a strategy for pursuing a particular campaign or situation. No detail is too minute. The more specific you are about goals and expectations, the easier it will be to keep everyone on track. *Third*, whether you have formalized yourself as an organization or not, draft a written agreement that all advocates sign and must follow regarding appropriate and expected behavior. *Fourth*, assign duties according to the strengths of each advocate and have a written description of what each duty entails. If one advocate is shy and not well-spoken publicly but enjoys computer work, assign that advocate to record keeping, the website, or other administrative work. If another advocate is well-spoken and makes a good appearance, or has an impressive career or place in the community, have that advocate be the official spokesperson of your group. Assigning specific tasks to each advocate will avoid duplication of effort and prevent advocates from feeling like their work is being overshadowed by someone else. And lastly, choose your leader wisely. Not everyone is suited to lead a group of ardent advocates. The leader should be levelheaded; respected by other advocates; able to see both sides of the issue; able to remain respectful, calm, and resilient in the face of adversity; aware when a campaign is not working and willing to reassess a new strategy; and capable of motivating others to continue when the campaign runs into difficulties. A good leader will praise good deeds and prompt others to get action when needed.

If a situation arises where two or more advocates are beginning to quarrel or simply not work well together, intervene immediately to mediate the situation. If one advocate is simply unable to follow the goals of the group or is too disruptive to other advocates, then consider removing that person. Having a well-written volunteer agreement will help you to rely on a document that was signed by the disruptive advocate. But it is more important to resolve the situation than simply remove volunteers, because a disgruntled volunteer could engage in rash and improper conduct that could harm the overall advocacy campaign or mission.

It is important to have as many advocates as possible working collaboratively on the issue. The opposition may be strong in your community or state, so having a sufficiently large group will give you strength in numbers as well as allow for division of assignments so that burnout is avoided. If you do not have a large group to rely on, it is important to recognize the signs of burnout or compassion fatigue so you can remain strong for the long haul.

Compassion fatigue is a type of emotional exhaustion from observing suffering and trauma. It comes from a source of caring and feeling helpless when things do not go as planned. It is common for animal shelter workers and others who help animals to suffer from compassion fatigue at some time. Burnout, on the other hand, can result from any form of constant stress, not necessarily related to caring for others, including animals. Compassion fatigue or burnout can come from continuous stress, exposure to euthanization of shelter animals, pound seizure occurring with shelter animals, and struggles with shelter staff or lawmakers.

The following are some helpful tips to avoid burnout or compassion fatigue:

- Keep your expectations in perspective. Realize that you will not be able to protect all the animals, at least not immediately. Campaigns are a process, and you need to maintain a clear head in order to prevail.
- Set daily, weekly, monthly, and yearly goals for your advocacy efforts. For example, when I volunteered at an animal shelter with a low adoption rate and pound seizure, one of my goals was to ensure that every cat that entered the shelter's cat room was safe. Each day, I would check over the list for the cat(s) that had been there the longest and then work on securing an adoption (through placement of adoption ads in the local newspaper) or foster care (by contacting other animal organizations). I kept a list of all the cats that were saved from pound seizure and made it safely out of the shelter. At the end of each week and month, I would review the list, and it would energize me to keep going. Those assisting the shelter dogs also kept a list, and together it empowered us all, even during difficult times.

- Celebrate small victories. If you are advocating within an animal shelter, those may include each shelter cat and dog that is adopted from the shelter, each new advocate that joins the cause, each donation received, each lawmaker that supports your efforts, and each media story that positively supports your goal.
- Keep a scrapbook of photos or articles supporting your advocacy. If you collect photos of animals that you helped, during dark days it is soothing to look back on the faces of all the animals that are now safe because of you and your organization. Today I still enjoy the photo albums of cats that I helped over the past decade.
- Have animal-free time. Animal advocacy, especially in life-and-death situations, can be all consuming. I know; I have been there. Be sure to have other hobbies that do not involve animals or even your animal friends; spend time with family, go out with friends, and/or exercise. It is important that these outside interests don't involve your work with animals. You need to take a break every now and then to rejuvenate. Too often I find that conversations with friends turn toward animals during a time when I want to focus on other positive aspects of life. Be diligent in maintaining a healthy boundary so that you can be effective for the animals. One hobby that helped me keep balanced during my first pound seizure campaign was West Coast swing dancing. Several times a week, I would meet up with my dance friends, and we would dance for hours. It would instantly lift my spirit, was great exercise, and reenergized me.
- Pamper yourself. If your advocacy results in frequent visits to a struggling animal shelter, the smells and noises at the shelter can have a toxic impact on your state of mind. Surround yourself with beauty at least once a week, if not more. Go for a walk in nature (especially if you have dogs); lie on the grass, sand, or woods to have direct contact with Mother Earth; burn beautiful-smelling candles; take bubble baths or Epsom salt baths scented with essential oils (Epsom salt is believed to clear out negative energy); sit with and love your animals and appreciate all that they bring to your life; laugh, play, and pray. Cats and dogs know how to live in the moment and enjoy life, so consider mimicking their behavior. I often find that I feel better if I follow the lead of my cats: resting in a pile of fluffy blankets, cuddling, and staring off into space (to daydream). Or with dogs, going for a walk or a run and rolling around on the ground.

- Meditate. Many people cringe when they hear the word *meditate*. But meditation can be very simple, and it is a healing method to calm your mind so that you can think clearly and receive inspired thoughts. Meditation can involve something as simple as spending ten minutes per day sitting in silence. Sometimes this is best done as you wake in the morning or before going to bed at night. Stay in bed, sit with your back straight, and let your mind remain in that place between sleep and alertness. End the silence by setting your intentions for the day. A good intention could be to remain strong and resilient and to enjoy one success that day. Intentions should also be stated positively rather than using negative words such as *not*. Gradually increase the amount of meditation time each week. A realistic goal might be to meditate for thirty minutes straight at least four times per week. Afterward, I always find that I have new ideas and strategies and feel more empowered. It helps to clear my mind of clutter, too.
- Protect yourself from the despair of others. We all know people who are negative, toxic, and always have something to complain about. If you are working with an advocate or have a friend who fits this description, make efforts to avoid or limit exposure to this person. Being around negative people can bring down your energy level. When advocating for animals, it is important to keep your energy uplifted. Associate with people who make you feel good and inspired, and this will spread to others.
- Read about and understand the Law of Attraction. Simply put, the Law of Attraction is a universal law where you receive what you put out. For example, if you constantly complain about situations and are negative about life, you will receive more negative things to complain about. You will receive whatever you put your attention toward. However, if you are happy (which can be easy if you focus on the small victories each day) and truly believe that your goals will be achieved (you may not know how you will succeed, but you just know that you will), then that changes your energy, and you will receive more experiences in line with those beliefs. Good things will start to come your way, which then increases your positivity and allows for more good events to occur. If you can remain positive, this will spread to others and your group dynamic will benefit. As a certified Law of Attraction Counselor, I think this information is very important to keep in mind. The foundation for the Law of Attraction

is "ask and you shall receive." If you are interested in learning more about this practice, visit my website at www.manifestedharmony .com.

- Publicly recognize the work of yourself and others, and do so frequently. A pat on the back and some genuine heartfelt praise can motivate everyone to keep going.
- Seek the help of a professional counselor if feelings of despair about the animals are overwhelming. It takes a courageous person to ask for help, so do not feel embarrassed to receive guidance. Or have a support system of friends and family that you can talk to when a situation becomes difficult or if you lost a beloved shelter pet to pound seizure or euthanasia. Do not keep your feelings bottled up inside.
- For additional information on compassion fatigue involving animals, a good resource is *Compassion Fatigue in the Animal Care Community* by Charles Figley and Robert Roop.

For most people, change can be difficult and uncomfortable. You may question and not understand why others are so determined to maintain the status quo, especially if it is harmful for animals. Change can be frightening. When pursuing a cause that you deeply believe in, let your belief be your guiding light. There will be dark days during your advocacy where the opposition seems stronger and more educated than you, where shelter cats and dogs are dying, where incidents of cruelty seem on the rise, and where others you are advocating with start to bicker and quarrel about strategy. But there will also be days of joy for each animal that you help, when you locate another kindred spirit to help in your advocacy, and when an unknown donor appears out of nowhere to help you fund your efforts. In the end, if you keep your focus on a positive result, you will be rewarded.

Lastly, I would like to share the Smudgie Award for Resiliency. Smudgie is an exotic-looking calico cat who was surrendered to the cat orphanage where I volunteer. Smudgie was about seven years old and was surrendered with her feline sister, Serendipity, in January 2007. The prior owner informed the orphanage that Smudgie and Serendipity did not need to be adopted together because she did not believe that they were bonded. She was wrong, but we did not know that. Within a few days, Serendipity was adopted and Smudgie quickly went into a deep depression. She then started to have quivering in her back legs that caused her difficulty in jumping and walking. A few weeks later, she had her first seizure. The veterinarian put Smudgie on antiseizure medication that caused lethargy and walking difficulty. A volunteer and I shared foster care of Smudgie because both of us had employment that required travel. After three months on the antiseizure medication Smudgie had increased difficulty in walking and a questionable quality of life, so I decided to consult with a homeopathic veterinarian. This veterinarian was able to wean Smudgie off of the antiseizure medication and use homeopathy to help Smudgie through the grief she was suffering over the loss of Serendipity. Smudgie was grieving and was literally shaking/crying from the inside out, thus causing seizures. Through homeopathy, Smudgie was nudged through a grieving process that included a "healing crisis," where it appeared she was getting worse after suffering a significant subsequent seizure; yet that was a good sign, and Smudgie never had a seizure again.

Smudgie is now in a new home and is reported to still be seizure free. Throughout Smudgie's ordeal of heavy medication with antiseizure drugs, ultrasounds and an MRI, acupuncture with needles sticking out of her head, transitioning between foster homes and eventually her permanent adoptive home, Smudgie remained sassy and resilient. Although Smudgie needed a little help in processing her grief, she was always a highly spirited kitty who was talkative and spoke her truth. She remained resilient during a difficult time that almost resulted in her death. Why am I telling you the story of Smudgie? I have taken Smudgie's story and turned it into an award that I give to people who are able to stay strong and resilient in the face of adversity when helping animals. So for you, I hope you will find the Smudginess in you to stay strong and resilient to be the voice for animals.

CHAPTER 4

Humane Education: Kids Helping Animals

Babies and young children have a natural affinity toward animals. Children are surrounded by animals from their first breath: their blankets and clothing feature teddy bears, giraffes, and ducks; their first gift may be a stuffed animal; their nursery often contains animal images such as the cow jumping over the moon; the mobile spinning above their crib likely has animals dangling to soothe and entertain; books and movies feature animal characters such as Clifford the Big Red Dog, Blue's Clues, Big Bird, Garfield, and Nala and Simba. Even songs like "Old MacDonald" feature animals. It is natural and healthy for children to grow up with pets and to learn the proper care, treatment, and respect for living creatures.

If you have raised a child, you may already have experienced the joy that a child has when they see a pet or an animal in the wild. Taking a child to the state fair sometimes makes the child want to bring home a goat as a family pet, or if there is an animal adoption event occurring where cute kittens and puppies are on display, your child may not only run to be near the cute pets, but also beg to bring one home. A research study found that 99 percent of children between the ages of three and thirteen want a pet.[1] This is a natural response that should be nurtured.

Regardless of whether you have a pet at home for your child, raising children to be kind to animals is our hope for creating future generations of compassionate and caring adults. Every day through the media we hear of despicable acts of cruelty and neglect committed against animals. So how do we get people to be conscious about compassion toward animals in their everyday living? We start with the children.

HUMANE EDUCATION

"A Humane Educator is anyone who teaches and promotes humane attitudes toward people, animals and the environment. This includes, but is not limited to, anyone who teaches animal welfare, animal rights, animal behavior, environmental concerns, character education, cultural studies and any combination of the above."[2] Humane educators, in addition to parents, are in a powerful position to reach children and provide information and tools on appreciation and care for animals. A variety of professions within a community contribute toward humane education, such as staff at an animal shelter, volunteers with an animal welfare organization, animal control officers or humane investigators, police officers, veterinarians and veterinary technicians, community leaders, clergy, community business owners, teachers, zoo staff, dog trainers, and anyone that can deliver a positive message to children about respect and responsibility toward people, animals, and the environment.

Humane education is a growing field with many excellent resources available, especially on the Internet. The Association of Professional Humane Educators (APHE) is composed of professional members who are making a difference to bring humane education to America's children and youth. APHE has many programs and tools available on their website, including a Summer Camp Resource Manual and CD that is available for a small fee.[3]

Humane Education Advocates Reaching Teachers (HEART) is one of only a few full service humane education providers in the United States with numerous resources on their website.[4] The HEART staff of teachers conducts free multilesson humane education programs for students from kindergarten through twelfth grade in various venues in-school and after-school, as well as in summer camps in the New York City and Chicago areas. HEART conducts credit-bearing humane education professional development courses through the NYC Department of Education for schoolteachers and offers teacher training workshops for attorneys through the American Bar Association.

The Humane Society of the United States (HSUS) has programs for children, tweens, and teenagers to get involved in helping animals.[5] The HSUS *KIND News*[6] is a newspaper that has circulated to more than 200 million students nationwide and emphasizes proper pet care and appreciation of wildlife. Classrooms can receive *KIND News* through the Adopt-A-Classroom program where parents, businesses, civic organizations, and other community programs can select a classroom to sponsor. "A consistent part of a child's school year, *KIND News* keeps important lessons about animal protection resonating in the classroom long after students' last shelter tour or your last school presentation. Our surveys of teachers receiving the newspaper show that 99 percent think teaching children to care responsibly for pets is 'very important' or 'important.' *KIND News* gives teachers that opportunity throughout the school year. And our surveys show that virtually 100 percent of teachers who receive *KIND News* use it every month."[7]

The American Society for the Prevention of Cruelty to Animals has *ASPCA Kids*, an information-packed website specifically for educating children on animals and getting them involved.[8] And the Latham Foundation[9] works to educate all ages, including children, on the humane treatment and care of animals and has affordable publications and videos for purchase.

So how can you become involved in humane education and teaching the next generation to treat animals with kindness? To start, contact your local animal shelter or animal welfare organization to see if they have a humane education program and ask how you can become involved. There are currently no education or certification requirements for becoming a humane educator, which is why humane education is perfectly suited to a variety of different professions and different backgrounds. Distance-learning courses can be taken through the Humane Society University[10] and the Institute for Humane Education.[11] Moreover, the *Humane Education Guidebook*, created by the Federated Humane Societies of Pennsylvania Education Committee, is a resource for those just starting out in the profession.[12] A copy of the *Shelter Operations Guide on Humane Education* is a free download from American Humane Association and is a great tool for those considering starting a program.[13] Anyone interested in helping children become more caring and compassionate people would be well-suited to become a humane educator.

HOW KIDS CAN HELP ANIMALS

"Do not underestimate what children can do to learn about and protect animals,"[14] says Jane Deming, who has been a humane educator since 1978 and was previously director of humane education for American Humane Association. Jane explains, "Kids from an early age, about eight to nine years old, want to work in an animal shelter. They want hands-on opportunities with animals. However, this is a rare opportunity, since many shelters require children to be eighteen years of age or to come to the shelter with a parent. But we do not want to discourage children from participating with animals, so there are other ways to get them involved."[15] One such way is through summer camps with animals, which is a breakthrough concept occurring all over the United States. Jane explains, "When kids participate in a summer camp, it links them to other kids in the community that have similar interests. It broadens the fact that they are not alone and there are plenty of other kids out there with the same passion for animals. It also puts them all in the same room to discuss the same topics, to debunk a lot of myths, and to provide them with the absolute facts and how they can help. They also get to play and do crafts and activities to solidify and celebrate the idea that it's good to be humane."[16] Jane has found that kids are sometimes less receptive to their grown-ups telling them how to take care of animals or understand animal behavior; as an alternative, the summer camps provide the information to kids in a fun, interactive, and learnable way. "If we blanket the country with humane kids, it will make a real difference. When kids go home and tell their parents what they learned, it also educates the parents and helps them to be more compassionate pet owners."[17]

Sheryl Pipe has been a humane educator since 1999 and previously worked with the ASPCA and then with American Humane Association, where she served as director of The Link® and community outreach. She has seen that kids can help out in a variety of ways: "Penny Harvests, run by Common Cents, are a good example. There is a rather sophisticated process by which classes choose representatives, and these representatives evaluate nonprofit organizations to which the collected funds are donated. Animal welfare organizations consistently rank in the top ten among organizations to which Penny Harvest funds are donated. Young children can participate in fund-raisers for animal welfare organizations, create cat toys or adoption bandannas (with adult input on what is safe), or artwork for the shelter."[18]

Stacey Zeitlin is the director of education and community programs at San Diego Humane Society and SPCA, as well as the president of the Association of Professional Humane Educators. Stacey is involved in numerous activities for children at San Diego Humane. For younger children, they offer the Tots and Tales story-time program that introduces young children to humane and animal-themed stories. Birthday parties at San Diego Humane's campus are also another way to get children involved. For older children, the party includes a tour of the adoption gallery, games and crafts, and interaction with some of the animals. "For children ages five through thirteen, we offer our Animal Adventure Camp, which is a weeklong camp session filled with games, crafts, and animal interactions. All the campers have a wonderful time while learning about animal needs, responsible pet care, and careers with animals. Many campers come back year after year, and their families utilize our other programs such as adoptions, training programs, and fund-raising opportunities."[19]

For school-age children, San Diego Humane offers School Outreach and Home-School sessions, two programs aligned to school standards. Stacey explains, "Credentialed teachers present animal welfare lessons based on the standards that teachers and parents must address in life sciences, mathematics, language arts, critical thinking, and character education. The teachers value that the lessons are standards-based, and the children love to interact with and learn about our animals."[20] The facility also helps children to earn Girl and Boy Scout badges, such as Dog Care Merit Badge, Animal Try-It, Pet Care Badge, and Pets' Interest Project. Stacey elaborates, "We created our own patch that Girl Scouts can obtain called the Playful Paws Patch. This patch combines a tour of the facility with a community service component of making enrichment items for our adoptable animals."[21]

For children that need assistance with learning, San Diego Humane offers Listening E.A.R.S. (Education and Reading Success). Due to animals' nonjudgmental nature, the children read and study with animals, and the animals are a perfect audience for children to practice. This contributes to reduced anxiety and stress for the child. Animal ambassadors from the facility are also taken into inner-city facilities to introduce children to friendly animals.

Opportunities are also available for high school students through the coordination of job shadow experiences in animal welfare so that they can learn about careers as a humane educator, humane officer, veterinarian or medical staff, or animal trainer. It is a wonderful program to show youth that there are career opportunities to assist animals other than becoming a veterinarian. During the summer, the students can intern with the Animal Adventure Camp by assisting with art projects, interacting with younger campers, monitoring interactions with animals, all while being introduced to humane treatment of animals. This program is excellent for a college application or résumé.

For all ages in the community, San Diego Humane offers tours of their state-of-the-art facility that include lessons on safe interaction with animals and animal care. When asked to share a memorable story of children interacting with animals, Stacey shared the following:

"One of my favorites is that of Mrs. Benowitz's fifth-graders at Olivenhain Pioneer Elementary School in San Diego County. Each year, her class would create a business that would produce, market, and sell dog-related items, such as greeting cards, dog treats, doghouses, and more. They would research their potential market and what they could sell; they would create a budget to work within for the purchasing and fabrication of their items; they would take turns selling the items throughout the community and at local farmers' markets; they would organize an auction for some high-end doghouses that they designed, built, and decorated; and then they would submit a check, often over $2,000 for their nine months of work, to the San Diego Humane Society and SPCA in the name of their business, Red Dawg, Green Dawg. This lesson was valuable on so many levels for both the students and our animals. The students were learning real-life skills but also learning philanthropic values at the same time. They could have used that money for a class party or field trip, but instead they chose to support a local, nonprofit organization in its mission. Their check and letter was always written very humbly, and they expected nothing in return for their actions. We were thrilled to invite this year's class to present their check at our annual Telethon to celebrate their accomplishments and dedication to the animals of San Diego."[22]

An easy way for kids to get started in thinking about and helping animals is to participate in American Humane Association's Be Kind to Animals Week®, which happens annually each May and has been celebrated since 1915. Kids that have gone above and beyond to help animals can enter the Be Kind to Animals Kids Contest with a monetary grand prize of $1,000 in two age categories. The winner is announced in conjunction with Be Kind to Animals Week. There are also lesson plans and activities on the American Humane Association website for getting children engaged in kindness to animals.

Listed below are American Humane Association's "Ideas for Educators"[23] with a variety of ways for kids to get involved:

Elementary Grade (K–5) Activities

- Pennies for Puppies = Children can work together to decorate cans, distribute them among local merchants, and then use them to collect coins as a fund-raiser for a local animal shelter or animal/wildlife group in your area.

- Pet-to-Person Matching Game = A group can decorate a bulletin board with pictures of people and their pets. The purpose of the game is to correctly match the pets with their people. This game can also be used as a fund-raiser by asking participants to make a donation that will be contributed to a local animal shelter or animal/wildlife group.

- Make Pet Blankets = Following directions from an online resource, craft book, craft store, or other source, make a blanket for your pet or the pet of a friend, family member, or neighbor. You can also donate blankets to a local animal shelter or veterinary clinic in need of warm pet bedding. Another option is to donate blankets you've made to local animal organizations that could then sell the blankets to raise proceeds for the animals they care for.

- Make Homemade Dog/Cat Treats = Using a recipe from an online resource or pet cookbook, make dog or cat treats for your pets, for distribution to a local shelter, or for a fund-raiser. Profits can be donated to a local shelter or animal welfare organization.

- Build a Bird Feeder = Contact your local Audubon Society for directions on how to make a bird feeder that is attractive to birds in your area. Make the bird feeder, fill it with the appropriate seed, and determine the best place to display it. You and your students will enjoy observing the different types of birds that visit the feeder. Be sure to have bird identification reference books on hand to name the types of birds that are coming to the feeder. Essays, poems, artwork, and other projects can be created around the birds that visit the feeder. Also, charts and graphs of behavior, populations, and species variety can be created.

- Build a Kitty "Castle" = Decorate a cardboard box with nontoxic markers or paints. Close all the sides, but make sure there is an opening large enough for a cat to easily pass through. Place blankets or towels inside the box to create a soft bed and let your kitty enjoy this fun new castle. Castles can also be given to friends, neighbors, or relatives who have cats, or can be donated to local animal shelters.

- Make a Puppy Bed = Cut the top flaps and one side off a cardboard box, so you are left with a back, two sides, and a bottom. Decorate the box with nontoxic markers or paints and place blankets or towels inside to create a soft bed for your puppy or small dog. You can also give beds to friends, neighbors, or relatives who have puppies or small dogs, or to a local animal shelter.

- Make a Pet Dish Place Mat = Cut construction paper into strips that are 2 inches wide by 24 inches long. Place eight of these side by side to form the finished size of the place mat. Cut 12 additional strips 2 inches wide by 16 inches long and weave the first through the others that were already laid out. Glue the first strip in place and use paper clips to hold it securely while the glue dries so you can continue the weaving. After the weaving is complete, glue along the outside edges where the strips overlap. This place mat can also be sealed in adhesive-backed plastic (or laminated) to make it waterproof. Place mats can be donated to local animal shelters for a fund-raiser.
- Poster Contest = Have children make a poster that shows ways to be kind to animals. Hold a contest to choose the best poster. You can then have all posters on display in the school, a local pet store, an animal shelter, or a business during the week.
- Essay Contest = Have children submit essays on a topic related to kindness toward animals. The winning essays can be read to the group (troop, church group, classroom, school assembly, etc.) and/ or displayed. Suggested topics: ways to be kind to animals; what Be Kind to Animals Week means to me; how a special animal made my life better; a special animal in my life; and what it means to be kind.
- Show and Tell = Have children present a picture of an animal and explain how one should properly care for that animal. Have the child explain why it's important to be kind to the animal. The animal could be the child's pet, a class pet, a friend or relative's pet, etc.
- Visit a Wildlife Refuge or State Park = Arrange a trip to the local wildlife refuge or state park. Have children focus on the animals living in their community. Discuss what they learned from the trip on the way home.
- Draw an Animal = Have children draw or paint an animal and then draw or cut and paste pictures around it of what that animal needs to be happy and healthy. Pets or wildlife would be appropriate for this project.
- Supply Drive = Contact a local animal shelter, animal welfare organization, or wildlife organization and ask workers what supplies they need. Organize a drive with specific instructions as to the needs, gather those items, and then deliver them to the organization.

- Host a Guest Speaker = Invite a humane educator, wildlife rehabilitator, animal behaviorist, dog trainer, veterinarian, or other animal professional to visit your group. Prepare the children before the visit so that they have a variety of questions ready for the expert.

Middle School Activities

- Make a Wildlife Feeder or House = Contact your local Audubon Society or other wildlife organization to find out what type of house or feeder would be best for the wildlife in your area (see suggestions below). Using directions from your local wildlife organization, from online, or from a woodworking class, construct a house or feeder made out of wood (adult supervision is imperative). Hang the house or feeder in an appropriate area and enjoy observing the different species that visit. Be sure to have identification reference books on hand to name the species you see. Essays, poems, artwork, and other projects can be created around the wildlife that visits. Also, charts and graphs of behavior, populations, and species variety can be created. Recommended building projects: birdhouse or feeder, squirrel feeder, bat house, or butterfly house.
- Help Care for a Pet = Ask a neighbor, friend, or family member if you and a child can help them care for their pet. Walking, playing, feeding, brushing, and petting are great ways to help someone out. Be sure to always supervise the child.
- Design a Brochure = Have your students interview the director of a local shelter, wildlife organization, or other animal group to identify pertinent information to include in a brochure. Children can work together to design and distribute a brochure promoting the organization within their community.
- Make a Scratching Post = Research directions online on how to make a scratching post for a cat. You can give the post to your own cat or as a gift to someone you know with a cat. Another option is to build several to donate to your local shelter for sale or for the resident cats.
- Make a Dog Bed = Search online or in your local craft store for instructions on how to make a dog bed with fabric and foam. The dog bed can be used by your dog, a dog you know, or a shelter that houses dogs and needs supplies.
- Make Catnip Toys = Search online for ideas for making catnip toys. Make the toys and give them to your own cats or give them as gifts to

friends, neighbors, or relatives. Toys can also be donated to local animal shelters to give to their cats or to sell as a fund-raiser.

- Make a Pet Care Bin/Bucket = Using a bucket, basket, box, or bin, create a place to neatly store all your pet-care products, toys, blankets, and other supplies. Decorate the bin with nontoxic paint and use it for your own pet, give it as a gift to someone you know with a pet, or donate it to a local shelter for sale or use.
- Interview a Professional = Have students interview an animal shelter worker or volunteer, dog trainer, veterinarian, groomer, wildlife rehabilitator, or other local animal professional. The interview can be audio or video recorded and then turned into an essay or presentation. You can also edit it and submit it for use on a local cable TV show. Be sure to conduct research and prepare appropriate questions in advance.
- Newspaper Articles = Have students find and cut out articles relating to kindness and animals or kindness and the environment in a local, national, or international newspaper (not online). Ask each student to prepare a discussion of how the article shows kindness to animals. Encourage students to come up with ideas for how they could get involved, and then vote on one or two ideas. Follow through on the ideas for getting involved. Link this to civic responsibility.
- Classroom and Group Activities: PowerPoint, poster presentation; essay, poem, short story, research paper; skit, poster contest, drawing, collage, mural, posters; or web page. Have students use one of the modalities above to address a topic from the list below. Presentations and projects can be graded and put into regular classroom curricula. Contests can be held and winners can be presented to the group and/or put on display at school, a local pet supply store, an animal shelter, or a business during the week.
  - Science: Animals and their environments, niches, needs, etc.; pet care and responsibility; where our food comes from and how it is produced; pet diseases/illnesses, treatments, the need for veterinary care; spaying/neutering.
  - English/Language Arts: Write from the point of view of a pet or about a special animal; pet adoption; what it means to be kind; what Be Kind to Animals Week means; the role of animals in art and literature.
  - History: The history of animals in film, art, literature, movies; the history of animal laws; timeline of the domestication of animals.

◦ Math: Pet overpopulation; cost of having a pet; cost of operating an animal shelter.

High School Activities

- Build a Doghouse for a Dog in Need = Search online for instructions and, providing adult supervision at all times, construct a safe and weather-resistant doghouse for an outside dog in need. Be sure to get permission from the dog's caretaker before beginning the project.
- Organize a Fund-raising Activity = Team up with a local pet or wildlife organization to organize a fund-raising activity, such as a walk to benefit a shelter; a game (volleyball, basketball, baseball) of students versus faculty; a clean-up day (inside the building, on the grounds, in your community, etc.)
- Design a Pet Adoption Kit = Work with your local shelter to determine what the kit should contain. Suggestions include coupons from local businesses, list of veterinarians in the area, pet toys, pet care information, list of local trainers, list of local pet supply stores, healthy treats, etc.
- Volunteer Cleanup = Contact a local pet or wildlife organization and volunteer to help them clean up. Cleanup can be inside their facility, on facility grounds, in the community, or in wildlife habitats.
- Local Animal Professional Speaker = Contact a local pet or wildlife organization or professional and arrange for a speaker to visit your group or for a field trip to the speaker's facility. Ask students to prepare questions in advance.
- Newspaper Articles = Have students find and cut out articles relating to kindness and animals or kindness and the environment in a local, national, or international newspaper (not online). Ask each student to prepare a discussion about how his or her article shows kindness to animals. Encourage students to come up with ideas for how they could get involved, and then vote on one or two ideas. Follow through on the ideas for getting involved. Link this to civic responsibility.
- Debates = Organize students into groups of "pro" and "con" and have them research their assigned positions on one of the hot topics that follow. Be sure to focus on both sides of each issue. Schedule debates and facilitate informative discussions. Suggested topics: animal testing (cosmetic and/or medical); vegetarianism; factory farming; exotic

animals as pets; circuses; hunting; wearing fur; breeding cats and dogs; cloning pets.
- Classroom and Group Activities: PowerPoint, poster presentation; essay, poem, short story, research paper; skit, poster contest, drawing, collage, mural; web page. Have students use one of the modalities above to address a topic from the list below. Presentations and projects can be graded and put into regular classroom curricula. Contests can be held and winners can be presented to the group and/or put on display at school, a local pet supply store, an animal shelter, or a business during the week.
  - Science: Animals and their environments, niches, needs, etc.; where our food comes from and how it is produced; pet diseases/illnesses, treatments, the need for veterinary care; endangered animals in the community; unusual pets; pet care and responsibility.
  - English/Language Arts: Write from the point of view of a pet or about a special animal; pet adoption; what it means to be kind; what Be Kind to Animals Week means; the role of animals in art and literature.
  - History: The history of animals in film, art, literature, movies; the history of animal laws; timeline of the domestication of animals; animal fighting.
  - Math: Pet overpopulation; cost of having a pet; cost of operating an animal shelter.
  - Miscellaneous: Adopting pets; choosing a pet.

There are numerous ways children can get involved to help animals; children are only limited by their creativity. Jane and Sheryl shared the following additional ideas for getting kids involved in helping animals:

- Host a lemonade stand.
- Hold a Thon event (jump-a-thon, bowl-a-thon, walk-a-thon, baton-a-thon, read-a-thon, etc.) to raise money to help animals.
- If a child is having a birthday, bar/bat mitzvah, confirmation, or other party, ask guests to bring money or items for the shelter animals (such as toys, blankets, food) instead of a gift.
- If kids want to make toys for shelter cats, go to a thrift shop and purchase baby socks and fill them with catnip.
- Hold a car wash (and ask the shelter staff if a few adoptable shelter dogs can attend).

- As a parent, volunteer with your child at an animal shelter that allows children to socialize kittens and puppies.
- Collect newspapers for shelters to line cages or collect boxes for cats and kittens to play in or for litter boxes.

Jane remembers how one group of kids purchased large cheese pizzas and then sold slices during lunch at school and raised about $100 each month for the animal shelter. And a school art group made frames for cages at the animal shelter that would hold information regarding the animal. Each frame was decorated with cute sayings like "Adopt me" or "I need love." Jane believes, "Ideas are endless when you let your creativity take hold."[24]

KIDS WHO ARE MAKING A DIFFERENCE

Ciara Petronzio is an example of how to take action with a love for animals. Ciara and her "Pennies for Pups" program were featured in *The Latham Letter* magazine in summer 2010. When Ciara's golden retriever, Dakota, died in 2006 at just twelve years old, it left a void in Ciara's heart and life. She initially wanted another dog, but her family was not ready. She started volunteering with Rescue a Golden, where she helps with adoption events and even provides foster care for dogs. Through her volunteer work, Ciara learned about the tragedy of pet overpopulation in the United States, as well as animals that are abused, homeless, and hungry. Knowing that she could do more, she started Pennies for Pups to raise money to help animals in need. In her first fund-raiser, she hosted a book sale and raised $1,000 for Rescue a Golden. Knowing that many animal organizations needed help, too, Ciara hosted other events. "Funds came in from dog washes, booths at street fairs, lemonade stands, and wrapping gifts and she gives it all away. . . . Her latest project was a pet food drive that collected 2,000 pounds of dog and cat food for local shelters and rescues."[25] While many teenagers are spending time on Facebook or texting friends, Ciara spends her hours making a difference for animals.

American Humane's Be Kind to Animals Kids Contest winners in 2010 were Hannah Blaze (age 11, from Ohio) and Justin Strawser (age 13, from Pennsylvania). Both exemplify how a little effort can go a long way. Hannah was saddened by the conditions at her local animal shelter, particularly in the cat adoption room, which was windowless and crowded. She went by herself to a city council meeting to ask for change. Because of her advocacy, new fencing was installed for the dogs, and the cats were removed from their windowless room to a new building that has windows, more space, and even allows the cats to roam. This has increased the adoption rate for the cats because the cats are happier. For Justin, after he adopted a dog from Dogs Deserve Better, an organization that helps dogs often coming from outdoor confinement, he realized that his dog did not know how to play with toys. Dogs Deserve Better has a sponsor program for dogs during the holiday season. Instead of choosing one dog to receive a toy, Justin chose them all. Justin gathered spare change, his birthday money, and savings and bought items from the wish list totaling more than $600. He plans to do this annually to help out animals and has even started educating others about the proper care for animals.

Maya Alcala is thirteen years old and entered the eighth grade in the fall of 2010. She has been a volunteer with King Street Cats in Alexandria, Virginia, since 2007. In my volunteer work with King Street Cats, I have witnessed Maya's interaction with the orphanage kitties. She started volunteering so that she could interact with different types of cats and currently volunteers with her mom twice a month to feed the cats in the evening. Her favorite part about volunteering is socializing with the cats and seeing their different personalities. "They are like humans; some are really sweet. It's taking care of another being and having them interact and respond to me that I like."[26] Maya's volunteer work also involves fundraising to help the cats. Some of Maya's accomplishments include hosting a lemonade stand, plant sales, bake sales, and yard sales; each event has a jar for people to donate. She has also worked with a friend to conduct a supply drive with local businesses. "We collected cat food, got toys from Old Towne School for Dogs, and even the mayor donated food and paper towels. We also went to classrooms to collect food. We ended up collecting seven large bags of food, many rolls of paper towels, a lot of cans of cat food, toys, and $120 in donations."[27] In addition, each New Year's Eve, Maya sets up a hot apple cider stand at the Athenaeum in Old Town Alexandria with proceeds going to King Street Cats. Maya's volunteering and fund-raising for King Street Cats has helped her to obtain leadership points with her Girl Scouts troop. Although she has already completed the volunteer hours required of Girl Scouts, she plans to continue earning additional badges and awards, including visiting with a younger troop and telling them about King Street Cats and how to help animals.

Sheryl Pipe has these words of encouragement for adults and kids: "For parents and other adults . . . be good role models. Children learn through modeling our behaviors. If you are driving transports of animals from one area to another in which they have a greater chance for adoption . . . take your children with you. If you are writing a letter in support or opposition of something animal related, if the subject matter allows, discuss the issue with them and perhaps include their thoughts in the letter. Make sure there is time for your children not to be involved in helping animals too . . . everyone needs balance. For kids . . . never underestimate what you can accomplish. A twelve-year-old girl, Mimi Ashland, founded FreeKibble.com, which resulted in the donation of over 390 million pieces of kibble to feed hungry cats and dogs in shelters since April 2008."[28]

Stacey Zeitlin says, "Go for it! If you have an interest in helping others, find ways to make that happen. It might not be directly with the animals at the shelter, but there are so many other ways that you can get involved until you are able to have a more active role with the animals. Remember to always be kind to all creatures and to encourage others to do the same. And thank you for caring so much about others and for wanting to make a difference in the world! As for adults, nurture that kindness and compassion. Help your children find appropriate ways to assist animals and your community by contacting your local facility to see what they need and how children can get involved. Get involved with the education programs that your local facility offers. Role modeling is critical to help them learn humane values. Engage in age-appropriate conversations with children to help them think critically about important animal welfare issues. This will help them grow up into adults who think critically and question how their community treats its animals."[29]

Jane Deming sums up the importance of getting children involved with animals: "If we can get the kids in the next generation to be more compassionate about animals, it will make for a better world."[30]

You Can Do More

- For parents:
  - Allow your children to interact safely with animals. Teaching them how to properly approach, touch, and care for an animal will be a lesson that lasts a lifetime.
  - Allow and encourage your child to volunteer to help animals. If your child is under eighteen years of age, you will need to be present if volunteering at a shelter or with an animal organization. This joint-volunteer

effort is a good opportunity for you and your child to work together to help animals.

○ If you are unable to locate a shelter or organization that will allow children to volunteer, there are other ways for children to get involved, as outlined earlier in this chapter, such as setting up a toy drive, blanket collection, or food donation event.

○ Encourage your child to be creative on events and activities that will benefit animals.

○ If your home is ready for the pitter-patter of four feet, let your child (with your guidance) adopt a pet from an animal shelter or animal welfare organization. Be sure to educate your child on the proper care, feeding, and activities that the new pet needs. And ensure that your child follows through on caring for the pet, as these lessons will last a lifetime.

• For kids:

○ Make a promise to spend time every week to learn about animals. Considering writing stories about what you learn and sharing it with your class, civic groups, or your local newspaper.

○ If you are in Brownies, Girl Scouts, Cub Scouts, or Boy Scouts, find out what animal patches and awards you can earn and work toward earning as many as you can.

○ Check out the ideas listed in this chapter and at least once a year, have a fund-raiser for a cause that protects animals.

○ If you have a Facebook page, post your accomplishments or ideas about how everyone can care for and help animals. Doing this may inspire your friends to get involved.

○ Write letters to your local newspaper if you learn of a situation in which animals need help. Also write letters to local leaders and legislators about issues involving animals. Your voice can be powerful to get others involved.

○ Check out DoSomething.org, which has ideas and service opportunities on a variety of topics, including animals. There are also grant opportunities if you have an amazing idea and need a little money to get it started.

○ Read these books on how you can do more: *A Kid's Guide to Protecting and Caring for Animals: How to Take Action* by Cathryn Berger Kaye and the ASPCA[31] and *Kids Making a Difference for Animals* by Nancy Furstinger and Sheryl Pipe.[32]

Advocating for Shelter Animals: Ending Outdated and Questionable Shelter Practices

In the world of animal protection, it can be quite political and controversial to work or volunteer at an animal shelter. When dealing with the care of animals, you may be subject to the rules and restrictions of local government or a board of directors, while also receiving pressure from the community to change shelter practices. In the sheltering business, you can never make 100 percent of the people happy 100 percent of the time. It can be both rewarding and heartbreaking, all in the span of a day. It is also an emotional business that involves life-and-death situations every day. As an advocate striving to help a shelter and the animals, it is important to keep this in mind.

As in life, there are shelters that thrive, and then there are shelters that struggle. The thriving shelters are filled with workers and volunteers who are committed to the mission to save lives; are happy about their work, which results in good customer service; and they think "outside the cage" to come up with creative solutions to benefit animals. On the other hand, the struggling shelters may be run by people who outwardly appear not to care about animals; they may have limited resources and may not be inclined to change that; they may reject the assistance of volunteers or animal protection organizations; they may warehouse the animals in old, filthy, and cramped quarters with little or no comfort or attention; and euthanasia may occur in mass numbers every day, giving these pets little opportunity for a second chance. Some struggling shelters also continue to cling to outdated practices such as pound seizure and gas chambers, as well as failing to change the image of their shelter from a "pound" to an animal care center that works endlessly to re-home pets.

So which shelter do you want to volunteer for? Most people would choose the thriving shelter because it will be a happier experience. Thriving shelters and their animals absolutely deserve and need your help to keep the title as a thriving shelter. But what about the struggling shelters? What about the animals languishing in those shelters with little hope at life unless you garner up the courage and help? What about the shelters that do not have volunteers or foster homes and do not even have a website that features photos and stories of the animals for adoption? Do you walk away and take the easy route? Or do you roll up your sleeves and make a decision to help animals in the struggling shelters even if your help is not initially welcomed?

This chapter is dedicated to encouraging you to offer help to a shelter, particularly one that is struggling. Thriving shelters will be featured in the next chapter to show how they are making a real difference for animals so that those ideas can be passed on to struggling shelters by people like you who want to make a difference.

GETTING YOUR HANDS DIRTY

It can be rewarding and depressing to volunteer at a shelter that is struggling: depressing in the sense that you may witness droves of cats and dogs coming in on a daily basis with no place to house them and very few adopters knocking on the door, yet rewarding for every frightened and depressed animal that you can comfort, and every pet that you can help find a new home. I frequently hear people say, "I could never go into a shelter because it is too depressing and I'd want to take all the pets home." My response is, "Imagine having to live in a shelter, even for just a few short days, in a cage or kennel, with no blanket or toys, with the smell and sounds of fright and death hanging in the air. Wouldn't you want someone to help you? Those animals did not choose to end up at a struggling shelter, yet they still need our help." It is easy to turn the other way and hope that "someone else" will help animals at a struggling shelter, but it is not the right thing to do if you truly care about helping.

For more than three years, I volunteered at a shelter that was struggling. It was not the worst shelter that I have seen and it did have some redeeming qualities. But overall, it was a depressing shelter. I first visited the shelter in January 1989 when I adopted my cat Chyna. The shelter was old, with cold ceramic tile walls and floors, steel cages without the comfort of a blanket or toy, animals sitting in their own filth, food bowls covered in mold, and jail inmates cleaning cages and feeding the animals. The sights, sounds, and smells plagued me, but I did not know how to make a difference, other than to adopt Chyna and save her life. The shelter did not "allow" volunteers at the time, so I walked out feeling defeated. When I returned almost ten years later, in December 1998, to adopt Oscar and shortly thereafter to adopt Lucy, the shelter had not changed. It was obvious that the shelter did not have volunteers and did nothing to make the shelter appealing to visitors or comfortable for the animals. Again, I did not know how to help. For Christmas that year, I took some plastic ball cat toys and dog treats to the shelter. The staff looked at me in disbelief as if no one had ever brought gifts for the animals. A few of the staff were thankful, but others looked at me as if it were a joke. Everything changed in January 2000 when I heard that the shelter was accepting volunteers. So I joined in and finally felt encouraged that something could be done to help the animals.

Many of my experiences at the shelter, both good and bad, are scattered throughout this book. I quickly became entrenched in the shelter and took on the task of working to safeguard the cats, doing whatever it took to save as many cats from euthanasia, dying of illness or injury in the shelter, or being sold for research. It became all-consuming and I was soon spending twenty to forty hours per week to help the animals, in addition to my stressful career as a prosecuting attorney. When I started, the shelter took in 4,000 animals yearly and was only adopting out approximately 400 per year. After a while, I found it difficult to sleep at night and often had nightmares about the pets at the shelter because there were too many to help, and not enough volunteers. Most of the shelter staff was not supportive of the volunteers' efforts and treated us like we were interfering. All we wanted to do was bring good publicity to the shelter, make it nicer for people and pets, increase adoptions and reduce euthanasia, engage more animal protection organizations to help out, advertise the pets through the local newspaper and a website, and raise money to cover expenses not within the shelter budget. It seemed like a noble cause that anyone would welcome with open arms; instead, we were treated like intruders.

It was difficult to go into the shelter every weekend or during lunch if I had a break from my court docket. But what inspired me were the individual cats that I met, named, photographed, and loved. They were all wonderful and worthy of living. My first adoption in 2000 was a black cat that I named Dimitri. I placed an advertisement in the local newspaper, with my own money, and received a call within a few days from a family that wanted to adopt him. I met the family at the shelter, explained the adoption process, and as they walked out the door with Dimitri, they thanked me for making the experience positive. I was on a high with happiness and started working toward my next adoption "fix." Within a few months, I had my first taste of being a foster home for a four-week-old tortoiseshell kitten that I named Annabelle. She was so tiny, alone in a huge cage, and needed to be bottle-fed. Worried about leaving her home alone, I took her to work one day, and one of the office clerks quickly bonded with her and adopted her. That was the start of fostering more than seventy cats and kittens over the three-and-a-half-year period.

As I write this, I can see the photo albums sitting on my bookshelf with thousands of photos of cats that I helped to get adopted from the shelter or placed in foster care until adopted. Of course, there were cats that I lost to euthanasia, illness, or research. Those were heartbreaking, especially when I begged the shelter director to let me take into foster care a particular cat or kitten that was being taken into the euthanasia room or being led out the back door to a research facility, and was denied. It was those cruel moments with the director, who seemed to take pleasure in watching me and the other volunteers suffer, that fueled my fire to work even harder. Even now, I try to look upon the director and staff through kinder eyes knowing that they worked in a facility of death. In the end, the volunteers not only increased adoptions by more than 400 percent and eventually were re-homing almost half of the animals, but we brought positive publicity to the shelter as well as much-needed extra funds, and we ended pound seizure.

My story is not unique. For almost a decade, I have counseled and commiserated with others who try to help struggling shelters. For example, a county animal control shelter in mid-Michigan had been gassing animals to death in a metal chamber for decades. In April 2010, the county commissioners voted to stop the gas chamber for that shelter. In spite of media publicity announcing that the shelter was transitioning to humane injection euthanasia, the shelter did not transition and instead opted to close its doors effective January 1, 2011. In the time span before the closure, citizens believed that the shelter had stopped gassing and were taking animals there in hopes they would die humanely. They were unaware of the truth. The county humane society, which is a volunteer-run organization, worked endlessly every day to get as many cats and dogs out of the shelter before they were gassed. After a cry for help, I became involved in helping the humane society reach out to advocates and animal protection groups across the state, especially after learning that a cat who was in labor was gassed in the chamber. As difficult as it is, I can only praise the volunteers with the humane society for going into the animal control shelter every day to get as many cats and dogs out to safety as possible, yet knowing that they cannot save them all and having to walk away. The work they are doing is spectacular and deserves recognition. That humane society organization is featured later in this chapter, and they have since taken over operations of the shelter, including the immediate dismantling of the gas chamber.

Although it was difficult to volunteer at a struggling shelter where efforts were unwanted and some cats that I named and loved never made it out alive, it was some of the most rewarding work I have ever done. You may believe that you can never go into a shelter because you love animals too much, but you will be surprised at how strong and effective you can be if you just take that first step. If you love them, you cannot turn your back and hope that "someone else" will get involved. If making a difference were easy, everyone would chip in and the world would be a better place. Making a difference can be difficult, yet it is the right thing to do, and you will be rewarded in so many ways. For every cat and kitten that left the shelter through the front door on its way to a new home or foster home, I could truly count that as a life saved. I even kept a list, which I still have, so that on dark days I could look at all the lives that I helped to save. And one by one, the lives saved started to add up, for both cats and dogs, and even a few ferrets and birds, and an iguana named Fred. Ten pets saved quickly turned to fifty, and then a hundred, then a thousand, and it kept growing. Although very rewarding for me, it completely changed the lives of those animals and gave them a second chance. And it completely changed me in the process. To this day, I still exchange Christmas cards with a few of the cats that I helped find new homes, and it brings me joy to know that my efforts not only saved that pet but brought years of joy to the family who adopted the pet.

That is why volunteering at a struggling shelter is necessary. If you don't, who will? If you truly love animals, you cannot turn away from the plight of animals at a struggling shelter. You may worry that if you become involved in foster care for animals, you will end up keeping them all. I had that worry but simply made a promise (to myself and my three cats) that if I kept even just one foster cat, it would prevent me from helping in the future. So I set boundaries and stuck to them. To this date, I have fostered more than one hundred cats and kittens. Had I kept any of my fosters, all of those cats and kittens would have surely died because I would not have had room to foster them. So by promising yourself that you can help far more animals through fostering them than through adopting them, you will be amazed at how well you can keep your promise.

Thriving shelters are featured in the next chapter to give you ideas of what can be done to help a struggling shelter. Their programs and facilities are innovative. And if you join others, your advocacy can change the lives of animals, one at a time, and change a shelter into a thriving shelter.

Let me share a few words of advice if you want to help a struggling shelter: approach the staff with kindness and understand that their work is difficult and most often unappreciated and criticized; accept that they may initially treat you with suspicion or hostility and recognize that it could be a coping mechanism; offer assistance rather than criticism or pointing out what they are not doing; ask the staff what they need to improve at the shelter for staff, visitors, and the animals; make a list of what you (and other volunteers) can do to make the shelter a better place; and even if your efforts are initially not welcomed, keep trying. After all, the animals are counting on us to help.

ENDING OUTDATED OR QUESTIONABLE SHELTER PRACTICES

One of the first things you can do to help a struggling shelter is learn about their practices. If the shelter engages in a practice that does not benefit the animals, you should first work to end that practice. It can hamper efforts to improve a shelter, and improve its image, if the shelter engages in practices that are not for the benefit of the animals and are frowned upon by the community. If the shelter will work with you to end a questionable or outdated practice, that is the best scenario; if the shelter resists your efforts, then this section will provide you with the tools to make changes to protect the animals.

Communities are outraged when they learn that their local animal shelter is engaging in practices that seem inhumane or questionable. Although the term *inhumane* has always intrigued me because it can mean so many different things, there are two shelter practices that most people in a community deem inappropriate, unwanted, and inhumane: pound seizure and gas chambers. Another practice often results in the immediate euthanasia of animals entering a shelter: labeling animals with behavioral problems.

Pound Seizure

Pound seizure, or pound release, involves shelters providing cats and dogs to U.S. Department of Agriculture Class B dealers (animal brokers), research facilities, or educational institutions for purposes of experimentation. Most people in America do not know that pound seizure occurs in this country, yet it has existed since the 1940s. I call it "America's dirty little secret" because shelters that engage in pound seizure do not advertise the practice to their community. People surrendering their pet, or a stray that they found on the streets, often do not realize that the pet could end up in a laboratory.

Many pound seizure laws were enacted as a reaction to the expanding pet overpopulation problem and a desire to utilize unwanted animals for research rather than breed more animals for research. In essence, why euthanize an animal if that animal could be used in research to help better the lives of humans and animals? Minnesota was the first state to pass a law requiring pound seizure in 1949. But with advancements in non-animal-method research, the need for animals, particularly cats and dogs from shelters and unknown backgrounds, is declining at rapid rates.

So why do some shelters still engage in pound seizure? The answer is still unclear. What I do know is that shelters engaging in pound seizure are most often struggling shelters that do little to promote the adoption of animals and instead euthanize a majority of their animals. In their mind, they may believe that sending the cat or dog to research is providing some overall benefit to society rather than euthanizing the pet. What these shelters fail to recognize is that cats and dogs that are socialized to be in homes are not well suited to be research subjects. Since laboratories prefer animals that can be handled, the obvious choices for cats and dogs would be those that came from a home. However, those pets are not accustomed to being in a cage; being handled by numerous strangers; being deprived of their family, love, and affection; or being deprived of the ability to behave naturally. Yet some shelters still cling to this outdated practice that has been legislatively rejected by seventeen states[1] and countless communities nationwide.

Pound seizure is on the decline, and legislative efforts are working toward abolishing the practice. Currently, thirty-three states allow pound seizure: Alabama, Alaska, Arizona, Arkansas, Colorado, Florida, Georgia, Idaho, Indiana, Iowa, Kansas, Kentucky, Louisiana, Michigan, Minnesota (mandatory), Mississippi, Missouri, Montana, Nebraska, Nevada, New Mexico, North Carolina, North Dakota, Ohio, Oklahoma (mandatory), Oregon, South Dakota, Tennessee, Texas, Utah, Washington, Wisconsin, and Wyoming. Minnesota and Oklahoma mandate pound seizure, which means that the shelter staff cannot deny a Class B dealer or research/ educational facility from taking a cat or dog. The other thirty-one states leave it to the discretion of the shelter or local government to decide whether to engage in the practice.

In my book titled *How Shelter Pets Are Brokered for Experimentation: Understanding Pound Seizure*,[2] I detail the complicated issues regarding pound seizure and why it is inhumane, and now outdated. There are two primary concerns related to pound seizure: First, due to the secrecy of the practice, it results in a betrayal of trust for communities who view and rely on their shelter to be a safe haven for pets. Depending on whether a shelter is an open-admission shelter (and must accept all animals) or a limited admission shelter (and can decide which pets to accept), the broad understanding by Americans is that all shelters, regardless of their name (animal control, humane society, SPCA) or their status (municipal/ government shelter, private shelter), are temporary safe places for pets. Even with people understanding that euthanasia may be an outcome for a shelter pet, it is the practice of pound seizure that makes shelters unsafe for pets and for communities.

Most states have stray dog laws that require people, or animal enforcement officers, to take stray dogs to the shelter so that their families can find them. Advocacy campaigns have encouraged citizens to report animal abuse and neglect so that the animals can be removed from those homes and placed at the shelter for possible adoption. And when you see a stray cat or kitten, you take it to the shelter to keep it safe while it waits for a good home. However, if you act as a Good Samaritan and take a stray dog or cat to the shelter, or report a case of animal abuse or neglect, can you be sure that the pet will not be sold or given away for research? What if you go away on vacation, leaving your pet in the hands of a neighbor or pet sitter, and your pet gets outside and becomes lost? In the summer of 2010, I experienced the loss of a cat that escaped from a shelter, and within minutes he was gone despite of my best efforts to chase after him. Luckily, he was safely found three weeks later. But for most pets, they run away and may enjoy the freedom or are scared and run to a hidden location, thus making it difficult for you to find them. Can you be sure that your pet won't end up at a shelter that engages in pound seizure and be sold or given to a dealer or facility before you return from vacation? That happened to a dog named Conan.

Conan was a young, black and tan, neutered male pit-bull mix who was very loved by his family. In September 2002, Conan's family from lower Michigan went on vacation and arranged for a neighbor to care for him. Like any playful and curious dog, he escaped from his yard unbeknownst to the neighbor and ended up at the animal shelter in a neighboring county. The shelter engaged in pound seizure at the time. The neighbor did not realize that Conan was in a neighboring county shelter. Conan was held at the shelter for the minimum five days before being sold to a Class B dealer. When his family returned from vacation, they searched everywhere for Conan but it was too late. Conan was sold with his identifying rabies tags still on him. Yet no one had contacted the family to retrieve Conan. His family eventually tracked him to a research facility in New York where Conan was utilized as an experimental subject and subsequently killed. The family was devastated.[3]

An even worse scenario involves people struggling with the current financial downturn that must give up their beloved cat or dog because they lost their job and/or their home and cannot afford even the basic necessity of pet food. Imagine taking your longtime companion to the shelter, filled with remorse, but believing that the shelter will find your pet a new home because your pet is friendly and loving. The shelter fails to tell you that they engage in pound seizure, and when you call a week or two later to check on your pet, you learn that it was sold for research. Or worse, the shelter attempts to cover up pound seizure and informs you that your pet has been "re-homed" or euthanized when it may actually be sitting at a Class B dealer facility waiting to be transported hundreds or thousands of miles to a research facility. I have personally observed those scenarios play out.

The second primary concern about pound seizure is the potential presence of Class B dealers at your shelter. Class B dealers are licensed by the U.S. Department of Agriculture to acquire random source animals for resale. A random source animal means any animal that comes from a shelter, auction, or from someone who did not breed or raise the animal.[4] There are more than 1,000 Class B dealers licensed in the United States. However, as of 2010 there are only nine Class B dealers that broker live random source animals for experimentation. These B dealers are located in Indiana, Michigan, Minnesota, Missouri, Ohio, Pennsylvania, and South Carolina.[5] It is these dealers that sometimes troll willing animal shelters for their next supply of cats and dogs that will be resold at a profit. Some dealers have been known to engage in quid pro quo arrangements with a shelter whereby the dealer gets the pick of the shelter cats and dogs in exchange for providing free carcass removal or other "free" services to the shelter. Through these relationships, I have witnessed some shelters prefer to give an animal to a Class B dealer rather than getting it adopted or retrieved by an animal protection organization. It makes me wonder why. What is concerning about the Class B dealer system is not necessarily the system itself, but what has occurred within the system.

For decades, USDA has struggled with the problem of regulating this very small number of licensees, many of whom are repeatedly cited for violating the laws that regulate them. As of 2010, seven of the nine dealers were under investigation for violations of the Animal Welfare Act.[6] Dr. Robert Willems, assistant regional director, eastern region, for USDA/APHIS Animal Care, shares these concerns about shelter cats and dogs used for research purposes:

> There is a very basic problem that I believe is inherent to the business of supplying random source dogs and cats for use in research. That problem is simply this: finding a steady, reliable, and constant supply of dogs and cats that is also legitimate. If the research community is going to use a dealer (vendor) as a supplier of these animals, that dealer must be able to meet the needs of his customers and be able to fill their orders. Finding sources of these animals is not always that easy. Finding legitimate sources is even more difficult. Historically, [random source B dealers] RSBDs have had problems complying with many of the other sections of the Animal Welfare Regulations—housing, veterinary care, feeding, etc. Proper and adequate recordkeeping seems to be the biggest problem the RSBDs have as a group. What seems to be unique to the RSBDs as a group, when compared to any other group of licensees, is a high rate of acquisition of animals for resale coming from non-legitimate sources.[7]

Dealing Dogs was a documentary featured by HBO depicting the undercover investigation of Last Chance for Animals' infiltration into the world of Arkansas Class B dealer C. C. Baird.[8] As a result of that investigation, Baird was arrested, criminally prosecuted, and convicted, and his business was shut down. Historically there has been concern about dealers brokering stolen pets, which is why the USDA has instituted a strict trace-back policy whereby these nine random source dealers undergo quarterly on-site inspections that require tracing of certain animals back to their origination source. Since dealers are not allowed to accept stray animals, or animals from people who did not breed or raise them, the trace-back process is catching a number of violations. USDA is also concerned about a group of individuals called "bunchers," many of whom are not licensed by the USDA but round up animals from a variety of sources (including free-to-good-home advertisements and strays) and sell them to the dealers. It is concern about bunchers that has USDA putting significant resources into attempting to regulate, with little success, a small class of individuals.

The issue reached a level of crisis when Congress ordered a study on the use of random source animals in government-funded research. In May 2009, a report on the *Scientific and Humane Issues in the Use of Random Source Dogs and Cats* was issued by the National Research Council of the National Academies of Science.[9] After months of testimony and information gathering, the council concluded that random source Class B dealers are not needed for providing random source animals for National Institutes of Health–funded research projects. The report, which is available online,[10] details the committee's concerns regarding questionable and illegal conduct of dealers, inhumane conditions at some dealer facilities, as well as the USDA's difficulties in enforcing compliance.

Although the problem with pound seizure and Class B dealers is discussed in great detail in my book, *How Shelter Pets Are Brokered for Experimentation: Understanding Pound Seizure*, is this a practice of a thriving and quality shelter? Is this a practice that a community will support? In a 2009 survey by the American Humane Association, more than 3,000 animal welfare professionals and advocates were asked about pound seizure. More than 97 percent indicated they would not take a stray animal to a pound seizure shelter and would not donate to a shelter that engages in pound seizure.[11]

Many states do not keep exact numbers of animals that become victims of pound seizure. However, USDA records for a one-year period covering

November 2007 through November 2008 showed that 947 dogs and 230 cats were obtained from shelters by Class B dealers.[12] That may seem like a small number, and the numbers are declining every year; however, for those 947 dogs and 230 cats, their life as a family pet was over. Most states do not require shelters to report their annual intake or disposition numbers and do not track pound seizure numbers. However, Michigan shelters are required to report pound seizure data, and the practice has declined from approximately fifteen shelters in 2004 providing 2,344 cats and dogs to Class B dealers to only two shelters in 2009 providing 321 animals. Yet in spite of the significant decline, a 2009–2010 bill that I authored to end pound seizure in Michigan was met with extreme opposition. The opposition from the three Michigan Class B dealers was predictable; however, the opposition from the Michigan Farm Bureau, Michigan Veterinary Medical Association, Michigan Department of Agriculture, and Michigan Association of Counties was shocking and disturbing. Why those organizations wanted to cling to an outdated practice that had been rejected by all Michigan shelters except two was beyond anyone's comprehension.

For more than three years, I volunteered in a shelter that engaged the services of a Class B dealer. After successfully ending pound seizure, I now help advocates in other pound seizure communities to eliminate the practice. My personal experience with dealers is that they pursue what I perceive as suspicious and secretive activities. I have witnessed dealers creating relationships with the shelter staff or even community politicians so that those individuals refuse to listen to their constituents about concerns regarding the presence of a dealer at the shelter; where the dealers refuse to engage in open disclosure about where they resell the cats and dogs; and where shelters have provided preferential treatment to the dealer rather than allowing an adoption or rescue by an animal protection organization. Some shelters allow a Class B dealer to enter and obtain cats and dogs before the shelter opens. Some of the pets are first eligible for adoption on the day that the dealer arrives. These pets have not even had one minute to be available for adoption, and it should cause us to question why this is being allowed. I observe too many shelter animals being caught in the struggle between the dealer, a shelter clinging to the practice of pound seizure as if it were a lifeline, and the community and animal protection organizations wishing to get cats and dogs safely out of the shelter.

To help with advocacy to end pound seizure, appendix A contains key points to assert and facts to back up those assertions. It is fortunate that the practice is declining because one by one, advocates are getting involved and standing up against this practice. In Michigan, there were fifteen pound seizure shelters in 2003 and only two in 2010. This is all because people like you cared enough to get involved and make a difference.

Pound seizure is questionable because of the secrecy of the practice, and it is outdated because research is moving away from animal models toward more technologically advanced practices. The betrayals are end-less when dealing with the pound seizure. For a detailed account of pound seizure in the United States, including stories from advocates winning the war against pound seizure, and specific techniques on how to advocate to end the practice in your community, read *How Shelter Pets Are Brokered for Experimentation: Understanding Pound Seizure.*[13]

Inhumane Euthanasia

You may be surprised to learn that some shelters end the lives of animals in a way that a majority of people would question. Although the practice is on the decline, some shelters still use carbon monoxide or carbon dioxide gas chambers to kill shelter animals. Some shelters even shoot shelter cats and dogs.[14] This section will focus on ending gas chambers.

For clarification, I use the word *euthanasia* when discussing the injec-tion method, which is the most approved and commonly used method to end the life of an animal. I use the word *kill* only as it relates to gas chambers, drowning, and other inhumane methods, because killing, to me, involves a violent and painful end of life. Euthanizing an animal, when done properly, is a gentle, painless, and compassionate way to end life. However, when dealing with outdated methods, such as gas chambers, I have no problem labeling that method as *killing* an animal.

Why do I make this distinction? Ending the lives of shelter pets is an unfortunate symptom of society's improper care of animals and puts the burden on shelters to handle the problem. Although there is a movement in the United States to rename all euthanasia as killings, I feel doing that in relation to humane injection methods mislabels an already tragic situ-ation and condemns shelter workers for doing something they have little control over. Providing the harshest label for ending the life of a shelter animal may get people's attention, but I fear that it actually deters people from helping those shelters and provides a self-fulfilling prophecy ending in the death of those animals. Entire books have been written about this topic. However, this section narrows the debate to focus on advocacy to end gas chamber killings, an outdated practice that has been rejected by a majority of shelters.

When gassing an animal to cause its death, the gas is pumped into a metal chamber that is sometimes filled with more than one animal at a time. Some gas chambers are nothing more than steel barrels (similar to an oil barrel). Testimonials from shelter workers and experts say that the animals are terrified to be locked in the chamber and scratch and claw to get out; they may even fight with each other. It can take up to twenty-five minutes for a dog or cat to die in a gas chamber. And there have been some instances where the animals do not die, yet are tossed out with the dead bodies. That happened to a dog named Davey who was put into a gas chamber in the Davey County Animal Control shelter in North Carolina in 2005. Along with dogs that were dead, Davey was dumped in a landfill and presumed to be dead. However, he was still barely alive and was found wandering around. He was rescued, has since been adopted, and is the namesake behind attempts to legislate the ban of gas chambers in North Carolina.

Although no one wants to think about a shelter pet having to be euthanized, it is a sad fact that 3 to 4 million shelter pets per year have their lives ended because they were not adopted and the shelters ran out of space.[15] Although it is easy to be upset with shelters that euthanize, or have high euthanasia rates, we need to keep in mind that the shelters did not cause the pet overpopulation or pet irresponsibility problem in their community, yet they are left to deal with the aftermath of too many pets and not enough homes.

If an animal needs to be euthanized, the most humane and preferred method is to use an injection after the animal has been sedated. This is what occurs if you have a gravely ill or injured pet; you take your pet to the veterinary clinic, and they are gently put to sleep. So why should a shelter animal have any less consideration? It is sad, and sometimes unthinkable, for people to get involved in campaigns for more humane euthanasia. After all, if you love animals, you do not want to see them euthanized solely because the shelter has run out of space and adoptable homes. But given the reality that too many shelters still engage in gas chamber killings, we owe it to those animals to get involved in this issue and advocate for them to have a humane end to life.

Euthanasia by injection (EBI) is the method endorsed for shelter cats and dogs by the National Animal Control Association,[16] the American

Veterinary Medical Association,[17] the Association of Shelter Veterinarians,[18] American Humane Association,[19] American Society for the Prevention of Cruelty to Animals,[20] and The Humane Society of the United States.[21] Yet it might surprise you to learn that some state veterinary medical associations have lobbied against legislation that would ban the gas chamber because the American Veterinary Medical Association Guidelines on Euthanasia lists instances in which gas can be used on a cat or dog.[22] For example, the American Veterinary Medical Association (AVMA) states that carbon dioxide and carbon monoxide is only suitable for *most* small species.[23] However, old, neonatal, and injured animals are often biologically unable to absorb the gas as readily as larger or healthier animals, which prolongs trauma and stress.[24] The question then becomes, what is considered a small species and what weight of dog would be considered too large for gassing? Efforts to change the AVMA recommendations to prohibit gassing of cats and dogs began in 2010. But in the meantime, the veterinary associations are powerful advocates that have blocked some legislative bills from banning gas chambers. That occurred in Michigan with the 2009–2010 bill that I worked on, through American Humane, to ban gas chambers in shelters.

EBI is not only the safest, gentlest, and most humane way to end an animal's life, but it is also safer for the people working in a shelter. With EBI, loss of consciousness occurs within three to five seconds, and death within five minutes; whereas animals in a gas chamber may be in the chamber for up to twenty-five minutes and only lose consciousness and brain function after their vital organs first shut down, causing prolonged suffering and distress. Referring to the horrors of carbon monoxide, Doug Fakkema, the nation's animal euthanasia expert, has stated, "[t]he animal is in a warm or hot box, usually with other animals. They don't know what is going on. They get dizzy, and then they panic. Fights can break out, and animals' calls can sometimes be heard."[25]

There have been too many reports of shelter workers being injured or killed because of a faulty gas chamber. Carbon monoxide poses a danger to humans because it is colorless, tasteless, odorless, and highly explosive.[26] A gas chamber must be constantly checked and maintained to ensure there are no cracks in the structure or failing seals. When carbon monoxide is released in a confined area, it can cause asphyxiation, kidney damage, or induced coma. In 2008, an explosion in the Iredell County, North Carolina, animal services' gas chamber revealed that the equipment in the vicinity of the chamber was not explosion proof. A shelter worker was in the room at the time, and other personnel were nearby. Photographs taken of the interior of the gas chamber showed that the insides were charred from the flames. There were dogs inside the chamber at the time of the explosion. In 2000, a shelter worker in Tennessee was asphyxiated while operating a faulty gas chamber, and in 1997 a shelter veterinarian in Illinois was severely injured while operating a gas chamber. In contrast, there are no documented reports of any shelter worker being killed from an accidental injection of sodium pentobarbital.[27]

When shelter workers have to euthanize an animal, regardless of the method, it can cause serious physical, emotional, and psychological trauma for that worker. It is also a moral stressor, especially for those who entered the animal sheltering business to help animals.[28] This can cause shelter workers to displace their guilt and frustration on the public and to those who are relinquishing their animals.[29] When you compound those issues with gas chamber killings, the trauma may be enhanced. This might help to explain some of the perceived resistance in shelters with high euthanasia rates and/or that employ the gas chamber.

In a 2008 study to address euthanasia-related stress, more than three hundred shelter workers involved in euthanasia were surveyed on what would help them handle the stress of euthanizing animals. Some of the responses included being supportive and encouraging support from others (including making sure that noneuthanizing staff or people do not criticize those who must euthanize); providing counseling and support groups; rotating staff; providing better communication as to why euthanasia is occurring with certain animals; making the euthanasia room more peaceful (which I believe would be difficult to implement in a shelter with a gas chamber); taking time to pay homage to the animals that were euthanized; and making efforts to prevent euthanasia.[30]

Although some people may think that it is easier for a shelter worker to simply load the animals into a gas chamber, flip the switch, walk away and not have to witness what occurs, no human being would be able to block out what happens to the animals in the chamber. Physically walking away is not the same as psychologically walking away. So ending gas chambers is a small step toward making shelters better for both people and pets.

To help with advocacy to end gas chambers, appendix B contains key points and facts to assert. Assisting a shelter in removing some of these outdated practices can take time, due to restrictions from the local government, financial restrictions, or support for this practice. While you are working on this issue, the best way to help the animals is to help the shelter increase adoptions and mobilize animal protection organizations and adoption partners. Chapter 7 will provide you with the tools to be successful in rescuing and transporting animals for re-homing options.

Pets with Negative Labels

There are still some shelters across the United States that engage in a practice I believe is outdated and unnecessary: immediately euthanizing a pet that comes to a shelter with a negative label. I first discovered this practice in 2002. Garbo was a beautiful gray tabby with sparkling green eyes. She was also very pregnant. I removed Garbo from the shelter where I volunteered and brought her to my home, where she gave birth to eight healthy, beautiful kittens that were all adopted in pairs when they were three to four months old. One pair, Gumby and Gretel, were victims of negative labels. A few months after they were adopted to what I believed was a loving family with two young girls, I received a cell phone voice message that they were in trouble. After a long day in court, a fellow volunteer had left me a voicemail that the family had taken Gumby and Gretel to the local humane society shelter (a different shelter from where I volunteered) because the kittens were not using the litter box. As I frantically drove to this shelter, about twenty miles away from where I was working, this volunteer informed me that the humane society shelter frequently euthanizes pets upon intake if they have a behavioral issue, such as not using the litter box. As I was driving ninety miles an hour trying to get to the shelter before it was too late, I tried to phone someone at the shelter in hopes of intervening and saving their lives. I kept getting an answering machine and was not able to speak to anyone. When I arrived at the shelter, completely out of breath and trembling with fear, I was informed by the shelter director that Gumby and Gretel had been euthanized within five minutes of arriving at the shelter. I was inconsolable and kept asking why they called a volunteer with my organization about Gumby and Gretel but did not allow any time for us to retrieve them. The shelter director simply informed me that it was their policy to euthanize animals with behavioral issues. Gumby and Gretel were only six-month-old kittens, and any so-called behavioral issue, I believed, could be quickly corrected. I then called the adopter to find out why she violated the adoption contract and took them to a shelter rather than return them to me. The tone of her voice made it clear that she did not care, and she stated that the kittens were afraid of her children. Once she told me that, I knew that was why they had stopped using the litter box. So rather than having the children educated on how to treat kittens with kindness, Gumby and Gretel lost their lives. This occurred in September 2002, and I have never forgotten what happened to them. I still have their photos and cherish one particular image of gray-white Gumby at four weeks of age sitting in my hand and looking up with his big blue eyes.

Gumby and Gretel's premature death broke my heart because it was unnecessary. Unfortunately, this practice still continues in some shelters today, even shelters that I would label as thriving shelters. While writing this book in October 2010, I received a phone call from the president of the cat orphanage where I volunteer. She informed me that she had been at a nearby shelter having one of our found cats scanned for a microchip when she observed a family coming in with their cat. She overheard the family explaining that the cat had nipped at their new baby. The shelter staff informed the family that if they left the cat at the shelter, it would be immediately euthanized because of the label that it had bitten a child. Understandably, our orphanage president was very distraught hearing that this shelter condemns animals that check in with a behavioral problem. She spoke with the shelter staff, who said that there was nothing they could do regarding their policy. When she conveyed the story to me, it brought back images of Gumby and Gretel, and I felt compelled to add this outdated and unnecessary practice to this chapter.

In my volunteer work with cats, many cats that I have met over the past ten years that were given up due to a behavioral problem (usually litter box issues) no longer had the problem when they were in our care or adopted to a new home. I have come to believe that some cats and dogs may engage in negative behavior to get our attention and to let us know that they are unhappy. Having accidents in the home, or engaging in other negative behavior, is an excellent method to get our attention. If it is not a medical issue causing the problem, then it may be the pet's message that they are unhappy and may need to be re-homed. And I have seen this successfully done with many cats.

I have also come to believe that when people are surrendering their pet to a shelter with a negative label, shelters need to create an environment where people will be honest about their pet. Some people who surrender their pets to a shelter may not provide an accurate reason for the surrender; they may not want to be judged by the shelter staff for giving up a cat because they grew bored of the cat or did not bond to the cat, or they are giving up a dog because they cannot admit that they failed to properly train the dog. So some people create a reason that is more socially acceptable, such as the cat is peeing outside the litter box or the dog bit someone in the home. The animal should be given the chance to enter the shelter with a clean slate, and then the shelter staff or volunteers can assess whether the label is accurate. For all we know, the dog may have bitten someone during an incident of domestic violence in the home and while trying to protect its caregiver, or the cat may be peeing outside the box because the family has not cleaned the box in weeks. Neither scenario is the fault of the pet, and we should aim to give the animal the benefit of the doubt.

For those animals that truly have behavioral or medical issues, shelters may argue that they do not have the space to care for or rehabilitate animals with behavioral issues, or the funds to help with medical disorders. But this is where you can help. For animals that intake with medical issues, such as broken limbs, injuries from being hit by a car or attacked by an animal, cancer, or other ailments that will require expensive medical care, offer to raise money specifically to help that animal and offer to find a foster home or adoption partner to take on the pet. If it were your own pet, you would want to provide the necessary care, right? If a family does not have the funds to provide medical care and surrenders their pet to a shelter, that animal should receive the care to heal and be adopted to a new home.

For pets that intake with behavioral issues, do not condemn them with a label given by their former family. Take the time to assess the pet and determine if the behavior is true and what caused the behavior. If the pet was reacting negatively to a new baby, then adopt the pet to a home without young children (or the possibility of future children); if the pet was surrendered because it hides and does not interact with people, consider adopting it to an older couple or a home that is calm; if the pet was surrendered because it bit another pet or person, consider that something may have happened to cause that reaction and have an animal behaviorist assess the pet. For every issue, there is a solution. By offering your help for these animals, in the form of raising funds, providing foster care, locating an adoption organization to take on the pet, or working with the pet at the shelter, many of these animals can be saved from automatic euthanasia.

TWO ORGANIZATIONS MAKING A DIFFERENCE FOR STRUGGLING SHELTERS

Although countless animal organizations are working to end question-able practices in their local animal shelters, I wanted to feature two groups I know, and support, to demonstrate that even though they are advocating for change, they are still making progress, albeit baby steps each day.

Help Furry Friends (Gratiot County, Michigan)

Help Furry Friends[31] is a nonprofit organization in mid-Michigan that has been advocating to eliminate pound seizure and gas chambers from the Gratiot County Animal Control shelter for many years. Gratiot County Animal Control is a rural shelter that intakes approximately 1,500 animals yearly. The group involves the advocacy of four individuals, including Maria Lott, who agreed to be interviewed. I have been in awe of the unwavering dedication that Help Furry Friends has in helping the shelter animals and steadfastly working to encourage the shelter toward better practices to help the animals.

I have always been fascinated with how people become involved in serious animal advocacy causes. For Maria, it involved the tragedy of her cat, Ozzy, escaping a few weeks after moving from Phoenix to Alma, Michigan. She searched for Ozzy but never found him. "A few years later I found out that our local shelter had a contract with a dealer who took live, stray animals from the shelter for research. I also found out that our shelter euthanizes by gassing. I want to save everyone's 'Ozzy' from meeting such an end. It is very important to me personally that everyone in our county is aware of the practices of our local shelter and to get them stopped. Being involved with Help Furry Friends has helped me toward that goal."[32]

At the beginning, Maria read as much information as she could find about pound seizure. She also searched for other advocates with the same passion. As others became involved, they shared ideas, developed stra-tegic plans, and saw things change from a unified movement. However, her organization was discouraged by the lack of response from the county commissioners, who are the local decision makers involving the shelter. "No matter how prepared we were, they continue to ignore facts as presented. They seem to be entrenched in 'that is the way it has always been done' and were often unwilling to try something different. We have found that often the public and media involvement has more power than does reason and detail when it comes to persuading politicians on any level."[33]

Though they struggle against the clock every day, knowing that the Class B dealer or gas chamber awaits the cats and dogs at the shelter, they keep on working and have made a difference for hundreds of animals since January 2009. Maria shares these words of advice: "Find others that are passionate about making changes happen in your community. Join forces, get organized, establish goals, and figure out ways to get them accomplished. There are so many caring, compassionate people and organizations that want to make a difference and are willing to help."[34]

In December 2010, I traveled to Gratiot County for an event featuring my book on pound seizure. I was pleased to see the shelter director and another county official attend the event and learn more about why pound seizure is harming their community and animal shelter. I left the event with hopes that change will occur soon for the shelter animals.

The Humane Society of Midland County (Midland, Michigan)

Neil Wackerle is the president of the the Humane Society of Midland County and has been assisting the animals at the Midland County Animal Shelter, a county-funded municipal shelter, since 1982 and more officially since 2008. The Humane Society of Midland County is composed of volunteers and foster homes and also offers transport services to relocate animals from the animal control shelter to animal welfare organizations. In January 2011, the group took over operations of the Midland County Animal Shelter, which is now known as the Humane Society of Midland County shelter.

Neil and his volunteers work countless hours each week for the animals; an estimated sixty to eighty hours per week for Neil. He is motivated to work long hours each day because the animal control shelter uses a gas chamber to kill its animals, a practice that keeps Neil awake at night.

Before taking over operation of the shelter, Neil and his volunteers spent many hours each week directly interacting with the shelter animals, including walking the dogs, cuddling the cats, cleaning and disinfecting cages, speaking with potential adopters, and even having their own volunteer veterinarian provide care to the sick and injured shelter animals. The number-one goal of Neil and the Humane Society of Midland County was to get as many pets as possible into foster care or to other organizations while advocating to end the outdated practice of gas chambers. Neil explains, "I have witnessed an animal die in the chamber, and the visions haunt me daily."[35]

In April 2010, the Midland County commissioners, the political body with oversight on the animal control shelter, voted to ban gas chambers at the shelter. As explained to me by one of the commissioners, the vote was a recommendation to the shelter and was not a mandate to change. Even with an offer from American Humane Association to provide the funds to transition the shelter from gas chamber to injection euthanasia, including free training, free supplies, and a buyback of the chamber, the animal control shelter did not make any effort to transition. In the end, and for several reasons, the commissioners voted to close the shelter effective January 1, 2011, and the Humane Society of Midland County has taken over the shelter, though without any county funding to support their efforts to care for an estimated 2,500 animals yearly.

When asked what struggles they encounter, Neil explains, "My biggest problem is the politicians with no compassion. The next would be the uneducated people that do not understand the importance of spaying/neutering their pet. Third, again, would be the uneducated people that believe an animal is a possession and not a commitment."[36]

Throughout 2010, I have communicated back and forth with Neil regarding issues with the animal control shelter's gassing practices as well as efforts to remove animals from the shelter and transport them to safety. I will never forget one conversation in the summer of 2010 where Neil told me how many cats, including pregnant and nursing cats, needed to get out of the shelter within the next day. It does not take much effort to empower me to call on my network to help animals, but when Neil informed me that a pregnant cat in labor had been placed in the gas chamber the previous day, I could not get that image out of my mind and it motivated me to find as many local organizations as possible that could help out. The efforts were successful for that day, and approximately twenty cats were taken from the shelter. But for every successful day, there is the next day when more help is needed. It is truly never-ending to try to help animals at a shelter that engages in outdated practices.

The work is exhausting for Neil and his volunteers, yet they keep going while finding rewards for what they accomplish each day. Neil shares one particular story that stands out in his mind.

"We rescued a senior female Lab once. Shortly after rescuing her, she gave birth to thirteen puppies. Two puppies died, and all the rest had issues that we found out after we adopted them out. Some of the people wanted their money returned. Some chose to keep the dog with our financial help for veterinary bills. Most of the puppies had sight issues if they weren't totally blind. Some had balance issues. One of the first puppies adopted was by a family with an autistic child. The family kept in constant contact at first. They told us how the boy had always fought going to bed and then would not sleep anyway. After they got Dexter the puppy, the boy and the puppy slept together, peacefully through the night. When the puppy started having the health issues, they spent thousands on him to no avail. They finally contacted us to return the dog. The child did not understand and told his parents if they returned Dexter, he would run away. They kept Dexter.

At an event later in the year, I was standing at the bottom of the stairs, waiting to go on stage to speak. They were having a contest for dogs, and as the trainers and their dogs came down the stairs, I noticed one young boy and his dog struggling with each step. The dog had one eye, and both the dog and the boy had trouble negotiating the stairs. Before I went on the stage they announced the winner; the young boy and his Lab won. Up they came, struggling with each step. I then realized it was Dexter and his young boy. They went up each step, accepted their prize, and struggled even more. I couldn't decide which one to carry down the stairs, Dexter or the young boy. They didn't want help. I had a huge lump in my throat and had a hard time speaking, but it was such a great feeling that I had for the both of them."[37]

Neil has countless stories of animals in desperate need of help. Although not all have been saved over the years from the gas chamber, there are those joyous moments where an animal, particularly an injured animal, is given help. In one situation, Neil learned that there was an "old Lab" in the isolation ward, a location where Neil and others were not welcome. Neil was taken to the dog, who was only about two years old and was in agony from a compound fracture of its right front leg. Neil explains, "When I opened the cage, she limped out and was so happy to see me. She wagged her tail so hard that it hurt my leg. She allowed me to examine her and never even cried, growled, or expressed anything but happiness for the attention she was getting. Finally she sat down as best as she could, looked up at me, and her eyes expressed, 'are you going to help me?'"[38] Neil did help this dog, who later became known as Bree. He could not let her lie there in agony only to be put in the gas chamber. A member of the Humane Society of Midland County raised money through one of her classes to help pay for the surgery. Once Bree was mended, she and Neil visited the class at an assembly to thank them for their generosity. "Bree dragged me up and down every aisle in the auditorium and thanked each student individually."[39] Bree was eventually adopted by a veterinarian due to her need for follow-up care from her broken leg. Neil still sees Bree every now and then; she runs up to him with her funny gait, sits at his feet, looks up with her big brown eyes, wagging her whole body and saying thank you.

So why does Neil spend a majority of his waking hours each day working to help the animals at this one shelter? It is because of animals like Bree and Dexter who need someone to give them another chance. He does so out of determination to make a difference in an animal's life, no matter how big or small. And that determination paid off in January 2011 when his organization took over operations of the shelter. The first order of business was to get rid of the gas chamber.

If you live in a community with a struggling shelter and/or a shelter with unnecessary practices that do not benefit animals, get involved. Neil advises to start by getting the community educated, aware, and on your side to promote change. Then you will have more power and a stronger voice to advocate for change. But at the same time, also be available to help the shelter. No one likes outsiders pressuring for change that are unwilling to step up and help. For Neil and his volunteers, they work every day to help the animal control shelter while also pushing for change.

You Can Do More

- Celebrate adopt-a-pet months throughout the year:
  - January = Adopt-a-Bird Month
  - February = Adopt-a-Rabbit Month
  - April = Adopt-a-Ferret Month
  - June = Adopt-a-Cat Month
  - September = Adopt-a-Less-Adoptable Pet Week
  - October = Adopt-a-Dog Month
  - November = Adopt-a-Senior-Pet Month

Visit www.petfinder.com to learn more about these special events and what specific things you can do to help promote adoptions.

- Be adventurous and create your own adopt-a-pet event, such as Adopt-a-Black Pet Week, Adopt-a-Kitten Month, Adopt-a-Special-Needs-Pet Month, and Adopt-a-Paired-Sibling Month. Create posters depicting photos of pets in the featured event that can be placed around your community or at adoption events.
- Donate to help your local shelter, and the animal protection organization helping the shelter, to save lives. Do not be hesitant to donate to a shelter that euthanizes animals or has a high euthanasia rate. Your donation could help save a life, especially if you designate the money to help save a pet.
- Donate items to the shelter from their wish list. If the shelter does not have a wish list, ask if you can help them create a list of items that are needed and not covered by the shelter budget. Items could include kitten or puppy food, canned pet food, mother's milk formula for abandoned kittens and puppies, blankets, toys, leashes, newspapers to line the cages, flea and tick treatment, and grooming supplies.
- Contact your local shelter(s) to ask how they euthanize animals or whether they provide animals to dealers or research/training institutions. If the shelter engages in gas chamber killing or pound seizure:
  - Ask the shelter if anything can be done to stop the practice. If the shelter is agreeable to stopping either practice but is precluded due to financial constraints or local government policies, ask if you can help them to advocate for change. Offer to help raise money to switch over to more humane practices, or research how ending these practices will benefit the shelter and the community overall.
  - If the shelter is accepting of pound seizure and/or gas chambers and does not want to change, then contact the unit of government that oversees the shelter and ask them to stop the practice. Reach out to your community to let them know of the practice and garner support. Attend local government meetings and publicly ask for the practice to stop.
- Volunteer at your local shelter to help animals. This can encompass providing foster care for needy animals, updating a website that features the pets, photographing the shelter animals and posting them on Petfinder.com or AdoptAPet.com, being shelter adoption counselor, or making the cages and kennels friendlier for the animals (with blankets, toys, welcoming cage cards). Volunteer options will vary based on the size of the shelter. Smaller shelters may have more opportunities and more need for volunteer help.

- If your local shelter does not have a volunteer program, offer to co-ordinate a program. The volunteer program can simply be a group of people who want to help the shelter or can be more formalized with a name, such as a "friends of the shelter" group, or even organized as a state nonprofit or a 501(c)(3) nonprofit. If the shelter is hesitant to have volunteers, find out why in a nonconfrontational manner. The shelter may simply have a misperception of what volunteers can do to help or concerns about liability. With any volunteer program, it will only be as good as the foundation it is created upon. So be sure to read about how to create a volunteer program, how to select volunteers that will be beneficial (and not cause conflict at the shelter), have volunteers sign a liability waiver agreement, and institute policies for the volunteers.
- Offer to create a foster care program to help the shelter with needy animals, such as pregnant and nursing animals, orphaned kittens and puppies, older pets, pets with medical or behavioral problems, or depressed or frightened pets. Be sure to interview foster homes to make sure they are appropriate for this volunteer work and are willing to follow policies and procedures (such as how to obtain veterinary care, when to bring the animals to adoption events, etc.).
- Offer to create and/or update a shelter website that includes photographs and descriptions of the pets. Pets can be posted on Petfinder.com or AdoptAPet.com. Petfinder also provides a free one-page website.
- Offer help to promote adoptions with cute marketing campaigns or low-cost adoptions matching senior pets to senior citizens.
- Offer to do laundry for the shelter.
- Create a pet sponsorship program where people can donate to help a specific animal.
- Create a "kitten kindergarten" class for those who adopt kittens from your shelter. Just as people who adopt puppies may go through puppy classes, they should also be educated about kittens, how to kitten-proof a home, how to train a cat not to scratch (to avoid declawing), cat behavior and how to correct a problem, and how to raise a wonderful cat.
- Offer to oversee the lost-and-found information submitted to the shelter so that people who found a lost pet, or people who have lost a pet, can be connected.
- Organize a community adopt-a-thon event. Seattle, Washington, hosts "Woofstock" and invites area animal protection organizations and shelters to bring their pets to be adopted. In Detroit, Michigan, there is

"Meet Your Best Friend at the Zoo" and "Pet-A-Palooza," where shelters and animal protection organizations come together for an adopt-a-thon.

- Start an affordable spay/neuter clinic in your community. Reach out to local veterinarians and ask them to donate even just a half-day, once a month, to provide free or affordable sterilizations.
- Start an affordable vaccination clinic. And consider making these clinics mobile so that they reach areas of the community that need the most help.
- If you are skilled at writing grants, offer to seek out and write grant proposals for a shelter.

CHAPTER 6

Models for Thriving Animal Organizations: Saving More Lives through Innovation

Many Americans dream of the day when animal shelters no longer have to euthanize healthy and treatable pets simply because of lack of space or lack of adoptable homes. The term *no kill* has gained popularity in recent years and is a concept that resonates with many people, especially those needing to relinquish a pet and wishing to do so at a shelter that will keep their pet until it is adopted. However, it is also controversial in the sheltering community and has not been fully embraced for a variety of reasons that go far beyond the scope of this book. So what does *no kill* really mean?

As I discussed in the previous chapter, the term *kill* has become a loaded word in the world of animal protection because, to me, the word implies a violent and painful death; but I think we can agree that most shelter workers do not get into the business for the purpose of killing animals. That is why the term *euthanasia* is preferred, as it describes a painless death when the injection method is used properly. However, a brief discussion of the no-kill movement is needed to understand its current place in society.

There are many differing views on what no kill actually encompasses. Tracy Coppola, formerly a policy and government affairs associate for American Humane Association, spent two years (2008–2009) researching and writing a paper titled *Examining America's Pet Overpopulation Crisis, Controversy and Solutions*. She states that the term *no kill* is starting to be examined by communities in response to euthanasia of healthy or treatable animals. "A shelter that is 'no kill' is ideally a shelter that is able to save all its healthy, adoptable and/or treatable animals from euthanasia, or 'killing,' which is the movement's preferred terminology. The term is often confused by citizens concerned about our nation's heartbreaking euthanasia numbers in that it appears to suppose that a 'no kill' shelter would not euthanize *any* animal whatsoever."[1]

U.S. shelters receive 8 to 9 million animals every year, with approximately 4 million being euthanized. Those numbers may be higher due to the 2008–2010, and beyond, financial crisis resulting in a record number of family pets being surrendered to shelters. The numbers are staggering and at times seem unnecessary. The No Kill Advocacy Center[2] was started to help and persuade shelters to rethink the process of housing and re-homing animals. The center has created its model for change, called the No Kill Equation, and educates others through conferences, drafting no-kill legislation, and publishing books, such as *Redemption*[3] and *Irreconcilable Differences: The Battle for the Heart & Soul of America's Animal Shelters*.[4] The No Kill Advocacy Center has also filed lawsuits to stop shelters from "killing" healthy, treatable, and adoptable animals.

Although the no-kill movement has been controversial and has come under fire from many in the animal protection community, one certain thing is that no-kill fever is sweeping the nation and Americans are growing more intolerant of senseless euthanasia and the epidemic of pet overpopulation. Yet it is Americans who have contributed to this problem by not spaying or neutering their pets and treating pets like disposable objects; it is not solely the shelters causing the problem, it is also the people in communities.

The phrase *no kill* raises the ire of the animal sheltering community that knows what a virtually unreachable goal it currently entails. I say virtually because communities can take positive steps to reduce and work toward eliminating euthanasia. Citizens love the concept of no kill yet have little realistic view of what is required to reach that status. I frequently hear people say that they will only donate to a no-kill shelter, will only volunteer at a no-kill shelter, and will only surrender their pets to a no-kill shelter. All of those are noble beliefs, and the shelters that are labeled no kill appreciate and need the donations and volunteer hours to maintain their good work. However, by adopting a "no kill or nothing" mentality, we are condemning a majority of shelters to solve a problem that they did not create, limiting their resources and chance at success, and condemning those shelter animals in the process. To put it in perspective, an animal advocate once told me, "You don't get mad at the American Cancer Society for creating cancer, so don't get mad at shelters who euthanize, because they did not create the pet overpopulation problem." So once we can gain a little perspective on how big of a problem our shelters are facing, we can then create a plan to work together to solve it. I do not profess to know how to solve the crisis of euthanasia in the United States, but small steps can be taken by everyone (and yes, that means you) to start walking down the path toward saving lives.

So why isn't every shelter in America taking this challenge to reduce euthanasia? Tracy Coppola explains, "The main struggle is the number of animals that enter an open-admission shelter each day, and the unpredictability of this number. Sometimes the struggle will lie in a misguided temptation to save each and every animal the shelter takes in no matter what. In many cases, this has led to shelters warehousing animals in subpar conditions, even if the animals are sick and dying. In turn, this takes away emphasis on strengthening other life-saving initiatives like spay/neuter and adoption. Another scenario is when a shelter struggles to meet a no-kill mandate set by local government; these mandates can be dangerous without additional government support and without the necessary resources in place."[5]

Dr. Mark Goldstein, a veterinarian and president of San Diego Humane Society and SPCA, has an innovative theory on how to handle the dilemma of animal care and protection and ensure that homeless animals find homes. As featured later in this chapter, San Diego Humane has not euthanized any healthy or treatable animals since 2001. Through its various programs, and including its investigation and animal field services work, this shelter has helped more than 38,000 animals per year, and Dr. Goldstein has earned his opinion on how to help animals and move other agencies to what San Diego Humane has achieved.

Dr. Goldstein believes that we first must improve the welfare of animals in communities, rather than focusing on increasing adoptions and reducing euthanasia. If you do the first, the rest will follow. Basically, focusing on adoptions and euthanasia numbers (a quantity issue) works on the symptom and not the underlying problem of how people treat their animals (a quality issue). He explains, "We want to create circumstances where people come to us to adopt out of love and not out of desperation."[6] If we are to be truly successful, we need people to take better care of their animals, to keep their animals and help them through health or behavioral issues that arise, and to make spaying and neutering commonplace regardless of locality.

Dr. Goldstein also explains that our goal should be to work toward a day when animals coming to a shelter are only seriously ill or dangerous, and therefore the euthanasia rate is 100 percent. But there are two sides to achieving that nirvana: we will significantly reduce healthy or treatable animals coming to a shelter because we have done a better job educating communities on animal welfare and taking care of their pets; however, we will always have animals that are the most challenged, seriously ill, or dangerous to other people or animals that are not healthy or treatable, and that should not be placed back into our community. When we get to that perceived "no-kill" state, the save rate will actually go down because at that point, the only animals that would be taken to a shelter would be those that are dangerous or need to be euthanized as the kind and humane thing to do to alleviate suffering. So those shelters will again be labeled "kill shelters," but in a different light than how they are labeled today. So it all comes back to improving the welfare of animals in communities.

Is preventing euthanasia of healthy and treatable animals truly achievable in the United States? It can be so long as shelters approach their work with the sole purpose and investment of all of their resources in saving lives while educating communities about animal care and welfare. This will encompass opening the shelter doors to allow the community at large to help and educating people about animal care. But as mentioned earlier, it also takes reframing the message in how we talk about shelters. The no-kill movement is a noble cause that will undoubtedly help many animals. Regardless of whether a shelter euthanizes or not, so long as we are tossing the label of *kill shelter* around, that shelter and those animals are doomed to a label that will turn away potential adopters, volunteers, and donors, all of which are needed to move a shelter toward reducing its intake of healthy and treatable animals and keeping those animals in their homes.

THRIVING AND INNOVATIVE ORGANIZATIONS FOR ANIMALS

The organizations featured in this section are to be commended for achieving and maintaining a status whereby no healthy or treatable pet is euthanized. Five different organizations, including two large metropolitan agencies, one rural open-admission animal control shelter, one sanctuary, and one limited-intake nonprofit organization, are featured in this section.

While more organizations are also achieving success in this area, there is still more to be done to reduce our nation's euthanasia rate for healthy and treatable pets. The stories of these facilities should provide practical tips and inspiration to help struggling shelters save more pets.

Nevada Humane Society

Nevada Humane Society in Reno made the decision in early 2007 to make their community "one of the safest communities for homeless dogs and cats in the nation."[7] In its January 2008 report, the number of dogs and cats euthanized in the county's shelters declined 51 percent for dogs and 52 percent for cats since 2006, the "save rate" for dogs was up to 92 percent and 78 percent for cats with a continuing upward trend, and the overall adoption rate increased 58 percent for dogs and 84 percent for cats.

How did Nevada Humane work toward reducing euthanasia and saving lives? They practice these ten tips for how shelters (and you as an advocate) can move toward no more euthanasia of healthy or treatable pets.

- **First:** Making lifesaving the number-one priority. Nevada Humane established four priorities: "Create lifesaving solutions for the animals; involve the community in our work; deliver quality customer service; and provide excellent care to the animals."[8]
- **Second:** Have the shelter staffed with employees who believe in and support the mission of saving lives. This may result in watching shelter staff leave or having to terminate them. Having staff at the shelter that are unsupportive or working against saving the animals will quickly defeat the efforts of others. But "when you have the right people on the team, a lot of things fall into place right away!"[9]
- **Third:** Review all programs and place all resources and efforts into saving lives, even if that means that other good programs are cut in the interim. Nevada Humane eliminated their retail store and turned it into a space for pet adoptions.
- **Fourth:** Make a public declaration of your lifesaving goals and ask the community for help. Create a volunteer program and have a wish list of work to be done and materials that are needed to make it easy for your community to get involved. Nevada Humane has more than 3,000 volunteers that help them reach their goals every day. Also

reach out to the media, frequently, so that your efforts stay in the news.

- **Fifth:** Focus on adoptions! Set adoption goals and celebrate with each pet going home. Nevada Humane posts the names of pets adopted on a board behind the adoption counter and rings a bell to celebrate each adoption. They believe that there truly is a home for every pet, regardless of the pet's medical history or behavioral or personality issues. Make the shelter accessible to the public through hours in the evenings and on weekends and allow visitors to interact with and touch the pets. This is not only healthy for the pet, but it allows potential adopters to make good decisions. Nevada Humane has cat colony rooms for people to walk in, cat cages in the lobby to greet people, and dogs that go for their walks with "Adopt Me" vests. They make it easy to adopt, with easy-to-understand forms and a welcoming shelter. They also host fun events to promote adoptions.

- **Sixth:** Spaying and neutering is important to reducing pet overpopulation in shelters. When people surrender kittens or puppies, Nevada Humane offers to spay the animal mom and dad for free. Creating a trap-neuter-return program for feral cats is also essential (and will be featured more in chapter 9). "Another mistake some people make is putting a lot of effort into mandatory spay/neuter legislation. While it can be a good idea to require shelters and pet stores to neuter all pets, the effort and energy that goes into passing legislation that focuses on individual pet owners can almost always be better spent ensuring that low-cost and free spay/neuter services are readily available and accessible to the people who need them most."[10]

- **Seventh:** Work to keep animals out of shelters. Nevada Humane does this through an Animal Help Desk that takes calls from the public and works to educate people about problems they may have with their pet. Educating people about animal behavior and care reduces needless surrender of pets to a shelter.

- **Eighth:** Help feral cats. Many well-intentioned people will trap and bring a feral cat to a shelter in hopes that it can find an indoor home. It is a death sentence to bring a feral cat to a shelter. Feral cats enjoy living outside. To do so safely, create a trap-neuter-return program to avoid unwanted litters ending up at your shelter. Consider creating a barn cat adoption program[11] where feral cats can be relocated to a barn rather than being returned to an unsafe area.

- **Ninth:** Partner with other shelters and animal organizations. Nevada Humane found it incorrect to assume that nonprofits are hesitant to partner out of competition for donor dollars. "Animal lovers are amazingly generous, especially when they feel that groups are working together to get an important job done."[12] Coordinating outside groups to assist the shelter is essential to saving lives.
- **Tenth:** Stay flexible, because there will always be challenges that require new and creative thinking. Situations arise where mass animals may arrive at a shelter from a hoarding situation, animal-fighting ring, or a natural disaster, or an injured animal may need expensive medical care. Be flexible and always remember to ask for help.

San Diego Humane Society and SPCA

San Diego Humane was established in 1880, and its mission is to promote the humane treatment of animals, prevent cruelty to animals, and provide education to enhance the human-animal bond. Through its various programs, and including its investigation and field services work, it serves approximately 38,000 pets annually and has more than 200 staff members and more than 1,050 volunteers. San Diego Humane is another organization that understands the critical importance of volunteers.

Dr. Mark Goldstein, president of San Diego Humane, honored me by being interviewed for this book. In a fascinating and lengthy interview regarding the San Diego community's animal "campus" (he prefers the term *campus* to *shelter*, as *shelter* does not include the vast educational programs and other services provided by this organization), he shared his views of how to reframe how we care for, speak about, and promote the welfare of homeless animals and shared what the San Diego Humane Society is doing to continue their track of not euthanizing any healthy or treatable animals since 2001.

As outlined in the foreword, Dr. Goldstein explains how we need to change the way we speak about homeless animals so that more people will be inclined to help, either through adopting, volunteering, donating, or working in the field of animal protection. For example, "low-cost spay/neuter" should be called "affordable or subsidized spay/neuter," because when something is labeled low cost, it does not have value and does not send out the correct message. *Animal control* should be relabeled *animal services* because we should stop focusing on the "control" aspect of animal welfare and refocus on services that humans can provide to help animals. Instead of using the term *kill*, we should use *euthanasia*, because no shelter worker, regardless of what we may think, wants to "kill" an animal; instead, they are required (for a variety of reasons) to euthanize an animal and frequently suffer a moral dilemma for ending its life. Killing does not cause a moral dilemma, but euthanasia most certainly does.[13] And *rescue groups* should be called *adoption partners*. Admittedly, this change was the most difficult for me to grasp, because I have been involved in animal "rescue" for more than a decade. But when Dr. Goldstein explained the need to shift from *rescue* to *adopt*, it made sense. For example, if I say that I rescued a cat from a shelter (even adding the words *kill shelter* or *high-euthanasia shelter*), I have certainly done a noble act for that animal, but I have left that shelter in the wake of negativity. Calling the shelter a *kill shelter* or *high-euthanasia shelter* where animals need to be *rescued* labels that shelter as a bad place. Admittedly, I do know of some shelters where animals are not safe for a variety of reasons. But for many shelters that try their best to care for the animals and are making efforts to re-home them, often with little or no resources or help, labeling their work as unsafe for animals just further impedes their efforts; it is likely that future adopters, volunteers, and donors will not want to help that shelter because it "kills." So although that one pet is safe and you can pat yourself on the back for being a rescuer, all the other animals left behind now have less opportunity to receive the loving care of a volunteer or the comforts of home from an adopter. The act itself may factually be a rescue for that one animal, but the aftermath of what we call it negatively impacts the remaining animals. Dr. Goldstein certainly caused me to think consciously of how I talk about this business of animal protection, and hopefully his words will cause others to do the same.

So why has the San Diego Humane Society had overwhelming success in placing all of their healthy or treatable animals since 2001? The first thing that is different about the San Diego Humane Society is the process of welcoming people and showcasing the animals. "It starts from the moment when you get out of your car and know that you are at the San Diego campus for animal care. We've gone from pound (jail), to shelter (which sells ourselves short because we do more than shelter), to village, to campus. The County of San Diego Department of Animal Services (formerly animal control) is on one side of the campus, and the Humane Society is on the other, working together in a great partnership. I wanted to call it a campus and people didn't understand why at first. But we have educational programs, just like a university campus. And the educational process starts the moment you walk through the doors."[14]

Dr. Goldstein explained that when you first enter the campus, you pass Rocky's Café and you can get a "yappacchino." I laughed when he said "yappacchino," and Dr. Goldstein asked me when was the last time I laughed when entering an animal shelter? Good point. He said, "It gets people to laugh, and that changes their mind-set about what and who we are."[15] He then described walking in and seeing a waterfall; Gandhi's statement about how we treat our animals is etched on the wall, and that is what they hope is the start of creating people's perception that they are in a place of positive energy. "When you open the door, instead of hearing what you expect, such as crying, odors, and screaming, the facility has been feng shui'd, to make it more appealing. To your right is a waterfall, the ground is a brown color, the blue-sky atrium is sixty feet high, the physical plant is inviting, the staff proudly wear name tags and are smiling, and we recognize that we want this to be a place where people come to fall in love, and not just take an animal to save its life."[16]

Dr. Goldstein explained that their care of animals is also different from what most people expect. The animals live in habitats instead of cages. They held a contest where professionals from the American Society of Interior Designers and design students competed to make over each habitat, with all the materials donated by local companies and organizations. Now the habitats look like showcases and are modeled after a more realistic environment that an animal can expect to live in once adopted. He explained that some people have complained that even though the transformation was free, they still see it as a waste of money because the space could be used to cage more animals, and the habitats take more time to clean. But shelters that warehouse animals in small steel cages are not allowing the animal to show its true personality or live in a comfortable way. And that can make the difference in whether that animal finds a home. The difference between a dog in a habitat room and a traditional dog run is dramatic, even though both are the same size based on square footage. "The dogs are lounging on the couch instead of pacing in a run. If we want people to stop housing animals in their backyard and place them inside the house, then we need to reflect that in how we house the animals. The traditional shelter today keeps animals in a situation (a cage) where the shelter would not adopt to someone who would keep the animal in the same housing situation."[17] Dr. Goldstein says we need to walk the talk.

Dr. Goldstein emphasized that although it is important to have a welcoming campus for visitors and a natural and comfortable environment for the animals, the staff and volunteers must not be forgotten. When staff and volunteers feel good about working at the facility, the animals react to that good mood. And when a visitor is making a difficult decision to euthanize their pet, they are welcomed to the soothing serenity room with a large, sunlit glass window and a wall mural of a rainbow to help people feel at ease. It is not a gray and depressing dungeon. When people come to use the serenity room for their own pet, they have a special parking space; they will walk through a garden with a waterfall, and their privacy and emotions are respected. When someone has to let their pet go, they talk with a staff member who does not judge what is happening; instead, the decision and person are honored for bringing the animal in and not harming the animal. Dr. Goldstein explained that if people surrendering animals for adoption or euthanasia are judged harshly, then that disrespect will spread throughout the community, and we risk losing the trust of the community and prevent them from wanting to come to us in the first place. It is important for San Diego Humane to provide a supportive environment. It should not be made difficult for people to surrender an animal (for adoption or euthanasia). Making it difficult will not cause people to change their mind because they have likely struggled with the decision for an extended period of time, and this may potentially guide them to less desirable alternatives. All you do is make it uncomfortable, which will not change the end result.

The Paws to Success program started in 2008 by the San Diego Humane Society began with the goal of ending euthanasia of healthy and treatable animals throughout San Diego County Coalition Partners. The first of this three-part program is to create a neonatal kitten nursery that operates 24/7 to house kittens from other organizations, the population of healthy and treatable animals most at risk of being euthanized. In April 2009, they opened their Paws to Success Nursery, which provides round-the-clock care to meet the needs of young and fragile kittens. In 2008–2009, they admitted 782 kittens under eight weeks of age, and 598 were adopted. The number has increased to 1,367 admitted in 2009–2010, with 1,266 being adopted, representing a 92 percent save rate. Some critics argue that money should be put into spaying/neutering instead of building a kitten nursery. Dr. Goldstein explains that when you have hundreds of kittens that need help, putting all of your money toward spaying and neutering will not help those kittens. So do they abandon the care of those kittens? He says no. Instead, it is okay for groups to take different paths and respect those different paths. San Diego Humane chooses to care for those vulnerable kittens while educating and promoting the importance of spay/neuter, and supporting those that are primarily focused on spay/neuter services. "Let's support and deeply respect each other's successes rather than criticize or judge each other. At the end of the day, it's the animals that ultimately lose when we disrespect one another."[18]

When Dr. Goldstein was asked what a struggling shelter can do to welcome its community to the shelter, thus benefiting the animals in care, he shared this vision:

"Good businesses show their best work. They develop a business plan and sell their plan to an investor. You must have a plan. Some shelters may not feel that they have the time to create a plan, but they must put aside some of their time to work on this. They must value that this is worth it. They need to know where they want to be in three years and select a reasonable but high goal. You have to present that plan on 'this is what we can do' instead of 'look at what we're up against.' Always do better today than yesterday, but do not hold yourself up to someone else's standard. Others will do that to you, and that is where we have hurt ourselves and are quick to pass judgment. Make sure that you build the physical foundation to be a healthy environment. Health, welfare, and safety come first. Get rid of signs that warn people of what not to do; get rid of the negativity that is seen by visitors and staff. Invest in your staff, train them, care for them, earn their trust every day, find out what tools they need, provide classes on compassion fatigue, and after that you can care for the animals. When you get the building and staff in place first, then you can help animals. When you have a broken-down shelter and demoralized staff, the first thing you need to do is empower the staff and make these foundational changes. Dream and build, then watch others get on board and the resources start to appear. Celebrate successes, learn from mistakes, and accept that humans are fallible; then you have created a culture that is unstoppable. This is not generally how people think in animal welfare. It has been more expected that it is quantity over quality, and that needs to be reversed if animal welfare organizations want to become proactive instead of reactive in the work we do. It takes time to make these changes. You must have a can-do attitude, an acceptance of celebrating your successes and not comparing yourself to someone else's standards. You can then face the challenges with the power of positive thinking—follow through with a successful program and then you have something of interest to show the next donor or 'investor,' as the San Diego Humane Society refers to them."[19]

Roscommon County Animal Center (Prudenville, Michigan)

When Terry MacKillop began volunteering at the Roscommon County Animal Control[20] shelter in 1998, he had no idea that he would end up as director of the shelter and president of the Michigan Association of Animal Control Officers (MAACO). Terry became involved as a volunteer because the shelter needed help; but most importantly, the animals needed help. The shelter was in a rural area with few resources, fewer adoptive homes, and some outdated policies that did not benefit the animals. In 1991, he was hired as an assistant animal control officer and chose helping the shelter animals as his career. Terry explains, "When I started, there were only eight dog kennels that went inside and out through shuttle doors and only one cat cage. The building smelled like death and had not been maintained in many years; it had only one purpose: to hold animals until they were euthanized, or if a pet was lucky, it went back to its owner. However, there was a good chance the animals were exposed to many shelter diseases such as kennel cough or parvovirus. The shelter had no operation hours for the public, nor were there volunteers or any type of animal adoption partners. There was no budgeting for medical care or immunizations for the animals, plus most cages housed four to five dogs, and they were emptied as soon as the minimum holding time was up. There were two animal control officers for my first year of employment with the county who shared all duties from feeding, cleaning, and running animal complaints. The euthanasia rate ran about 95 percent, and most of the rest were sent to an animal broker [Class B dealer], who also disposed of the county's dead animals."[21] The animals were only fed once a day, and cages cleaned only once a day. For a shelter that received more than 3,000 animals yearly, the situation was grim.

Terry knew that something needed to be done to turn things around for the shelter and the lives of animals in their care. In 1992, Terry was approached by a small group of concerned citizens who wanted to start a volunteer group for the shelter. The group would help clean cages and promote adoptions and would have hours available to open the shelter to the public. Then with the installation of a new animal control director who was willing to change past policies, the volunteer group formed under the name of Pets Are Worth Saving. With this volunteer group now assisting the shelter, at no cost to the county, progress started.

In 1993, Terry was appointed as animal control director and quickly implemented several important improvements, including writing a new animal ordinance that banned pound seizure (Class B dealer taking animals for experimentation), adding cats to the licensing process, and providing for increased penalties for animal abuse. Terry clarifies how the changes were well received by the community: "We started to see such a positive change in the public perception that we received a donation which allowed us to make repairs and put an addition on the old shelter that included a laundry room and cat room separate from the main shelter, and eight more kennels were added. When the volunteer group disbanded, the county hired several to maintain the shelter seven days a week from 8:00 a.m. to 4:00 p.m. Adoptions started to increase, along with donations, and new ways to place the animals along with the use of outside animal protection organizations and a low-cost spay and neuter program for cats. We started using many media outlets locally and through the Internet, like Petfinder. We purchased a trailer and took our adoptions mobile, including Meet Your Best Friend at the Detroit Zoo twice a year. We are very fortunate our donations grew to over $100,000, and we were able to build a new state-of-the-art shelter in 2008 thanks to the people of Roscommon County who approved a millage. My motivation was simple; it has been and will always be about the animals."[22]

The millage from 2005 allowed the shelter to expand from a 900-square-foot facility to 8,400 square feet on 20 acres, and averaged about $7.00 per household.[23] Instead of being known as an animal control shelter, it is now the Roscommon County Animal Center. Terry designed the center himself with an eye toward comfort for the animals and ease in cleaning for the staff. The new center can now care for sixty to eighty cats, compared to thirty at the prior facility; and the dog runs have doubled from fifteen to thirty. Every room is easy to clean and contains a floor drain. The new building has improved the lives of the shelter animals as well as provided a more comfortable and friendly environment for staff, volunteers, and visitors.

When Terry became the shelter director in 1993, the euthanasia rate hovered around 95 percent. Today, the euthanasia rate is close to zero.

In 2009, the shelter took in 542 dogs and only euthanized two, and accepted 713 cats and euthanized 59, many of which were sick, aggressive, incapable of rehabilitation, and unadoptable.[24] The reduction in the euthanasia rate did not happen overnight, but the steady changes made at the shelter did make an immediate and noticeable impact for the animals. For a shelter labeled an "open-admission" shelter, which must take every animal that arrives at its door, and located in a rural community within a state that has suffered more than most in the financial downturn, how can the euthanasia rate be slashed so dramatically? As someone who has accomplished that feat, Terry shares this advice: "Open your doors to help; be honest with the public and the people you work for; use every resource out there. The public will help if you present your case and allow them to help. Make sure that you have adoption hours on the weekends; seek sponsorship for your animals in your local papers; use Petfinder.com; send out notifications by e-mail of animals needing help; use purebred rescues and any other rescue that meets state guidelines; and never ever settle for less."[25]

The shelter places a high priority on returning lost pets to their owners, and opening the shelter seven days per week allows for families and pets to be reunited. The shelter also sterilizes feral cats and returns them to their colony if someone is available to maintain the colony. This has helped to reduce the number of feral cats being euthanized. The website for the shelter, hosted at no cost through Petfinder.com, outlines the dedication that the shelter has toward keeping the euthanasia rate low and adoptions high.[26] Through Petfinder, the shelter features the pets available for adoption, including naming each pet (and avoiding posting animals with just their intake number), displaying a photo, and describing the pet. The website also features a shelter program that offers affordable spay/neuter for cats at $30 for males and $40 for females; encourages families to bring their dogs to the shelter to meet their new buddy and ensure that the adoption will be a success; has future plans to offer microchipping for $20 per pet so that more lost animals can be reunited with their family; and, the newest addition, a pet food pantry for families who are financially struggling to afford pet food. The website also actively solicits volunteers to help keep the shelter running at optimum levels.

For the Roscommon County Animal Center, the millage certainly helped by providing funds for a larger facility to accommodate the best interests of the animals; but maintaining the adoption success rates is directly attributable to dedicated staff, community support, and volunteers. As mentioned previously in this book, allowing volunteers to assist a shelter is crucial to success in re-homing more animals and working with the community on proper care of animals. For municipal shelters that believe they are constrained by budgets and other limitations, the Roscommon County Animal Center demonstrates that opening the doors to volunteers and the community, while implementing efforts for the primary benefit of the animals, can make a substantial difference in the environment at the shelter and the life of the animals.

Rolling Dog Ranch Animal Sanctuary (Lancaster, New Hampshire)

In 1998, Steve Smith and Alayne Marker took the leap of purchasing a ranch in Montana that would help disabled animals. The intent was to keep their careers at Boeing in Washington State and slowly build the sanctuary with the end of goal of taking early retirement in fifteen years. However, as with most people who get involved in helping animals, the cause becomes all-consuming. "Once we bought the property in Montana, it seemed like we spent every waking moment thinking about being there and getting the sanctuary started. We realized that early retirement was a long, *long* way off, and that the need for a sanctuary like ours was *now*. It occurred to us that working for another fifteen years in the corporate world would have left us financially very well-off for the rest of our lives . . . but during that time a lot of disabled animals would have been left without any options. So we finally decided to quit our jobs in Seattle and move to the ranch to open the sanctuary."[27]

Although they continued with side employment for a few years by working from home offices at the sanctuary to maintain some income, Steve and Alayne invested their life savings into starting and sustaining Rolling Dog Ranch Animal Sanctuary[28] and now work full-time at the sanctuary to maintain their vision. With some media publicity early on, and their website catching the eye of a producer of the *Today* show, donor support now fully sustains their mission.

Rolling Dog Ranch Animal Sanctuary helps disabled dogs, cats, and horses that are blind, deaf, three-legged, or have neurological or orthopedic issues. This sanctuary is unique in that they focus solely on disabled animals. On their website, Steve and Alayne explained that they chose the name because on trips to the ranch from Seattle the first couple of years, their personal dogs would roll around on the ground in joy as soon as they arrived at the property. In 2010, Rolling Dog Ranch moved its facility and animals from Montana to New Hampshire. The move was not only a feat on its own, but moving approximately fifty disabled animals takes a strategic plan, patience, and a lot of love. They relocated for several reasons, but a major one was to be closer to services like veterinary clinics.

Why do they focus solely on disabled animals? Steve states, "From the beginning we wanted to focus on disabled animals because it seemed to us that these were the most vulnerable animals in our society. While there were some organizations like Best Friends that did take in some special needs animals, we didn't see anyone focused exclusively on the disabled. That's where we felt we could make the biggest difference, both in terms of providing a sanctuary for them, and in helping to change the perceptions that many people had about disabled animals."[29]

Rolling Dog Ranch receives disabled animals from all across the country, almost all coming from shelters or animal welfare organizations. They transport them by ground and air. In most cases, Rolling Dog Ranch covers the travel expenses due to the limited resources of the originating shelter or organizations. Although they house approximately fifty animals at the sanctuary and enjoy ten adoptions on average yearly, they have the heartbreak of turning away needy animals every day. Steve explains, "We went into this knowing that we wanted to create a true home-style environment, and not have it feel like an institution. We also wanted to make sure that we never had to compromise the care we provided because we were stretched too thin financially. That means keeping the number of animals to a very specific, manageable limit. So we recognize that turning away animals is simply a necessary, if heartbreaking, consequence of maintaining the kind of standards we have."[30]

Now located on 132 sprawling acres in northern New Hampshire, Rolling Ranch has settled among the forest, fields, a pond, and a facility large enough to accommodate people and animals. Steve and Alayne share their 3,600-square-foot home with their furry family. The large dogs are housed inside the "dog wing" on the first floor with a solarium; smaller dogs are housed on the second floor. There is also a special indoor area for incontinent dogs. The dogs receive plenty of time romping around outdoors, and disability ramps were included at all entrances for dogs that need a little extra help getting outside. There is also a 7,200-square-foot, three-story fully renovated barn on the property. A fifteen- by twenty-foot room on the second floor of the barn houses the cats. It is heated and insulated, with linoleum floors and plenty of windows for sunbathing. The horses are in corrals with run-in sheds at night and out in the pasture during the day.

Rolling Dog Ranch has had several advantages that have helped to sustain the sanctuary. Sufficient funds to open the sanctuary and cover the costs was instrumental. "We thought it was really important to show any potential donors down the road that we had committed our own savings to get the sanctuary established and to develop a track record before we could or should ask anyone else to contribute."[31] Having a business background was beneficial, creating a professional website was a must to feature the animals and the work that was being accomplished, and having faith and enjoying some luck also contributed.

The primary struggle with operating a sanctuary is balancing the demands of your time and energy. Running a sanctuary involves long hours, every day, and not being able to take days off. Steve explains, "Our work day begins at 7:30 a.m. when we let the dogs out for the first time, and it doesn't end until we finish putting them up for the night at 9:30 p.m. Somewhere in there we have about ninety minutes to ourselves for dinner and a brief moment to unwind, but then we start that second—or is it third?—shift. And it's seven days a week. You can't just hire a pet sitter so you can go away for the weekend when you have that many animals. And if you have horses, it gets even more complicated. Yes, you can have volunteers to help and you can hire employees if you have the resources, but at the end of the day, you're still the one who is responsible for making everything happen and for ensuring standards of care are met."[32]

It is clear for Steve and Alayne that nothing is more rewarding than helping the animals in their care. They love what they do and where they live, and they are reminded every day of the positive impact they are making on the lives of the disabled animals they have grown to love. But Steve cautions that before leaping into the world of creating an animal sanctuary, decide if it is the life for you. "You know, a lot of people tell us, 'you are living my dream.' Well, if your dream includes scooping poop from forty dogs three times a day, no matter what the weather is doing, more power to you! But seriously, I think many people who want to do something like this have no idea what the day-to-day job is really like."[33]

Steve has these words of advice if you are considering creating an animal sanctuary: "To begin with, we'd recommend taking the 'How to

Start a Sanctuary' workshop at Best Friends. If you can't afford either the money or time to take the workshop, you're in no position to start a sanctuary. Then spend a lot of time volunteering at a sanctuary or animal shelter. Make sure this is really something you want to commit your life to. Figure out *why* you want to do this, and then *how* you're going to do it. Make sure you have sufficient personal financial resources to sustain the enterprise and yourself, at least initially. This is a business, and you need to plan accordingly. Hopes and dreams still need assets to become real."[34]

If you want to support those who are doing the work in sanctuaries, Steve says that monetary donations are the best way to help to cover veterinary costs, food, utilities, and other operational costs. Donors are absolutely indispensable to running a successful sanctuary for the long term.

King Street Cats

Located in Alexandria, Virginia, this is the organization where I have volunteered since 2004. King Street Cats (KSC) is a unique cat orphanage and adoption facility where approximately thirty to forty cats free-roam. KSC does not euthanize any cat or kitten for lack of space or behavioral issues. The few times that a cat or kitten is euthanized, it is in the final stages of life and is let go to alleviate suffering. For many years KSC was located on King Street in the heart of Old Town Alexandria. The orphanage at that time was only 350 square feet. KSC moved to a new location in July 2009 and now has more than 800 square feet.

KSC does not call the orphanage a "shelter" because it is set up and manned differently than a traditional shelter. Because all of the kitties have been orphaned in one way or another, the "orphanage" label just fit. KSC is completely volunteer run and funded through donations. They happily house more than 250 cats and kittens yearly that are re-homed through a thorough application process. There is no time limit on how long a cat can remain in the orphanage. Cats are welcome to live with KSC until their perfect home is found. KSC also insists that any cat or kitten adopted be returned, no matter when, if the adopter is unable to keep the pet. KSC has had cats returned after nine years and welcomed them back with open arms.

The orphanage is divided into the main "fun room," which has a kitchen and a sink that the kitties love to play in, and the "quiet adoption room," which functions as the intake room for newly arriving kitties and for kitties that need a calmer room with fewer cats. KSC does not allow kittens under four months of age in the orphanage as a precaution to keep them healthy; instead they are placed in foster care to be raised in a home environment. KSC prides itself on being a free-roaming facility, though there are spacious cages available to house new arrivals, kittens visiting for adoption events, and cats receiving medical care. Cages are also available for the rabble-rousing cat that simply needs a time-out, or kitties that enjoy snuggling in enclosures.

The orphanage caters to the needs of the cats by having many cubby-holes for the cats to sleep in, tables and shelves with comfortable bedding, sunny windows with cat trees for sleeping in the sun, as well as a wall with a three-level cat walk where cats can climb, sit, or sleep. Because cleanliness is next to catliness for KSC, the volunteers go to great lengths to clean the room every morning, provide washable toys and wooden cat trees with perches for the cats to sleep on that are easy to wipe down, and they host a monthly Big Clean where the entire facility is scrubbed from top to bottom.

The cats and kittens live in a quasi-home-style setting, with volunteers coming in and out throughout the day to feed, play, groom, and socialize with the cats. We find that the cats are happier and healthier this way, which then makes them more adoptable. KSC traditionally takes in cats that would not thrive in a traditional shelter environment. For example, we take pregnant and nursing moms and orphaned bottle babies into our foster care program. We also take in senior kitties, cats with behavioral issues, cats with disabilities (including blind, deaf, and three-legged kitties), and bonded pairs who need to be adopted together. KSC receives cats from shelters that struggle to increase save rates, including many local shelters, but also the St. Croix Animal Welfare Center and an animal organization in West Virginia. Although KSC is a limited-admission shelter and cannot take in all the cats seeking to enter, it works to take in the cats that are in the most dire situations. KSC has taken in numerous friendly stray cats (especially during colder weather), cats caught in the foreclosure crisis, and cats living in hoarding situations. Since some cats come to us with behavioral issues or are traumatized by losing their home, the volunteers go to great lengths to comfort and provide a healing space for each cat. Some cats rebound within a few days, whereas others grieve the loss of their home and owner for months. KSC has the luxury of giving them time and space to heal.

KSC boasts that they have the "cat-friendliest cats in town," because even cats that arrive with hissy attitudes soon learn how to live peacefully among the other felines. KSC also has a high bonded-pair adoption rate and will turn down requests to adopt one cat from a bonded pair and wait for the pair to be adopted together. In addition to adoption events every weekend at the orphanage, KSC also has a mobile adoption program, including the KSC Kitten Purrlooza[sm] adoption events at local dog bakeries, pet food stores, and bookstores. By getting out into the community, KSC has increased awareness, which has resulted in increased donations, adoptions, and volunteers.

Due to the unique nature of relying solely on volunteers to run this organization, KSC is proud to have a volunteer and foster care program of approximately eighty people. We enjoy having children volunteer with their parents and find that they can soften even the grumpiest of cats. KSC hopes that more volunteer cat orphanages will be created throughout the country, since many shelters are overcrowded with cats that do not fare well in a caged environment.

SOLUTIONS

"As the economy struggles, more shelters are reaching out to one another to collaborate on a more regional basis versus approaching their struggles on a more insular and county-by-county basis. This is encouraging because no shelter should feel alone in the overpopulation crisis,"[35] says Tracy Coppola. Tracy recommends that shelters extend their partnerships beyond other shelters, local governments, and advocates and embrace the help of the private sector, such as veterinarians, public health professionals, foundations, and so on. Pet overpopulation is a public health issue, so everyone in every community has an opportunity to get involved.

More can be done. Tracy states, "At the same time, I suggest that shelters need to be as honest about euthanasia as possible, in order to highlight the problem and the need for assistance as well as to foster honest communication with the public. We want to move away from an 'us against them' approach. This can be very difficult, however, because the shelter system currently lacks a standardized system of reporting statistics like euthanasia rates and intake numbers. The lack of a standardized reporting system sometimes makes the exact reasons for euthanizing animals and how euthanasia rates are calculated unclear to the public. For example, if a shelter goes no kill and/or limited admission, its corresponding animal control agency's euthanasia rates may increase, not necessarily because its practices worsened, but because its intake numbers increased. This type of scenario should be reflected when examining the data. The paper also strongly suggests that more national organizations—even those beyond animal welfare—need to get proactively involved. Sometimes I feel that the problem is so enormous that national groups feel they need to take it all on at once, and this can lead to something of an 'analysis paralysis,' if you will. This is why I feel it is very important for the larger welfare groups to approach the overpopulation crisis step-by-step, listening to local citizens on a grassroots level, in order to develop a robust and practical understanding of what resources are available and needed in struggling communities."[36]

Organizations housing homeless animals in the United States can reduce euthanasia rates and save lives if they expand their reach outside the walls of their shelter. It is crucial that shelters allow volunteers to assist, create a foster care program, welcome adoption partners, and set up accessible and affordable spay/neuter facilities to the community. If we each take one small step in the right direction, this can be achieved.

YOU CAN DO MORE

- Donate to help innovative shelters to stay in business and to be a model for other shelters.
- Share the concepts of innovative and thriving shelters with a shelter in your community that may be struggling. Offer to help implement small changes that will benefit the environment for the animals.
- Check your shelter's wish list and take them items that they need. Do not assume that the shelter will accept old linens or any type of pet food. Always ask or check the wish list.
- Volunteer at your local shelter to help save lives. This can encompass providing foster care for needy animals, helping to create or update a shelter website, photographing the shelter animals and posting them on Petfinder.com or AdoptAPet.com, being a shelter adoption counselor, making the cages and kennels friendlier for the animals (with blankets, toys, welcoming cage cards).

- Offer help to promote adoptions with cute marketing campaigns or affordable adoptions to match senior pets to senior citizens.
- Create a pet sponsorship program where people can donate to help a specific animal.
- For large renovations at a shelter, consider a fund-raiser that allows large donors the naming rights to the renovation. For instance, if a cat room or outdoor dog run area is being installed, allow the largest donor toward the project to have the right to name the project.
- Help with an enrichment program at the shelter to benefit the cats and dogs. Fund-raise or ask pet supply stores to provide items at low cost. Some ideas include:
  - Cats. Whether cats are caged or free-roaming, the goal is to create a stress-free environment where cats are not fearful, anxious, depressed, or sick.
    - Create fewer opportunities for cats to be moved within a shelter. Moving cats from intake to observation to adoption rooms increases the chance for stress and sickness.
    - Isolation wards should not be the worst housing in the shelter. If a cat is in isolation, often due to sickness, it needs a soothing and happy environment to recover.
    - Volunteer to play with, cuddle, groom, and talk to the cats to keep them happy and healthy. Make notes of what cats need extra attention so that the next volunteer knows who needs a little more TLC.
    - Purchase larger cages with portholes that can be opened and expanded to cover two cages, or create free-roaming rooms.
    - For cats in cages, check out the Hide, Perch & Go™ box, which consists of a lower box with two entries where a cat can sleep on a blanket and an upper hoodless box where a cat can perch. The box also turns into a carrier so that it can go with the cat when adopted. The San Francisco SPCA uses these boxes. Or put small hammocks or shoe boxes in cages to give cats a place to hide, which will reduce stress.
    - Cats need horizontal and vertical space. Cat trees and perches help (preferably with wooden bases and minimal carpet for easy cleaning).
    - Make sure each cat has at least one toy to play with and one blanket to call their own. Be careful not to change out blankets too frequently. Cats will mark their scent on the blanket, and washing or changing it frequently will cause stress.

- Get creative about toys that are inexpensive, such as paper rolls, wine corks, toothbrushes, pipe cleaners, Ping-Pong balls, plastic eggs, empty pill bottles, milk or bottle caps, or paper bags. All of these items are inexpensive and can be tossed out when used.
- Thread twine or rope through a toy ball and string it to the top of the cage to create a dangling toy that will provide hours of fun.
- Equip cat rooms with televisions that can play videos featuring birds, mice, and other sounds of nature. Bringing nature inside makes cats happier.
- Place a small radio in a cat room and play soothing classical music.
- Add a cascading waterfall that cats will invariably want to drink from or play with. Washington Animal Rescue League in Washington, D.C., did that, and the cats love the soothing sounds.
- Offer to paint the cat room with bright, appealing colors to attract visitors.
- For a free-roaming facility, offer to build a cat wall with multiple shelves so that cats can climb, perch, and observe from high.
- Place furniture with tops (old dressers, etc.) in a cat room and allow the cats to sleep on top or burrow in a dresser drawer.
- With cat adoptions generally being less than dog adoptions, reorganize the shelter to place cats up front, near the entrance so that people walk by and view the cats before seeing the dogs. Animal Friends, Inc., in Pittsburgh did this and it worked to showcase the cats.
- If the shelter is not putting L-lysine, an immunity supplement, in the cats' food, offer to donate it to the shelter. It can be purchased in bulk from most vitamin and health food stores. It is fairly inexpensive yet will save the shelter on veterinary costs by keeping cats healthy.
- If the shelter cat room has windows or cat doors can be installed, consider building an outside cat run that is completely screened in and allow the cats to jump in and out of the window and enjoy the fresh air and sunshine. SPCA of Central Florida in Orlando created an outdoor cat run.
- Offer to do laundry for the shelter.
○ Dogs
  - Volunteer! Volunteer! Volunteer! Volunteers can be the backbone of a thriving shelter operation and can provide extra care to dogs.

- Volunteer to walk dogs at the shelter. Walking dogs is essential to their good health and well-being, all of which helps to promote adoption. Dogs should go outside at least once a day, and volunteers are needed to help.
- Volunteer to socialize dogs with each other and form doggie play groups at the shelter. If a play group area is not available at the shelter, brainstorm ideas with shelter staff on how to create an area for dogs to socialize. Or think of ways to create a safe and secure outdoor dog run so that once a day shelter dogs can get fresh air and run around off leash.
- It is important for dogs to avoid boredom so that they show well to potential adopters. Offer to help change out toys frequently, install classical music in the kennels, pair up dogs to have kennel mates (based on compatibility and size), and provide Kongs (with peanut butter if tolerated) to keep the dogs busy with an activity. Also establish rotating shifts with dog walkers to give the dogs exercise.
- Dogs are natural foragers and hunters, so have them work for their food. Put their food inside Buster Cube, Kong Wobble, Kibble Nibble, or Tug-A-Jug and the dogs will enjoy the activity of retrieving their prize of food. Be sure that the dog knows how to work this system.
- Organize a toy and treat drive in your community, or a fund-raiser during Adopt-a-Dog Month.
- Offer toys for sale in your shelter lobby and encourage visitors to purchase one for a shelter dog (and allow the person to give a dog a toy).
- If you are a dog trainer, volunteer your services to help dogs at the shelter become more adoptable.
- If your community shelter has small kennels for dogs (where they sleep, stand, and urinate in the same location), offer to raise funds to create larger kennels where dogs can sleep and urinate in different areas.
- If space is available, think big when it comes to housing dogs. Housing dogs in chain-linked kennels can teach a dog that barking and eliminating in their living space is appropriate. Consider kennels that mimic home living environments with couches, chairs, maybe even a radio or television. Dogs that live in real-life rooms show better and are more adoptable. According to American Humane As-

sociation, "A lot of shelters think real-life rooms require too much space, but they actually take up less space overall and the dogs have more individual space than in traditional runs. Real-life rooms cost no more than runs, but they have tremendous advantages."[37]

○ For other shelter pets such as rabbits, guinea pigs, hamsters, reptiles, mice, and so on, peruse the Internet for species-specific examples of how to make the shelter environment more comfortable and pleasing. Also check with your local shelter and ask what you can donate to help these special pets during their time at the shelter.

CHAPTER 7

Saving a Life: Transporting Shelter Animals

Anyone who loves animals does not want to see them languish away in a shelter and then be euthanized because the shelter ran out of space and an adopter did not arrive in time. We see commercials played out on television showing the sad and soulful eyes of cats and dogs behind cage doors waiting for a loving home, with the plea to spend just a few dollars a month to help them find a new home. Although that tactic has helped some organizations to raise millions of dollars to benefit animals, it may also have the unintended effect of sending a message about shelters that do not have the resources to save every animal, which then causes people to shy away from helping those shelters. But knowing that those sad and soulful eyes are in shelters every day, hoping for a second chance, it is an amazing feeling to save the life of an animal that is in a less-than-optimal situation. I have lost count, but I suspect that I have been involved in re-homing more than a thousand shelter or homeless animals since 2000. Yet the work is never done.

I have been involved in many transport situations, including removing animals directly from shelters and taking them into foster care at my house or transporting them to another organization, flying a cat home to Washington, D.C., with me from the island of St. Croix, receiving cats arriving by plane from St. Croix, as well as connecting people and organizations with animals that need to be transported out of a situation. Sometimes the transport may be only a few miles away from the originating location, whereas other transports may be hundreds or thousands of miles.

Some people question why animals should be transported from one location to another, and for me the answer is simple. Some locations in the United States do not have the benefit of adoption organizations to help them place animals in homes, and they are isolated in an area with insufficient adoptive homes. Other areas may have hundreds of adoption organizations available to assist overcrowded shelters, and millions of local, potential adoptive homes. And while those overcrowded shelters may not have every animal transported to a different location for re-homing, at least they have numerous resources and possibilities available. Other distant or rural locations may have no local resources and must rely on moving the animals across state lines to help them find homes. Some areas also have fewer issues with pet overpopulation, such as the Northeast, because of successful efforts with spay/neuter enforcement and education campaigns on proper pet care. So transport programs should not be viewed as taking the space of a local animal in need, but instead should be viewed as accepting that animals do not choose where they are born and left homeless, and we as humans can help to relocate them to an area that has room to accept them and possibly even a demand for their particular breed.

PetSmart Charities has created the Rescue Waggin'® Program,[1] which is considered the gold standard for pet transportation. As of fall 2010, the program has transported more than 38,000 pets from high-euthanasia shelters to high-adoption shelters across the United States, while providing almost $600,000 in grants to shelters to promote spay/neuter programs and help improve shelter operations so that more pets can be adopted within the community.[2] The Rescue Waggin' operates in four regional routes — East Coast, South Central, Midwest, and Great Plains — with four temperature-controlled vehicles offering space for fifty to sixty dogs. The vehicles provide the comforts of lullaby music, and video cameras allow the driver to check on the animals from time to time. The Rescue Waggin' Program ensures that no local animals are displaced when animals are transporting to a new community. The goal is simply to allow overpopulated shelters to move their animals to locations that have demands for specific breeds or puppies.

This chapter features those on the front line, like the Rescue Waggin' Program, who are working every day to save and transport shelter animals to places where they can await their new adoptive home. Although this can be exhausting work because there is always "just one more" that needs help, it is some of the most rewarding work you will ever do. Read on, be inspired by these unsung heroes, and learn what you can do to help save a life.

TRANSPORTATION PROGRAMS MAKING A DIFFERENCE

Pets from Paradise Program (St. Croix, Virgin Islands)

I have had the pleasure of receiving long-distance transports coordinated by Donna Cascarelli with the St. Croix Animal Welfare Center's Pets from Paradise Program. Donna works with off-island organizations that are willing to accept transported animals from the St. Croix shelter. She is also working with Love Is in the Air, a pet rescue program that is part of the Humane Learning Center, a nonprofit organization working under the St. Croix Foundation. The St. Croix shelter receives approximately 3,500 pets annually; however, being landlocked limits the number of adoptive homes and the availability of animal welfare organizations to assist. Donna shares that it can be challenging to ask a mainland organization to accept a St. Croix cat or dog, especially when pet overpopulation, and the inability to save them all, is present throughout the United States.

However, Donna and the staff with Pets from Paradise spend their days working with the St. Croix shelter staff to determine which cats and dogs are eligible for transport, while also coordinating with mainland organizations that are willing to accept a St. Croix pet. Their goal is not only to help shelter pets leave the island to find a new home on the mainland, but also to transport a pet that is a good match to the receiving organization. And through the new collaboration with Love Is in the Air, which was created in 2010, even more island pets are destined to fly to new homes.

So why should shelter pets be transported to other locations? Simple. Some areas are not as overpopulated with pets, or they have a demand for certain breeds of animals. As written in the introduction, the St. Croix cats that arrive at King Street Cats, where I volunteer, most often have unique Oriental shapes and markings and are adopted more quickly than our other cats. Donna elaborates, "Many of our partner organizations adopt out our pets within forty-eight hours of landing, often because of a demand for smaller-breed dogs, which they don't have many of—and we have plenty of them!"[3]

Donna has been amazed that some areas do not have pet overpopulation issues due to strict enforcement of spay/neuter laws. Accepting a transfer from a shelter in need discourages people from purchasing a pet and supporting puppy mills. "It can, and has been, argued that many areas have their own overpopulation issues and therefore should not accept pets from transfer programs. They all deserve a chance, no matter where they come from. Just because Haiti has a need for adoptive parents doesn't mean people should be discouraged from adopting a child from Haiti. It's the same thing."[4]

Donna counts the most successful strategy for running a long-distance transport program as knowing the people at the partner organization. "Don't rely on e-mail—speak to them on the phone, know what kind of pets are easiest for them to adopt, ask for permission, with specifics, if there is an animal with any special needs you want them to place."[5] Because of Pets from Paradise's success in finding mainland partner organizations, the number of animals transported doubled in 2009 and will double again in 2010. The most immediate struggle for the program has been funding. Many of the partner organizations ask for the pet to have all veterinary work completed before travel (which is an added incentive for advocating to accept a pet from a faraway land). And then there is the cost of travel, which can range from $100 to $125 for a carry-on pet to $150 to $200 for a checked pet. Moreover, the pet travel bags and kennels are expensive to purchase on the island of St. Croix and can be expensive for partner organizations to mail back. So many of the carriers are not returned and need to be replenished.

Another challenge can be the weather. Donna explains, "The airlines prohibit any animals traveling under the plane when the temperature is below 45 degrees or above 85 degrees anywhere en route. That means in the winter months when it's cool enough on St. Croix to send as many as we can, it's too cold in our northern destinations for them to be accepted. Then by the end of May it becomes too hot on St. Croix for checked pets to be allowed. We have just started sending some out through Puerto Rico on Continental's Pet Safe climate control flights, but that is an expensive and complicated process, and not something we can do in great numbers."[6] So the program relies on travelers, who can carry one pet per person as a carry-on item. That is what I did when transporting Whisper the cat.

So why does Donna coordinate transports? "The Pets from Paradise Program is important to me because it offers hope in an otherwise hopeless situation. Anyone who works with a shelter with a high rate of euthanasia will understand that it is the element of hope that helps make the tragedies bearable and provides the motivation to continue working to save that 'one more' even when the tragedies do become unbearable."[7]

When asked to share a success story or two, Donna explained that there have been so many. I have enjoyed keeping Donna, and the St. Croix shelter staff, updated with stories and photos of all of the "Cruzan kitties" living in their new homes. But one story that stands out for Donna involves a dog named Pluto who went to a partner organization on Martha's Vineyard. "We didn't know when we sent him that he was deaf, and certainly would have asked for permission to send him or chosen a fully healthy animal to travel. Our Martha's Vineyard people were great about it, but had a hard time placing him because no one wanted the extra responsibility of caring for a deaf pet. We then got the news that Pluto was adopted and went to a family who had another deaf dog, and they were taking him to training school to learn sign language. Another great story is Duke, who was flying to the Cleveland Animal Protection League in Ohio. The traveler had offered to deliver Duke to the shelter rather than have a volunteer meet her plane. So she brought Duke to the APL and as she was leaving, the family who was sitting behind her on the plane was coming to adopt him. They'd fallen in love with Duke in midair—so he was essentially adopted before he even landed."[8]

Before starting or volunteering with a transport program, Donna recommends keeping these words of advice in mind. First, make sure you are matching the animal with the right adoption organization, especially if the pet is going into a foster care situation where children or other animals are in the home. Second, research the receiving organization to make sure that the animal is going to a place where an adoption, and not euthanasia, is the only outcome (unless a dire health issue arises) and the level of care is high. And most important, don't give up!

Donna recommends getting involved in transporting animals or providing foster care for an animal in transport or arriving at the final destination. Or consider supporting a transportation organization with monetary donations, donating travel carriers, or volunteering your time to help with travel coordination and follow-up after transport. Support those organizations that are saving an animal from another location, and support them by adopting from them.

Rolling Rescue Program (Michigan)

For as long as I can remember, Laurel Barrick has been the go-to person for coordinating animal transports in Michigan and beyond. She started transporting animals in the mid-1990s while working for a small owner-operator trucking partnership and locating a new group of volunteers called Rolling Rescue.[9] After joining Rolling Rescue, she began by working mostly with West Coast rescuers and then was introduced to Michigan transports when a national breed rescue organization started moving their dogs out of Michigan. Within a year, she inherited the Rolling Rescue list of volunteers.

After taking over the volunteer list, Laurel's first transport coordination efforts usually involved emergency situations, including assisting an organization in northern New Mexico that needed to move out their animals as a result of a fire. Laurel helped locate organizations to take the animals, coordinating transport of eight dogs into Montana and dropping off dogs with approved organizations along the route.

Now Laurel's work focuses on transports within and outside of Michigan. "There are many weeks when there is a daily need to move animals. Some of those are foreseen and planned, but there are always the last-minute transports; a death-row dog finds an eleventh-hour reprieve across the state or in a surrounding state and you have to move immediately. The presence of pound seizure in Michigan adds a desperate dimension to an already daunting task, even in good economic times. But for three years now, Michigan's shelters have been in crisis. Our economy here in Michigan has left us with increasingly more and more owner surrenders."[10] Laurel typically spends twenty to thirty hours per week coordinating transports, but that can increase to as high as fifty hours per week.

What does it entail to set up a successful transport? Laurel shares these recommendations: (1) Know the organization to which the animal will be transported. Do not rely on word of mouth; instead, check references, get photos of the location, and possibly visit the location. "People are so eager to help when they read, 'Help, Fido will die Tuesday without this transport' that they will jump to help anyone. They have no idea of some of the dangers that await animals sent into unscreened situations."[11] Transport coordinators must screen the receiving location to make sure it is not a hoarding situation, a backyard breeder, or an irresponsible person who has been placed on a do-not-adopt list. Those fates can be worse than death in a shelter. If you are transporting directly to an adopter, the animal must be spayed or neutered and the home fully screened. And whether the receiver is an organization or a private individual adopting, get it in writing that they are able to accept the animal and are accepting financial responsibility for any medical needs the animal may have or that may arise en route. (2) Collect all the information on the animals being transported, such as breed, age, size, temperament, medical history and records, including a health certificate for out-of-state transfers, and special needs. For out-of-state transfers, make sure vaccinations are completed. Unweaned animals must be transported with the mother and without other animals on the transport. Never transport the babies and leave the mother behind. And be cautious of groups that only want puppies or pregnant dogs. (3) Determine any medical issues that need to be addressed before or after the transport, especially if the animal has fleas or needs medication. (4) Locate drivers that have appropriate vehicles, crates, and the physical ability to load an animal. Make sure the transporter can handle the specific animal, especially large dogs or animals that remain in containers or crates that must be carried from vehicle to vehicle, such as alligators or potbellied pigs. (5) Gather the contact information for all transporters and people on the sending and receiving ends. For instance, find out what hours the animal can be picked up or dropped off and how far the sending or receiving location will travel for the transport. (6) To be efficient with transport volunteers' time and money, more than one animal is usually transported at a time. Laurel says, "We have to network! We have to plan to move as many animals as we safely can at the same time. Big emphasis on 'safely.'"[12] (7) Map out the route and determine if temporary foster homes along the route are needed, especially for long transports or for situations where the transport cannot happen immediately. "A number of our transports are 'feeder runs' where dogs from various shelters move to collection points and head out together from there over to a main route before splitting off to different destinations."[13] (8) Post the information to the network of drivers to see who can help. "We work with various lists and with our own file of contacts. I do as much as possible by e-mail, but when you have a last-minute situation or an e-mail is not bringing in a response fast enough, then you have to hit the phones."[14] (9) When drivers offer to help, a run sheet is put together to document the transport route, schedule, meeting times and places, and contact information for each driver. Each driver receives a copy of the run sheet. And (10) when the transport is occurring, the coordinator is on standby to accept calls from transporters who have completed their leg of the route, and to handle any issues.

Struggles involved in coordinating transports of animals include finding enough drivers to complete a transport, especially drivers during the weekdays, and locating credible organizations to take in the animals, provide the needed veterinary care, find appropriate homes, and be available to assist after the adoption. But the number-one struggle is keeping up with the demand for transports.

Laurel has countless success stories of moving animals to locations where they are now thriving, such as a pit bull that was forced out of Ontario as a result of a breed ban that made national headlines and went on to become a drug dog for the Washington State Police, or two dogs that were close to being euthanized at a shelter who are now in a home; both have movie and television careers, including recent roles in the Adam Sandler film *Grown Ups* or the NBC series *Undercovers*. But the transport that stands out in Laurel's mind involved a Labrador mix from Osceola County Animal Control in Michigan who was so active that he drove potential adopters away and the shelter staff crazy. He was transported to a temporary foster home downstate, and when the adoption organization lost a permanent foster space for him, he was shown to Leader Dogs for the Blind in Rochester, Michigan. After his evaluation they accepted him into their program, and now he is benefiting the life of someone who needs his eyes to help them navigate the world. Laurel says, "I am convinced that there are certain dogs out there who are meant to be with a certain person. They have a mission, whether we know it or not. We are part of a process that we don't always see the whole of. But the harder, more complicated the transport, the more likely we are to hear back, somewhere down the road, what an amazing difference that dog made in someone's life."[15]

Laurel has lost count of how many animals she has helped relocate to new areas for re-homing, but it is in the thousands. Laurel is motivated to coordinate transports because most shelter animals are adoptable and simply need a little time, more resources, or a new location to find a home. For her home state of Michigan, "finding rescues for animals facing the prospect of life in a research facility or an inhumane death in a gas chamber, and getting them prepared and transported to safety, is a pretty compelling undertaking."[16]

Getting involved in animal transports can be very rewarding and can give you a sense of accomplishment. Laurel suggests locating an established network to join. Yahoo groups has many transport groups, and you may be able to find one in your state.[17] If the transport is well planned, you will enjoy the process and come back to help again. But be sure to look for a transport group that screens its volunteers and has rules for transporting that are enforced. Laurel explains, "If you can join a group without being asked for your name, address, phone number, and references, look elsewhere. Those 'anything goes' lists are not safe places for the animals and certainly no place to expect to learn the transport ropes."[18] Your private information will not be shared, but it is important for the coordinator to be able to contact you. Besides being involved in the physical transport of animals, you can assist by being a temporary foster home along the route, or being a foster home for the receiving organization.

If you want to help but cannot drive or provide foster care, consider becoming a coordinator. To start, find a mentor, like Laurel. "No one is born knowing how to do this; there are no college classes in how to do it. We raise up new coordinators with an old-fashioned apprenticeship program."[19] What does it take to become a successful coordinator? Being a team player, being organized and having good communication skills, ability to work under pressure, and the ability to use a map and routing software. And lastly, donations are always needed in the form of gas cards to help subsidize the volunteer drivers who may have the time and desire to help but may lack the funds to pay for gasoline. There are many ways to help, from big to small, and the end result is relocating an animal to a location where a new and happy life and can be started.

Going to the Dogs Program (New York)

Melissa Henchen, founder of Going to the Dogs[20] in New York, had an interesting beginning in the world of animal protection and transport. "I actually got involved in rescue because I had a litter of pit bull puppies that I had bred my two adults for and was selling them on Craigslist. Someone who was a hard-core rescuer e-mailed me and explained to me (really chewed me out) about what I was doing was bad for the breed and that so many dogs were dying due to people like me who are uneducated. I invited her to my home because she thought I was a horrible person and I thought she was just crazy, but in the end she was right. After hearing only one in six pit bulls actually makes it out of a shelter alive I realized I needed to do the right thing for my dogs. I immediately got all three of my dogs altered and started joining any forums online dealing with rescuing pit bulls."[21]

Melissa created Going to the Dogs to help transport dogs for better opportunities at finding homes. Although it is a new organization and currently working on a smaller scale than the two previous featured programs, she primarily coordinates shelter transports from Michigan to New York and a few from Missouri to New York. She has even driven to Texas to perform a transport. Melissa spends about ten to twenty-five hours per transport to coordinate drivers and sending/receiving organizations. Besides putting together the "run sheet," e-mailing requests for volunteer help, and monitoring the transport, there is more to getting dogs safely to their next destination. Melissa explains, "The most important part of setting up a transport is making sure that the dog is healthy and legal enough to be transported, and that the receiving rescue/shelter/foster/adopter has been properly screened to ensure the dog is going to a better situation than they are already in. All dogs being transported must have a health certificate, and spaying/neutering is a big aspect, but most make exceptions for puppies or those who have no time to get an appointment before coming to safety. Once those details are all set, the run sheet is put together, typically consisting of one- to two-hour 'legs' of a volunteer driving the dog from point A to point B. Each leg the driver is responsible for calling the coordinator of the run, food/water the dogs, walk/potty the dogs, and ensure the utmost safety when letting dogs in and out of each vehicle."[22]

In addition to coordinating transports, Melissa has fostered more than eighty dogs in her home since 2007, some of which are part of a transport leg. Like Donna Cascarelli, Melissa finds that all the transports are special, but one in particular stands out. "We received a senior dog that was nine years old and had been hit by a car, and when the veterinarian refused to put the dog down for the owner who did not want to deal with the cost of help, we stepped up to take him from Missouri. This dog was adopted within one month of arriving at its destination. We have taken dogs with broken limbs, heartworm, blind, mange, and many more. The thought that people really don't understand the commitment of a dog is just very sad, and that makes our transports special with all of us volunteers knowing what we were able to do for this dog."[23]

Melissa has a few successful strategies for starting and running a transport program. "Attention to details, and be very big on keeping a great reputation with other great organizations. Without overwhelming yourself, make sure you are specific on your ethics and rules for the road. If you stray and allow exceptions, oftentimes you pay the price with your name/reputation with other rescuers."[24] As for struggles, Melissa says that finding good volunteers to do the transports is an issue. It is difficult to commit to helping a dog that needs a transport, and not being able to find volunteers along the route to help. The dog either sits in a shelter for another week, or could be euthanized if the shelter does not have space.

For people who have difficulties volunteering directly at a shelter, transporting is a great way to help save lives. On the Road Again is a system used by many people to find qualified and trained transporters. Melissa also suggests being a foster home for an animal in the middle of a transport that needs a place to rest, or providing foster care for an organization that helps animals in need.

What motivates Melissa each day to help coordinate transports? Knowing that some dogs, solely based on where they are located, have less of a chance at life. It just does not seem fair to Melissa, and she knows that she can do more to help change the lives of dogs, one at a time.

If you are unable to find a transport program, such as those featured in this chapter, there are ways that you can help transport animals in your community. For example, locate an animal group in your area that obtains pets from shelters and offer your assistance. Assistance may involve driving to a shelter to pick up and transport an animal, even just a few miles, to a local foster home or veterinary clinic, or to be a foster home for one of the animals. These short-distance transports are occurring in most communities across the country and can be an easy way to get involved without having to invest too much time or money.

And then there are transports that may take only an hour or two. King Street Cats, where I volunteer, helps locations and shelters that are the most needy. We coordinate with Potomac Highlands Animal Rescue in West Virginia, which is about three hours away by vehicle, and they often have weekly transports to the greater D.C. area to drop off dogs and cats at various approved receiving organizations, like King Street Cats. In the summer of 2009, I was assigned to meet the transport van from West Virginia. When the van arrived and opened the back door, there were three dogs inside along with six carriers filled with cats and kittens. They maximized the space in the van, while ensuring that all the pets were safe for transport. After leaving the six carriers of cats and kittens with me, along with veterinary paperwork, they went on to drop the dogs at another location. They created a simple and smooth transport process and have saved countless dogs and cats in the process.

Depending on your time availability, there are different opportunities for you to get involved in transporting animals. Just make sure that you receive an orientation before transporting animals and have the provisions in your vehicle to transport certain animals. With just a little planning, transporting an animal to a new location and new life can be the most rewarding work you can do as an animal advocate.

You Can Do More

- Locate a transport organization in your area. Check the Internet and Yahoo groups to find a group. Or locate an animal welfare organization that may need the services of a transporter for just a few miles to a new location. Volunteer and become trained in transporting animals out of or within your state. Each travel leg is usually only an hour or two of your time.
- Open your home to provide temporary foster care during the transport process, or become a foster home for an organization that receives transport animals.
- Support transport programs by donating gas cards to help subsidize the costs and allow for more animals to be relocated.
- Support animal organizations that accept transported animals by adopting from them, volunteering to help the animals, or donating to support their efforts.
- If your community shelter struggles with locating adoptable homes, offer to locate organizations that would be available to receive the shelter animals for re-homing, and offer to coordinate those transports.
- If you are unable to drive or foster transport animals but still want to help, locate a transport coordinator and ask to be mentored on how to become a coordinator.

CHAPTER 8

Preventing Cruelty and Neglect of Animals

Why are some people cruel or neglectful to companion animals? For those who love animals, it is unfathomable how someone could intentionally harm or overtly neglect a pet. Yet it happens every minute of the day. The American Society for the Prevention of Cruelty to Animals (ASPCA) estimates that an animal is abused every ten seconds. The mind-set behind animal cruelty is complex. When an adult is cruel to animals, it may be to threaten or intimidate someone (particularly a family member or partner). It may be based on a prejudice against a species; an attempt to retaliate against the animal or control it; for sexual gratification; for amusement; to shock other people; a rehearsal before committing violence; or a form of sadism. When a child is cruel to animals, it may be all of the previous list, plus lack of knowledge of how to treat an animal, curiosity or exploration, depression, peer pressure, fear of the animal, being coerced by another, reenacting the child's own abuse and/or an attempt by the child to regain power after being abused, or to protect the animal from other abuse.

Animals can be abused or neglected in many ways: animal fighting (dogfighting, hog-dog fighting, cockfighting); physical trauma (hitting, slapping, kicking, burning, poisoning, shooting, stabbing—the list is endless); hoarding (where too many animals are suffering from lack of food and/or medical care); puppy mills (where dogs are crammed in tiny cages, often in filthy conditions, and forced to breed until their bodies wear out); and abandonment (being locked inside an abandoned or foreclosed house, being chained up in the backyard of an abandoned house, or being dumped on the side of the road). Then there are other gray areas where people may differ as to whether this is cruelty: tethering (when dogs are chained in the backyard for a majority of their time and receive little human interaction);

cropping dog tails; declawing cats; unhealthy pet diets that cause obesity and health problems; dogsledding; and then there is the gamut of animals used in research.

This chapter will feature what is being done to tackle the epidemic of animal cruelty and neglect and provide tips on what you can to do help an animal that is in an abusive or neglectful situation. Regardless of your chosen profession, everyone can get involved to prevent cruelty and neglect of animals.

EDUCATING TO PREVENT CRUELTY AND NEGLECT

Randy Lockwood is the vice president of forensic sciences and anti-cruelty projects for the ASPCA and has been with ASPCA in that position since 2005. Before that, he was with The Humane Society of the United States for twenty-one years. I have known Randy since 2004, and he is truly knowledgeable on a broad range of issues to protect animals. Trained as a psychologist, Randy is now involved in veterinary forensic sciences and front-line efforts to investigate and prosecute animal abuse and neglect, as well as prevention efforts. In my work with national animal protection groups, I have come to respect that all of them have their areas of specialty. For ASPCA, I have found that their expertise is particularly strong in the proper handling of cases of animal abuse and neglect, while also working to educate and prevent maltreatment before it happens.

Dr. Lockwood approaches cruelty prevention through a holistic approach. "I think too many organizations think that they can stop cruelty just by passing a piece of legislation. We see that as just the beginning, but the laws are sometimes not enforced. Other places have moderate laws but good enforcement. This process starts with having good laws and awareness of those laws by both the general public and law enforcement. The next step is to get the general public to report as they see and recognize cruelty."[1] As part of this holistic approach, Dr. Lockwood and the ASPCA place their focus on training the professionals who are responsible for enforcing animal cruelty laws, such as prosecuting attorneys, law enforcement officers, and judges. If law enforcement officers are trained in responding to animal cruelty, the allegation will be pursued; if prosecutors are trained in how to put together an effective animal cruelty prosecution, it is less likely to be dismissed; if veterinarians are trained on what to expect in a courtroom situation, then they can provide valuable testimony; and if judges understand the nuances of animal cruelty and provide appropriate sentences, then that sends a deterrent message to society.

One of the best ways to spread a societal message about the proper care of animals is to connect people to the story of an animal that has suffered or died and frame cases of cruelty or neglect in terms of "what if this was your pet?" Dr. Lockwood explains, "The message is to help people to relate to the animals as individuals, and animals as victims. And that means recognizing that animals have interests, a life of their own, and should be appreciated for being sentient like humans. But that potentially rules out caring about insects and invertebrates that require a move to an ecological consciousness that is difficult for people to embrace. It has been difficult to get people to care about birds and fish. But if you start with the assumption that 'if it hurts you, it probably hurts every other living thing,' then that is a good frame of reference and you can build empathy from that."[2] In basic terms, people who have empathy toward animals are unlikely to harm them.

But Dr. Lockwood says more needs to be done besides training the front-line professionals and educating the public. One such effort is following up on advocacy strategies to determine if change actually occurred. He clarifies, "In a lot of advocacy work there is a tendency to tell people what is going on then hope that things will change. This is not necessarily true. Human beings are very good at denial and rationalization. We have been telling people about battery cages and puppy mills for decades, and things have improved but not dramatically. We are now in a new phase of animal protection of embracing social marketing. As with other marketing messages, we have to look at the effectiveness of our efforts. What resonates with which audience, and which messages are productive? The most passionate advocates are not necessarily the best communicators except to their own supporters. I do think one of the problems in animal protection is that we spend a lot of time preaching to the choir, and that can be good for sharing strategies that have proven effective and it is good to get that out to the supporters. But what about everyone else?"[3] Dr. Lockwood advises avoiding getting stuck in debates with opponents whose minds you will not change. Instead, place your advocacy focus on those that have not heard your message and have not formed an opinion either way. "Given the fact that fewer than 10 percent in the country are vegetarians and fewer than 10 percent are sport hunters, most people fall in a range of liking animals, particularly their companion animals, yet often they do not think about these broader issues. They do not want to be made to feel guilty, but they may want to make choices that help animals. That has been my approach. It is not that I am less radical with age, but you win over more people by leading them to conclusions that they are already inclined to."[4]

The most memorable story in Dr. Lockwood's career has been assisting on the Michael Vick case and being involved in the assessment of the dogs. "At first I thought, 'I'm going to be seeing the instruments of a crime, potentially dangerous dogs,' yet these were lost dogs who were neglected, ignored, unsocialized, and abused. It was a relief when we realized that most of these animals might be salvageable. Within the first few hours, a few dogs were happy to see us; they were well mannered around the other dogs, and we recognized that these were dogs that had no interest in fighting other dogs. Had we not been there to help them, these dogs would have been killed because they were too friendly to survive a dogfighting enterprise. Many of the dogs have become loved companions; some of these dogs have gone on to become therapy dogs, canine good citizen graduates, and it galvanized our dedication to looking at these animals as victims and individuals."[5]

There are joys and frustrations in working to prevent animal cruelty and neglect. For Dr. Lockwood, the frustrations come in accepting that some people do not see the world the way we do, and that can cause compassion fatigue. "People who bring in a box of kittens to a shelter think they are doing you a favor in giving you kittens to sell. We then get frustrated in trying to have them bring in the mom cat to be spayed. That is sometimes more frustrating than the outright hostile person. If someone is ignorant, that is more frustrating, and there are so many people like that. Some of it is education, culture, human self-interest, or just trying to understand why someone has a dog if all they will do is chain it in the backyard twenty-four hours a day. I hear sentiments like this constantly."[6] On the positive side, Dr. Lockwood finds joys in watching children find a connection to animals, particularly young offenders who have never been previously exposed to the power of using love and reward to elicit good behaviors from a dog, a horse, or other creatures.

In the end, Dr. Lockwood believes that we need to keep working to change how people view animals, through humane education and through accepting that the main educational source for children is peers and not necessarily parents. And with that goal, everyone can get involved. If you see someone being outwardly abusive or neglectful to an animal, do something. Report it to the proper authorities, or if it is occurring in front of you, speak up. Be sure to keep yourself safe if speaking out to someone you do not know, but oftentimes simply shouting "stop" to the person and watching their behavior will end the immediate threat to the animal. However, be sure to then follow up with a report to the proper authorities, because the abuse may continue after you leave. Since the animals are unable to speak for themselves, except through their cries of pain, it is up to all of us to speak up for them.

PUPPY MILLS: MASS BREEDING ENTERPRISES

Puppy mills have become well known to Americans in recent years due to media attention to shocking undercover investigations. In 2008, Oprah Winfrey shined a light on the plight of puppy mill dogs by running her own undercover investigation with the help of Main Line Animal Rescue.

Puppy mills are mass breeding enterprises where animals are often kept in conditions of squalor, including being in wire cages for their entire breeding life; not having any human affection, toys, or treats; and often not receiving any exercise unless an exercise wheel is placed in the cage. Many of these dogs have never felt grass on their feet or been touched kindly by a human. These dogs often end up with a lifetime of medical and behavioral issues, and many with a significantly shortened life span.

The Humane Society of the United States (HSUS) estimates there are 10,000 puppy mills in the United States, producing two to four million puppies every year.[7] Knowing that three to four million pets are euthanized in shelters every year, imagine how that number could be drastically slashed through the elimination of puppy mills. Undercover investigations by HSUS indicate that most of these dogs end up in pet stores or sold on the Internet or through classified ads.[8] Although pet stores routinely claim that their puppies come from legitimate breeders, HSUS has uncovered that those claims are not necessarily true.[9] But sadly, many of these dogs die before ever knowing the kindness of a loving home.

How can you determine if a puppy mill is in your community? Kathleen Summers, manager of puppy mill campaigns for HSUS, describes these telltale signs. "It's sometimes difficult to tell because puppy mills are often located in rural areas far from public roads. But if you see a property where large numbers of dogs are confined to cages year round, that's a pretty good indication of a puppy mill. And if someone nearby is regularly advertising puppies for sale, especially several different breeds, that is a red flag. Reputable breeders breed very sparingly and usually do not specialize in more than one or two breeds of dogs. They typically do not need to 'hang out a shingle' in front of their house to sell puppies—they are very careful about meeting with prospective buyers to ensure that their puppies are going to good homes."[10]

Efforts are under way by national and state animal protection organizations to expose and close down puppy mills. HSUS is engaging in a multi-model approach that includes conducting investigations to expose the true nature of puppy mills, assisting local law enforcement with shutting down puppy mills and rescuing the dogs, and passing legislation to crack down on puppy mills. Such legislation includes 2010 successes in Hawaii, Iowa, Louisiana, Missouri, and Oklahoma; 2010 federal legislation known as the PUPS Act that would close the loophole in the Animal Welfare Act, requiring the USDA to monitor and inspect large-scale breeders who sell directly to the public; and ballot initiatives including the 2010 Missouri Prop B success. HSUS is also supporting litigation against sellers and businesses that perpetuate the puppy mill industry; puppy-friendly pet stores, encompassing almost 1,000 pet stores as of late 2010 that have signed a pledge to not sell puppies; and educating consumers about ending the financial support of puppy mills. Kathleen says that everyone can become involved by writing to their legislators, educating others who are seeking to get a puppy, and refusing to patronize pet stores or Internet sites that sell puppies. There are also opportunities to join protests and to become a local advocate to pass puppy mill ordinances in your community.[11]

With the ramping up of efforts to close down puppy mills, battles have emerged between organizations working to shut down puppy mills and breeders fighting to maintain their profitable business. What is the difference between a puppy mill and a legitimate breeder? Most often it is the number of breeding dogs that the breeder has, as well as the conditions in which the dogs are housed and raised. Efforts to pass legislation to ban puppy mills often target the number of breeding dogs allowable as a way of distinguishing smaller-scale hobby or home breeders from over-crowded commercial breeders likely to be puppy mills. Legitimate breeders may have a few breeding dogs that produce one or two litters a year, and the dogs and puppies are raised in a home environment and know the love of the breeder.

Kathleen explains why the breeding community has opposed legislative efforts to ban puppy mills. "The pet industry has conducted a fear campaign to scare small breeders into thinking that inspectors will soon be in their living rooms looking at their dogs. Nothing could be further from the truth. Small, reputable breeders who keep their pets in the home as members of the family are not the type of breeders we seek to regulate; in fact, they are the only type of breeders we recommend. Most puppy mill legislation is only aimed at large-scale breeders who have ten or more breeding females. Reputable breeders are already abiding by proper care standards, so they should not be threatened in any way by legislation requiring common-sense care standards for the care of dogs, standards that they already far exceed."[12]

As a result of the overproduction of puppy mill dogs, some puppies once purchased become gravely ill and die shortly thereafter, resulting in a new form of legislation called "puppy lemon laws." These laws protect purchasers from the financial hardship that accompanies many of these dogs, but they have many limitations, such as limiting the buyer to a refund of his or her purchase price, even if the dog's veterinary care was many times higher.[13]

Although it may be heartbreaking to walk away from the puppies in pet stores, especially those that look ill, it is crucial to end the demand for these puppies so that the puppy mills will stop overproducing dogs. If you "rescue" a puppy mill dog from a pet store or the Internet, the money you spent on the dog will go back to supporting the puppy mills in producing more dogs. Kathleen explains, "We cannot solve the puppy mill problem by buying all the puppies. Unfortunately, 'saving' a puppy from a pet store by buying him or her only pumps money back into the puppy mill industry and ensures its success. That puppy's mother and thousands like her will continue to spend their entire lives in a cage. If you see animals for sale who are being kept in cruel conditions, by all means report it! But never buy a puppy to 'save' him or her. The best way to strike a blow against puppy mills is to refuse to support them by getting your next pet from an animal shelter or rescue group and refusing to shop at pet stores or Internet sites that sell puppies."[14]

To help reduce the demand fueling puppy mill operations, adopt dogs and puppies from shelters, animal organizations, or a breed rescue group if you are interested in a specific breed. If you see a puppy or dog in ill health at a pet store, contact animal control or law enforcement authorities in your community so that they can investigate. If you purchase a dog from a breeder, insist on visiting the dog in the environment in which it was raised. Do not take as truth verbal or online claims that the dog was "home raised." Responsible breeders are proud to show you where their dogs are raised.

If you suspect there is a puppy mill in your community, it may not be illegal based on your state's animal protection laws.[15] But if you suspect cruelty or neglect of animals that may be part of a puppy mill or at a pet store, there are steps you can take. First, gather information including the name and address of the breeder or store, and if you purchased a puppy, provide documentation of the sale and/or veterinary records. If you visit the breeding facility, document the number of animals you see and a description of the conditions. Second, report what you saw to your local animal control or law enforcement agency or state department of agriculture. If you can determine whether the facility is licensed by the United States Department of Agriculture, also file a report with USDA's Animal Care Division.[16] And lastly, contact HSUS by calling the toll-free tip line at 1-877-MILL-TIP or report the information online at www.humane society.org/puppymills. If you purchased a sick puppy that you suspect may have come from a puppy mill, you can also file a complaint with HSUS.

HOARDING

The Hoarding of Animals Research Consortium (HARC) at Tufts University is the primary resource on animal hoarding and solutions to tackle this misunderstood behavior. HARC was formed in 1997 by a group of professionals that collaborated until 2006 when they published a manual on animal hoarding.[17] Now the HARC website provides valuable information on animal hoarding.[18]

Animal hoarding is a complicated psychological disorder and behavioral deficit that impairs people's ability to care for themselves or others. There may be other barriers that result in hoarding, such as a physical disability or financial constraint that inhibits obtaining proper care for the animals. What often begins as a caring effort to help animals can result in a need to control the animals, thus resulting in losing control over the situation and the well-being of the animals. Currently, two states (Illinois and Hawaii) specifically outlaw hoarding; but all states have laws against cruelty and neglect under which hoarding could be charged.

There are many misperceptions about hoarding. According to HARC, animal hoarding contains these four characteristics: "failure to provide minimal standards of sanitation, space, nutrition, and veterinary care for animals; inability to recognize the effects of this failure on the welfare of the animals, human members of the household, and the environment; obsessive attempts to accumulate or maintain a collection of animals in the face of progressively deteriorating conditions; and denial or minimization of problems and living conditions for people and animals."[19] HARC has also identified three types of animal hoarders: overwhelmed caregivers (tries to provide care but then eventual decline occurs), rescue hoarders (has a mission to save animals and does not know when to stop), and exploiter hoarders (obtains animals for their own self-need, lacks empathy for the animals, and is the most difficult to address). Each has its own unique approach toward resolution.

Animal hoarding is different from object hoarding, yet both share similar characteristics such as living in clutter and unsanitary conditions, denial of the problem, alienation from others, and not seeking help. Although under debate within the psychological community, it is believed that object hoarding is rooted as an obsessive-compulsive disorder (OCD), whereas animal hoarding does not have the same repetitive behavior as OCD. At the International Association of Human-Animal Interaction Organizations Conference held in Stockholm, Sweden, in July 2010, I attended a presentation by Dr. Akimitsu Yokoyama of Teikyo University of Science in Yamanashi, Japan, who theorizes that animal hoarding is related to Asperger's syndrome and not OCD.[20] The simple explanation is that those with OCD are conflicted about their repetitive behavior (they understand that they should not wash their hands eighty times a day), whereas this conflict does not exist with animal hoarding. Dr. Yokoyama believes that Asperger's syndrome is becoming mainstream in the psychiatric field for explaining a variety of mental health disorders. If animal hoarding is a form of Asperger's syndrome, the treatment for it is different than for OCD and may explain why some therapeutic interventions for hoarding are ineffective and recidivism for hoarding is almost 100 percent.

HARC explains that animal hoarding is a community problem and is about a person satisfying a human need to accumulate and control animals that supersedes the needs of the animals. Animal hoarding is a serious problem not only for the animals involved, but for people within the home and communities having to deal with the public health hazard. "It is cruel to animals, can devastate families, be associated with elder abuse, child abuse, and self-neglect, and be costly for municipalities to resolve. Without appropriate post-intervention treatment, recidivism approaches 100%. Increased awareness, leading to more comprehensive long-term interventions, is needed."[21]

Hoarding can be addressed through different approaches based on the type of hoarding that occurs, including psychological intervention, cooperative efforts with the hoarder, and criminal prosecution. There is no current standard psychological treatment for animal hoarders; thus, identifying other disorders is usually the approach to get started therapeutically. The overwhelmed caregiver is usually the easiest to work with on reducing the number of animals in a cooperative manner. The rescue hoarder may need a threat of legal action to gain compliance. And the exploiter hoarder most often needs criminal prosecution and forced removal of the animals.[22] According to HARC, the best approach is the multiagency type from mental health, social services, animal welfare, city zoning, public health, prosecution, probation, and police departments. Without this multiagency approach to address the complex issues of animal hoarding, it is no wonder that recidivism of hoarders approaches 100 percent.

There is no one type of person who becomes a hoarder, although public perception and some data support it involving older women living alone. Hoarders may be people who appear functional with good jobs; thus, they are leading a double life. Some hoarders have been veterinarians or people who started as animal rescuers with a legitimate organization. HARC states:

Our research to date . . . suggests that, similar to object hoarding, animal hoarding is likely a final common pathway from a variety of traumatic experiences which result in dysfunctional attachment styles to people and lead to compulsive and addictive behavior. . . . Animal hoarders' impaired judgment and actions, or failures to act, may arise from a variety of factors. These include difficulties understanding relevant information about animals' needs, inaccurate appreciation of a situation and its consequences, being unable to reason about treatment options and alternative courses of action, faulty self-governance, psychological defenses and behaviors in response to stress, as well as magical thinking, lack of insight, and other cognitive distortions. When these impairments become associated with functional deficits (e.g., failure to provide adequate food, water, proper sanitation, necessary medical care, and failure to recognize and attend to fundamental behavioral and mental needs of animals), incompetent care occurs and animal suffering results. [23]

So how do you know if there is a legitimate animal rescue person in your community or a hoarder? A legitimate animal rescuer will provide appropriate veterinary care, food, water, and shelter to all of the animals, and they will allow potential adopters to visit the location where the animals are housed. There is transparency when dealing with a legitimate animal welfare organization.

Stories about animal hoarding are becoming more prevalent in the news media, often being reported daily. Animal Planet's *Confessions: Animal Hoarding* show has brought the inner world of animal hoarding to mainstream America. But according to HARC, dozens of other hoarding situations are undetected and unreported everyday. So what can a person do to help animals caught in a hoarding situation?

Jenny Coffey (who is also featured in chapter 15) works with the Mayor's Alliance for New York City Animals. As a trained social worker, Jenny has assisted with more than one hundred animal hoarding cases in her career. [24] Jenny has truly seen it all when it comes to the hoarding of animals and what is needed to prevent hoarding and treat the offenders. Jenny believes that "it takes a village" to combat animal hoarding, and this includes accepting help from caring citizens as well as coordinating with mental health professionals, lawyers, and animal welfare responders. For the layperson (a family member, friend, neighbor, or colleague), Jenny says it is important to not ignore the problem or brush it off as an eccentricity. Address the person and try to encourage their agreement to receive help for their animals, such as veterinary care, spaying/neutering, vaccinations, or even re-homing; make sure that the person has a supportive network of people who can help but also be confrontational about the behavior; address other issues such as lack of electricity or water and work to fix those issues; and engage community resources. For those involved in professions that help people, such as social workers and mental health or community health professionals, Jenny recommends learning about hoarding and attending trainings on intervention in an animal hoarding situation. Training can be important to not only learn the different types of hoarding, but also to protect yourself while working with hoarders. Home visits are crucial when working with a hoarder. It is important to evaluate the animals and find resources to help with animal care, spay/neuter, and when possible the safe placement of animals for re-homing. It is also important to work with the client to identify and document all the animals in the home and begin to identify the animals that can be re-homed.

Jenny advises that working in combination with other community resources is important, such as the health department, mental health, child and adult protective service social workers, animal protection, environmental departments, agriculture department, building departments, code enforcement, prosecutors, and probation. Since animal hoarding involves more than the improper care and accumulation of animals, bringing together community partners to address the problem will help. It is also important to connect the client with community services such as aging services, housing services, eviction prevention services, and legal assistance. If you can gain compliance from the hoarder, begin to work toward interventions that include addressing the environmental conditions, cleaning the home, and re-homing the animals. If the hoarder is resistant to having the animals voluntarily surrendered, and the situation warrants this intervention, then as a last resort consider having legal intervention, including charging the hoarder with misdemeanor charges or cruelty and have the animals seized. As a former prosecutor, I know all too well that this "forced compliance" in prosecuting hoarders and removing their animals may result in their accumulating more animals. So working with the client through a multiagency effort, while cleaning the home and removing the animals, is the best scenario for all involved. And afterward, close monitoring is needed. This is where family, friends, neighbors, and colleagues can help when official probation or social-working oversight is not available.

For professionals who work in animal protection, the hoarding case is becoming more prevalent. Responding to a hoarding situation is similar to responding to other disasters involving animals (see chapter 10 on disaster response for animals). Jenny advises that animal protection professionals be involved in coordinating efforts when addressing a hoarding situation, because specific supplies will be needed, such as carriers and crates, traps and netting, and hazmat suits. Coordination with local veterinarians will also be needed, especially to help the animals that need immediate medical care. Animal behaviorists should also be included to help assess the animals for re-homing. These responses can last several days, or even weeks, until every last animal has been removed. When an animal shelter or organization is involved in a large-scale hoarding situation, it can financially devastate the shelter as well as take up valuable space, thus displacing other animals in need. You can help by donating money or supplies to help with the effort, or offer to be a foster home for animals that need special care or socializing.

From Jenny's experience, she understands that no single community agency can resolve a hoarding situation; it takes a community response to address the behavior for the individual and provide help for the animals and community. Jenny recommends creating a hoarding task force within your community that brings the relevant professionals to the group, as well as support from citizens who can be on the watch for hoarding situations. For citizens, speak up when you suspect an animal hoarding situation. If it is a family member, try to work with the family member toward a resolution, but do not hesitate to seek the services of your community. Through early intervention and monitoring, animals can avoid being caught in a hoarding situation.

ABANDONMENT AND THE PLIGHT OF FORECLOSURE PETS

Although animal abandonment has been problematic for decades, abandonment has increased during the 2008 (and beyond) financial crisis in the United States. The terms "foreclosure pets" and "recession pets" are now commonplace among the animal protection community, as they involve family pets becoming victims of the recession. Foreclosure and recession pets are losing their homes at record rates because their owners are losing their jobs and their homes. According to a calculation that I created, anywhere from 24,700 and 41,000 animals *per day* are in jeopardy of losing their homes as a result of the financial crisis in the United States. This is based on an estimated 411 million pets in the United States (all forms of pets)[25] to 248 million pets (just cats, dogs, rabbits and small mammals),[26] 114 million U.S. homes, and over 11,400 homes per day entering foreclosure (based on August–September 2010 rates).[27] What is shocking about this number is that 10,000 pets a day are already being euthanized in U.S. shelters.

Foreclosure and recession pets are being turned in to animal shelters in record numbers. Since there is no animal intake recording system in place in the United States, exact numbers are unknown. But daily news reports across the country mention animal shelters that are struggling to handle the increased intake of animals, while also working against decreasing adoptions and donations. It is heartbreaking to think of the number of wonderful, healthy, and adoptable family pets being euthanized at a shelter simply because the economy has declined and potential adopters are hesitant to take on a pet.

However, those pets that are surrendered to shelters are the lucky foreclosure/recession pets. The unlucky ones are being abandoned outside with no ability to fend for themselves and few survival skills. Or worse, they are trapped inside an abandoned home or tethered in the backyard and may not be discovered by a foreclosure professional or real estate agent until weeks later. Many of these pets are starving to death or are on the brink of death when found.

In August and September 2010, I provided foster care to Luke and Leia, brother and sister cats, who were abandoned inside a home in Washington, D.C. No one knows how long they were in the house, but when the police seized them they were nothing but fur and bones due to severe starvation. They were likely within a day or two of dying. I struggled for months to get Luke and Leia to eat and gain weight. Both had difficulty adjusting to eating cat food, even high-quality, human-grade, healthy cat food, because of the trauma that they suffered. But throughout the ordeal, their sweet personalities remained intact. Lucky for Luke and Leia, they were rescued in time and were adopted to a wonderful home with four children, a mom, and a dad, who love them. Sadly, several months later, Leia passed away from complications believed to be associated with the severe neglect she experienced. Leia's story shows how even getting these abandoned pets to safety may still result in long-term health issues and even a premature death.

To help combat the epidemic of foreclosure and recession pets, Cheryl Lang, president and CEO of Integrated Mortgage Solutions in Houston, Texas, created No Paws Left Behind,[28] a nonprofit organization designed to help rescue and re-home foreclosure pets. I am honored to be the volunteer vice president of No Paws and am amazed at the number of animals in need, and the wonderful people who help them. No Paws Left Behind works to educate mortgage and foreclosure professionals on the growing issue of family pets being abandoned in and outside foreclosed homes. Mortgage and foreclosure professionals are not necessarily trained in handling pets being left behind, so No Paws Left Behind is helping to provide resources so that these animals can find placement with an organization. No Paws Left Behind seeks to place animals only with animal organizations that do not euthanize due to overcrowding.

Through a network of caring animal rescue people, e-mail alerts are sent out regarding pets abandoned at foreclosed properties. The goal is to find someone who is willing to rescue the pets and provide them with a safe place and medical care until a new adoptive home can be found. Sometimes it takes a few weeks or even a few months to locate someone who can help. In the meantime, No Paws Left Behind works with the foreclosure professional to care for the animals, including providing sufficient shelter, food, and water, while holding off animal control from seizing the pets.

Animals abandoned at foreclosed properties are often seen by neighbors. If you see a pet that has been locked inside an abandoned house, or placed outside, please contact No Paws Left Behind for help.[29]

REDUCING PET OVERPOPULATION TO REDUCE CRUELTY AND NEGLECT

Dr. Stacia Jung is a veterinarian on the island of St. Croix. Dr. Jung is featured in the next chapter for her work with feral cats; however, she is also motivated to prevent cruelty and neglect on St. Croix in a unique way. Dr. Jung's focus is to work on decreasing the pet overpopulation problem as a way of combating cruelty and neglect. She is doing this through a nonprofit organization she created called the Sunshine Foundation,[30] which provides affordable and high-volume spay/neuter services, the only program of its kind on the island of St. Croix.

Dr. Jung explains why this effort is helping to reduce cruelty and neglect. "By decreasing the number of animals that are roaming the streets in need of food, water, shelter, etc., we are decreasing the number of animals that may end up starving, sick, injured, neglected, and abandoned. By promoting our humane message of spay/neuter to the community about the importance of taking responsibility for their own pet's health and reproduction, we hope that we are also educating people to do the right thing for all of the needy animals on St. Croix. Education and awareness are often the first step. Many people on St. Croix are getting the message that there are too many animals on St. Croix and not enough homes. I believe that people respond to negative information (the facts about how many animals are euthanized, the facts about animal neglect and cruelty) by looking for positive ways to get involved and make a difference."[31]

To help with these efforts, Dr. Jung is exploring a working relationship with a new nonprofit organization on the island of St. Croix that is dedicated toward humane education. She is also working with Lucky Paws Foundation based on St. Thomas, which is promoting affordable and high-volume spay and neuter services. To provide more direct support for the animals, she has opened her veterinary clinic, the Sugar Mill Veterinary Center, to provide foster care to animals that have been maltreated. By addressing the prevention of cruelty and neglect in a multitude of pathways, Dr. Jung is hopeful that incidents of cruelty and neglect will begin to decrease in St. Croix.

As with any effort to protect animals, there are dos and don'ts to help you succeed. Dr. Lockwood has three main dos and don'ts: (1) People who are successful long-term in this business are able to keep their sense of humor and see the silly things that animals do to lighten the difficult moments. If you get disturbed because change is not happening fast enough, then you will burn out and not be able to help the animals. (2) Get a life. You must take care of yourself before you can help the animals. If you delay taking a vacation or even just a day off because there is one more animal to save, then you are suffocating yourself and will not be able to help in the long run. And do not self-medicate through caffeine, nicotine, or alcohol. Listen to your body and take breaks. And (3) you cannot save them all. Take pleasure in small victories and for each animal that you help. While you work on the bigger picture of getting people to change their behavior toward animals, celebrate each individual animal that you save.

So how can you help to prevent cruelty and neglect of animals? If you encounter a situation where you feel that an animal is being abused or neglected, do not walk away or second-guess your suspicions. It can be difficult to know for sure whether an animal is being abused or neglected. ASPCA's website has helpful information on how to identify and report animal cruelty. Because the behavior of an animal may not be sufficient to determine abuse or neglect, it is important to look at the surroundings of the animal. ASPCA has these recommendations:

Physical Signs
- Collar so tight that it has caused a neck wound or has become embedded in the pet's neck;
- Open wounds, signs of multiple healed wounds or an ongoing injury or illness that isn't being treated;
- Untreated skin conditions that have caused loss of hair, scaly skin, bumps or rashes;
- Extreme thinness or emaciation—bones may be visible;
- Fur infested with fleas, ticks or other parasites;
- Patches of bumpy, scaly skin rashes;
- Signs of inadequate grooming, such as extreme matting of fur, overgrown nails and dirty coat;
- Weakness, limping or the inability to stand or walk normally;
- Heavy discharge from eyes or nose;
- An owner striking or otherwise physically abusing an animal;
- Visible signs of confusion or extreme drowsiness;

Environmental Signs
- Pets are tied up alone outside for long periods of time without adequate food or water, or with food or water that is unsanitary;
- Pets are kept outside in inclement weather without access to adequate shelter;
- Pets are kept in an area littered with feces, garbage, broken glass or other objects that could harm them;
- Animals are housed in kennels or cages (very often crowded in with other animals) that are too small to allow them to stand, turn around and make normal movements possibly with too many other animals."[32]

So what do you do if you suspect an animal is being abused or neglected? Make a call to the proper authorities to have them investigate. Here is what you can do to be helpful in making a report: First, determine which law enforcement agency handles animal abuse complaints. In some communities, it may be the animal control shelter or it may be the police. Second, decide if you want to make the complaint anonymously or list your name. In my experience, if you make an anonymous complaint, it will not be acted on as quickly as listing your name. If you are afraid of retaliation or being wrong about what you suspect, tell that to the law enforcement officer. Third, write down what you observed and provide as much detail as possible, such as dates, times, location, abuse/neglect that you witnessed, noises heard (such as the animal howling), and people involved in harming the animal. If possible, take photos of what you observe and date the photos. If you know of other people who witnessed the abuse or neglect, ask them to write out a statement. Fourth, keep a log of the cruelty report, including who you spoke with and what information you provided. If you make a report of cruelty or neglect but then inform the law enforcement officer that you do not wish to get involved, including testifying to what you saw, that likely will be the end of the investigation. If people are unwilling to come forward with what they saw, including testifying if necessary, then there is no way to help an animal that is in an abusive situation. I have spoken with countless people who were afraid to come forward and testify, and what I always told them was, "what if you were being abused and wanted to get away from your abuser but could not, yet there was someone who knew what you were going through? Would you want that person to help, to make a call, and to get you to safety?" Animals that are in abusive or neglectful homes have no hope of surviving unless all of us stand up and do the right thing. Waiting for "someone else" to take action, or thinking that it is none of your business to get involved, is not how healthy communities will thrive. Fifth, follow up with the investigating officer. If you are not getting the answers that you need, or it seems like the investigation is taking longer than it should, do not hesitate to contact a supervisor. If you are still not getting the answers that you need, consider contacting the district attorney's office, local politicians, or, as a last resort, the media.

To keep your pet safe from being harmed by another person, keep your pet indoors or supervise your pet when outside. Even if you have a fenced-in yard, check it to make sure that your pet cannot escape, and always supervise your animal to make sure someone does not enter your yard and take your pet. Do not ever tether your pet to a pole or tree outside of a coffee shop or other store while you are shopping. This is just asking someone to take your pet and could result in your pet being harmed. Also get to know other pet-friendly people in your neighborhood. Together, you can watch out for each other's pets and report any suspicious people in the neighborhood.

If you suspect that someone has intentionally poisoned a pet, is breeding animals in a cruel and unhealthy manner, or is engaging in animal fighting, speak up and report your suspicions to law enforcement. The best way we can protect animals from cruelty and neglect is to be diligent citizens and report any conduct or behavior that appears wrong. After all, if we do not speak up for the animals, who will?

You Can Do More

- If you witness cruelty or neglect to an animal, do something! Make a call to the law enforcement agency in charge of animals or speak directly to the person abusing the animal if you can do so safely. If you see a pet that has been abandoned outside, provide food and water to the pet until they can be rescued. Or contact No Paws Left Behind or your local animal shelter to have the abandoned animal taken to the shelter, where it will receive food, water, and shelter.
- Support organizations that work to prevent animal cruelty and neglect. Monetary donations will help them to continue their work.
- Offer to become a foster home for a pet that suffered cruelty or neglect. Sometimes these pets need a little extra love and attention to thrive and find a new home.
- Support legislation to strengthen animal cruelty laws. Sign up for e-mail action alerts from these national organizations: American Humane Association, American Society for the Prevention of Cruelty to Animals, Animal Law Coalition, Animal Legal Defense Fund, Best Friends Animal Sanctuary, People for the Ethical Treatment of Animals, and The Humane Society of the United States. You may have state or local animal organizations that also send out e-mail alerts on state and local legislation that benefits animals. Getting involved by sending an e-mail or letter, making a phone call, or having a meeting with a legislator helps to pass animal-protection legislation.
- If you are ready to bring a new pet into your home, always adopt from an animal shelter, animal rescue organization, or breed rescue organization. Do not purchase animals from pet stores or the Internet, because you may be supplying the demand of a puppy mill.

CHAPTER 9

Protecting Feral Cats

According to Alley Cat Allies, the leading organization in the United States on the protection and care of feral cats, there may be as many as 90 million feral cats in the United States, equal to the number of pet cats living in U.S. homes.[1] What you may not know is that people have been living alongside feral and stray cats for 10,000 years. Alley Cat Allies educates people that feral cats are not a new phenomenon. "They are healthy and thrive in every landscape, from the most urban to the most rural."[2] Yet feral cats encounter two issues that may prematurely end their life: animal control policies that believe that stray and feral cats are better off euthanized and people who see them as a nuisance or as an animal that needs to be brought inside in order to thrive. Both could not be farther from the truth.

Stray cats can be feral or socialized. A socialized stray cat is commonly a domesticated family pet that became lost outdoors or was abandoned; whereas a feral cat is undomesticated, has not been raised with human contact, and is fearful of interacting with people. Feral cats can be any size, age, and breed. So do not be surprised if you see a feral Persian. The confusion between a socialized stray cat and a feral cat can actually result in a friendly cat being mislabeled as feral and missing out on an opportunity to get into an adoption program and find a home. The reverse can happen when someone sees a feral, believes that the cat may be a socialized stray, and they take the cat to a shelter in hopes of having it adopted. That often results in euthanasia of the unadoptable feral cat. When you see a cat outdoors, take the time to learn whether the cat is truly feral or whether the cat is socialized but may be temporarily scared. If the cat is willing to approach you after it has had time to know you, then the cat is likely a socialized stray who lost its home and can be re-homed.

There are many misperceptions about feral cats. Feral cats have a home; it is just outdoors. Feral cats can provide a real community service, especially when it comes to rodent control. As difficult as it may be to see a feral cat outside fending for itself, capturing it and taking it to a shelter to "find a new home" is a certain death sentence. One of the key messages in dealing with feral cats is to leave them in their chosen environment but sterilize the cat so that kittens are not born into the feral cat environment, thus allowing the cat to live a healthier and longer life.

In 2007, Alley Cat Allies conducted a national survey on how Americans view feral cats. The survey involved a national representative sample of more than 1,200 adults. The results were eye-opening, because 81 percent of Americans believe it is more humane to allow a stray cat to live out its life outdoors than to trap it and have it euthanized at a shelter.[3] When participants in the survey were asked if their opinion would remain the same if the cat would die in two years after being hit by a car, 72 percent still said it was more humane to allow the cat to live its life outdoors rather than be prematurely euthanized.[4] Yet the current practice in most American shelters is that it is more humane to euthanize a stray cat than to allow it to live outdoors.[5] And shelter euthanasia is the number-one cause of death in cats.[6]

The survey went on to address the myth that feral and stray cats live harsh lives and are often suffering from debilitating disease and injury. "A 2006 study found that of 103,643 stray and feral cats examined in spay/neuter clinics in six states from 1993 to 2004, less than 1 percent of those cats was euthanized due to debilitating conditions, trauma or infectious diseases. A small study conducted in 2002 examined the body weight, body condition score, and falciform fat pads of 105 mature male cats brought to a spay/neuter clinic in Alachua County, Florida. The study revealed that '[o]verall, the cats in this study were lean but not emaciated prior to neutering.' A study examining the infectious disease rates of feral cats in Northern Florida found that 'feral cats assessed in this study had similar or lower prevalence rates of infections than those published for pet cats in the United States.'"[7] While anecdotal stories may currently support the notion of trapping and euthanizing a stray or feral cat because a humane death is better than life on the streets, the research and opinions of Americans do not support that position.

Alley Cat Allies further clarifies why some cats enjoy and thrive living outdoors. They assert that it is erroneous to assume that "all domestic species are totally dependent on humans for their well-being. This notion of dependency may be true for some species, but it is not true for the domestic cat, *Felis catus*. In fact, 'nearly all domestic cats can . . . survive and even flourish on their own if they shift their core area or home base to a farm, a derelict building, or even land that is uninhabited by people.'"[8] This has been so for 8,000 to 10,000 years. And while we may like to believe that all domesticated cats enjoy the comforts of an indoor home, and many do, feral cats enjoy the freedom of outdoors.

Appreciating that feral cats enjoy living outdoors and have not been socialized to interact with people does not make them any less worthy of living an enjoyable life. There are ways that you can help a feral cat become a beneficial part of your neighborhood. Alley Cat Allies receives more than 45,000 calls yearly from concerned citizens who want to help feral cats but not have them taken to a shelter to be euthanized.[9]

Trap-neuter-return is an essential component of helping to protect feral cats. It is a process of humanely helping a feral cat thrive outdoors while reducing the feral cat overpopulation. According to Alley Cat Allies, trap-neuter-return improves the lives of feral cats, improves their relationships with people, and decreases the number of feral cats over time. There are numerous benefits to engaging in trap-neuter-return. Neutered feral cats become healthier, gain weight, live longer, roam less, are less aggressive and more affectionate toward each other, make less noise, and are less likely to end up at animal control to be euthanized.[10]

The process of trap-neuter-return involves setting a trap in a safe location, often with very smelly and appealing food, such as jack mackerel, which can be found at the grocery store, roasted chicken, or other appetizing food for a cat. Since cats tend to be nighttime creatures, traps are often set at night; that is when feral cats are most mobile and looking for food. If you are placing the trap in a public location, be sure to place a tarp or blanket over the trap to protect the cat until you can retrieve it. And placing a note on the trap to let others know of the trap-neuter-return efforts will help to avoid tampering. Whether in a public place or your backyard, be prepared to check the trap every few hours, or as often as you can. If you catch the cat in the middle of the night before your chosen veterinary clinic is open, have a safe location where you can keep the cat in the trap.

Before trapping a cat, be sure to have a veterinary clinic identified that is willing to handle a feral cat. Not all veterinarians are in a position to handle one. Once the cat is trapped, the veterinarian may sedate the cat immediately to avoid trauma. The veterinarian will examine the sedated cat for injuries, spay or neuter the cat, provide rabies and distemper vaccinations, "tip" the ear so that the next person will have a visible notification that the cat does not need to be trapped, and often will perform tests to determine if the cat has feline leukemia (which is a highly transmittable disease). The level of care during this one-time veterinary visit will depend on the amount of money available to be spent and what the veterinarian is able to provide.

While the cat is at the veterinary clinic, do not be surprised if you learn that the cat you have trapped is actually not feral, but a frightened stray that became lost from its home or was abandoned. I have found that some outdoor cats, once trapped, end up being socialized and adoptable cats. Due to the unpredictable nature of living outdoors, a socialized cat may become fearful and skittish of people; but once safely indoors, they blossom into wonderful indoor cats. So also be sure to have a plan in place if the cat is social and can be adopted. Identifying and working with feral cat organizations is a good first step to helping a socialized stray cat find an indoor home.

When the work on the cat is completed, you will want to give the cat a day or two to recuperate before being released to the original location. If you have a garage or other safe location at your house, be willing to give the cat a day or two to rest. Once the cat is ready, simply return the cat to the original location. Trap-neuter-return is essential to preventing the expansion of kittens born to feral cats, many of which end up in shelters that are already overcrowded. After you trap-neuter-return feral cats, they can become wonderful working cats in your community.

Some people may question why we should help to protect and care for feral cats. Some people complain that they are a nuisance; they hunt birds in the neighborhood and use gardens as litter boxes. If you have a feral cat in your backyard or neighborhood, chances are they are not alone. Seeing a stray or feral cat certainly tugs at the heartstrings of animal lovers. If you start feeding a feral cat and do not engage in trap-neuter-return, you will soon find litters of feral kittens running around your yard or neighborhood, and the population will continue to grow. So when feeding a feral cat, be sure to do so only if you are willing and able to perform trap-neuter-return or have someone else available to do it.

You may think that simply contacting your local animal shelter to have the cats removed will do the trick, but not so. Many animal shelters cannot retrieve stray and feral cats because of lack of laws that allow them to do that. For those that can, trapping and removing feral cats to a shelter will likely result in euthanasia. Removing the feral cats creates a vacuum effect whereby other feral cats will move into the territory and take over. It could result in even more cats coming to the area. Sometimes kittens born to a feral cat can be trapped and socialized if they are placed in an environment where they receive significant handling by humans at an early age. However, for truly feral cats and kittens, the most humane act that you can perform, and most beneficial act for your backyard or neighborhood, is to have them trapped, neutered, and returned. Once that happens, you can rest assured that those cats will not produce new litters of kittens.

I have two good friends named Kristen, both of whom are doing their part to help feral cats in their neighborhood. Kristen Flory lives in mid-Michigan and started a trap-neuter-return program in her backyard in 2008. Although her neighborhood has the Dickens-like appeal of tree-lined streets and beautiful older homes, it also appeals to a clan of feral cats that now consider her backyard a home. For several years before taking action, Kristen saw feral cats coming and going through her neighborhood. She explains, "Our family cats live indoors, and it was extremely hard to see these wild cats living outside in the elements—especially in the winter. I put out dry food and water, and occasionally, one or two cats would become regulars. Then those regulars would disappear, and we'd miss them terribly."[11]

In 2008, Kristen made a choice to tackle trap-neuter-return with full force so that the feral cat population in her backyard and neighborhood could be managed. She explains how it all started with a remodeling project at home and a Dumpster that sat in her driveway for six months. "I noticed two young ferals had taken up residence under the Dumpster for the winter. I think the workmen fed them, and eventually we did as well. That spring, I noticed the female feral was 'entertaining gentlemen kitties' in the backyard, and I panicked. Feeding a few feral cats wasn't a huge thing for us, but I knew how quickly two could become eight, then sixteen, and so on. On a whim, I set a Have-a-Heart trap in the backyard the next day, and within an hour, I caught the little feral female. I called my veterinarian and made arrangements to have her FeLv/FIV tested and, if negative, spayed and vaccinated. She was negative, so two days later, she was returned to me spayed and healthy. I kept her in a large dog crate in my garage for two days so she could heal, then I let her go. She ran from me in such a way that I assumed I'd never see her again. And I didn't for nearly six months! That was how I started my own tiny 'catch-spay-release' program."[12]

With her first successful trap-neuter-return effort completed, Kristen knew more cats would appear, and she prepared herself to continue her efforts until every feral cat was sterilized. As winter approached and she witnessed some of the feral cats shivering in the Michigan bitter cold weather, Kristen realized that the insulated doghouses she made available were inadequate. She opened her garage door a few inches, and the cats immediately took up residence in the loft of the garage. "We outfitted the loft with two old area rugs, multiple large dog beds, and eventually moved the insulated doghouse up there as well. They lived there, used a litter box, and ate their meals in the ground floor. When the worst of the cold was over, we started catching and spay/neutering each cat."[13]

During her attempts to trap a feral mom cat that had deposited two different litters at Kristen's house, she discovered that some of the kittens did not exhibit the typical feral behavior. At six to eight weeks of age, a few of the kittens sought affection from Kristen, swirled around her legs, and allowed Kristen to pick them up. While not intending to create her own adoption agency, Kristen now assesses each cat and kitten to determine if they can be socialized and adopted into a home. In two years, she has adopted four cats to indoor living situations, although one friendly male cat escaped from his new home on the first day and was never found. Kristen still grieves the loss of that cat and hopes that his survival instincts allowed him to find a new outdoor home.

Kristen knows the benefit of trap-neuter-return for feral cats because it helps to keep the feral cat population in her neighborhood under control. Providing inexpensive food, water, and litter boxes in her garage also helps to manage the cats so that they do not become a nuisance to other neighbors. Having visited Kristen's home on several occasions, I have seen how a little effort and money on her part has made a significant improvement in the lives of these otherwise toss-away kitties. Kristen also makes an effort to educate any neighbors who are not accepting of the feral cats. Due to Kristen's efforts to sterilize and feed the cats, these free-roamers are not a nuisance in the neighborhood. In fact, they are beneficial and help with rodent control, especially to scare away moles and groundhogs that enjoy burrowing in her yard.

Kristen has named all of her feral cats, keeps track of them to ensure their safety, and knows when a new cat has appeared that needs to be trapped. She has bonded with her outdoor feline family. And with that bond comes moments of worry, especially when one of the cats is sick or injured, or disappears for a length of time. "I worry for them, even though I know I'm doing better for them than if they were completely fending for themselves. I've seen them weather illness and injury, and on occasion we've watched a few disappear for days only to return. My husband and I try to reassure each other that we are doing the best we can for them, and at least are improving their lives. We do get attached to them and have a relationship with them that is kind of special. Despite the care that we do give them, we realize that the life of a feral cat is still short and often not kind. It is our hope that our actions make a difference to them."[14]

Since 2008, Kristen has trap-neuter-returned five cats and kittens and provides food to an average of eight cats every day. She encourages others to not turn away when they see a feral cat and hopes that her contribution will empower others to get involved. "I tell this story because I think about all the people I know that have a cat or two hanging around their yard, or living in their barns. If all of these people just made a little effort to catch and spay/neuter/vaccinate these cats, I think the impact would be enormous. It can be expensive, but there are many veterinarians that will provide low-cost spay/neuters for feral cats. My veterinarian set up a nonprofit organization specifically to help this critical population of animals. The surgeries are very inexpensive, and the amount I pay is tax deductible."[15]

My other friend, Kristen Brock, relocated from mid-Michigan to the island of Nantucket, Massachusetts, and laughs that feral cats find her no matter where she lives. Since 2005, Kristen has trap-neuter-returned a half dozen cats and kittens that were on her Nantucket property. Two of the kittens showed signs of socialization, so one has made his way into her home and the other was taken to the Massachusetts SPCA facility on the island so that she could be socialized with other kittens and find a new home. She also feeds the feral cats that stay on her property and has placed structures on her property to provide the cats a place to seek sanctuary during difficult weather. Because of her efforts, the feral cats in her backyard are manageable and not reproducing.

Kristen became involved in trap-neuter-return to stop the feral cat population in her neighborhood from growing. And she is not the only caring person on the island helping; she knows of another woman on the island who traps large numbers of feral cats and has them neutered. Kristen explains why she helps feral cats: "If there are too many feral cats, due to not sterilizing them, then there is not enough food for them. So my goal is to spay and neuter all the feral cats that I can so that those who are happier remaining outdoors will have sufficient food to survive."[16] Kristen knows that helping feral cats is not an insurmountable problem if everyone gets involved. "But if you do not want to get involved, that is okay; just ask for help because there are others, like me, who will help."[17]

TRAP/NEUTER/RETURN PROGRAMS MAKING A DIFFERENCE

Carol's Ferals (Grand Rapids, Michigan)

Carol Manos founded Carol's Ferals in 2006 to help reduce the feral cat overpopulation problem. Carol is a dedicated animal advocate who is eager to get involved to make a difference. I have seen Carol's work in action, and her tenacity is benefiting countless cats. In starting Carol's Ferals, her original goal was to solely work on trap-neuter-return efforts to reduce the number of feral cats and kittens breeding in the streets and thus entering local shelters. However, once she became known for helping feral cats, she was destined to receive calls from caring feral cat caregivers who need help controlling their burgeoning cat population. Though not intending to turn Carol's Ferals into an adoption agency, she has rehomed hundreds of friendly cats and kittens that otherwise would have been continually adding to the population of cats who eventually wind up euthanized at a shelter.

Carol became involved in trap-neuter-return and protecting feral cats once she realized the need. Initially, she possessed a few humane live traps for feral cats and began receiving calls from people who wanted her help. She quickly realized that if she could loan traps and train people how to trap, while assisting with funding, it would not be a financial hardship on people wanting to help and a greater impact could be made. Through this coordinated effort, she is also on the receiving end to get the cat ready for its sterilization surgery and provide a place for it to recover before being returned to the original location. "Knowing I was circumventing a great deal of suffering by fixing one homeless cat (an estimated 11,000 kitten breeding potential of an unfixed female and her mate over five years), I knew this was the kind of rescue work I wanted to do. It's a lot of 'bang for your buck.'"[18] Between February 2006 and August 2010, Carol helped about 3,500 cats through her trap-neuter-return efforts. The number of kittens that could have been born to these 3,500 cats is countless.

Carol has this advice on running a successful feral cat program: first, get educated on how to help feral cats. There are resources on the Internet, and you can connect with people already helping feral cats in your community. Second, be willing to fund the veterinary expenses or locate funding. Carol's Ferals finds that many caring people who feed feral cats do not have the funds for the sterilization process. Through the funding assistance of Vicky's Pet Connection,[19] Carol's Ferals is able to help people with trap-neuter-return efforts. Third, be determined to help educate people on the importance of trap-neuter-return. Carol spends hours on the phone daily educating people so that feral cats are not harmed. But the education expands to the greater necessity of spaying and neutering all animals, including the perils of advertising "free kittens" that may continue to breed or be abandoned outside unsterilized. Fourth, have a plan in place before you get started. A plan should include finding a veterinarian who will help and establishing how you will coordinate the trap-neuter-return efforts as well as re-home adoptable cats. Lastly, understand that you cannot help them all, but know that those you can sterilize and return to their environment will be happier.

Although focusing her primary effort on trap-neuter-return, Carol has assisted a few dozen cats and kittens over the past few years from local shelters or as strays. Carol explains, "One memorable cat was pulled from Montcalm Animal Shelter when I went to the commissioners' meeting one day to discuss how to get the Class B dealer out of the shelter. I was told that there was a feral mom and kittens there and they needed to get out before they were gassed to death. Of course, I knew nobody else would be able to help these cats since I was the only active feral advocate working on the project, so I took the mom and kittens. Turned out she was not feral at all, just scared. She and her kittens all found wonderful homes . . . a far cry from their horrible fate in the gas chamber for sure."[20] Carol has also taken several feral shelter cats and relocated them to be barn cats.

Carol struggles to educate people who simply want the feral cats removed and are uninterested in how trap-neuter-return works. Carol provides her philosophy to others on allowing feral cats to live and thrive. "I do not believe that a feral cat has a bad life. True, they suffer from fleas and ear mites and get diseases and die, but in general, so do many human beings. If anyone were to go up to a disenfranchised homeless person and say, 'We think your life sucks, and we think you'd be better off if we just killed you,' I'm pretty sure that person would fight for their life and try to defend themselves if it was tried. I think it's the same for homeless cats. The friendly ones need and deserve homes. But with the situation as it is in this country without enough homes for all the homeless pets, I feel better fixing the cat and allowing it back outdoors to be cared for by a feral caregiver than simply killing it because it might wind up with fleas or hit by a car. We can all be taken out by a car at any time. We still go outdoors, right?"[21]

For people who do not understand that trapping and killing feral cats only creates a larger problem, Carol educates them on the "vacuum effect." The vacuum effect occurs when a void is created in an existing feral cat colony. Since the goal of maintaining a healthy feral cat colony is to decrease, and not increase, the number of feral cats, simply trapping and destroying those cats actually harms those efforts. Feral cats congregate where there is a food source, such as discarded trash or a kind person putting out food. Since the food source will generally be there, removing feral cats from that location will invite new unsterilized cats to move in and multiply. If sterilized feral cats are returned to the location, they will not invite or allow newcomer cats to the area. If a cat is sterilized, the cat will not go into heat and will not attract a new cat. Sterilized feral cats, instead, will guard their food source and prevent the colony from increasing in size. If authorities go into a feral cat colony and "catch and kill" the feral cats, it will simply allow for a new group of feral cats to move in and multiply, thus thwarting the previous efforts at trap-neuter-return. Carol explains that efforts to "catch and kill" have been overwhelming failures; whereas trap-neuter-return is successful in maintaining a healthy and decreasing colony.

Although there are situations where re-homing a feral cat may be necessary (such as to a safer location, or to a home if the cat is socialized), trap-neuter-return efforts are the most humane and effective means to protect feral cats and decrease the number of stray cats on the streets or entering shelters. If you need to relocate a feral cat, Carol provides these words of advice:

"Relocating feral and outdoor cats is not as easy as physically placing them in their new outdoor home. Cats are very territorial, and if you simply place them in a new location, they will try to find their way back to where they came from, oftentimes killing themselves in the process. Fortunately, feral and outdoor cats can be acclimated to a new territory fairly easily and in a short amount of time. Place the cat in a large cage or kennel within the building they will be calling home. Give the cat a small, towel-lined carrier with the door held open with a small bungee cord, food and water, and a litter box. Clay litter is better than clumping in this environment, as clumping litter can get wet or in the water bowl, making a sticky mess that is more difficult to clean up. Clean the litter box and give fresh food and water daily. This can easily be done by closing the cat inside the carrier (the one you have bungeed open) to keep the cat safe while you are tending to its needs. After two to three weeks, you can open the cage door. Food and water should be kept both inside and outside of the cage. Once the cats leave, they may never want to go back into the cage. After two more weeks, the cats should be comfortable in their new home, and the cage and supplies can be taken away. Caring for your barn cat is as easy as providing fresh food and water daily. Some barn cat caregivers keep litter pans inside their barns, but often these are rarely used. Never rely on outdoor cats to sustain themselves on rodents alone; they need a nutrient-rich diet to sustain a healthy life."[22]

What motivates people to get involved in protecting cats? Carol Manos feels that while others are focusing on rescuing animals from shelters, she needs to focus on trap-neuter-return. "Currently the general public is not aware that there is anything that can be done to help a feral/stray cat that is skittish and does not come up to the caregiver for help. I am here to tell the world, 'Just because you cannot touch them, doesn't mean you can't help them.'"[23] Carol also knows that some of these cats end up being wonderful social cats. "I think of cats like Hook who came to me with wounds behind his ears so huge and bloody from scratching due to ear mite infestation. And I see what Carol's Ferals was able to do for him. We were even able to take him into our adoption program. He is deaf, has two different-colored eyes, and had a broken tail that looks like a hook, but he's the most loving little cat in the world. Knowing I could make a difference in his life is just the greatest feeling ever."[24]

Barnwater Cat Rescue (Denver, Colorado)

Kris Field does it all . . . she is the sole operator of a cat rescue organization, has a trap-neuter-return program for feral cats, and is trained in emergency services and disaster response for animals. Kris is always there for the cats, no matter the situation. I was first introduced to Kris around 2007 when a cat from my Michigan animal organization ended up in a Denver shelter. Kris did not hesitate to help out to make sure the cat would be safe. What I did not realize was the amount of work that Kris is doing to protect feral cats.

Kris became involved in helping feral and abandoned cats because, as she so bluntly states, "If you don't help them, who will?"[25] She explains, "They are out there because somebody has abandoned them, they have not spayed or neutered them, or sometimes people just do not care. Here are these little animals with little souls and little hearts and they have no one to take care of them and feed them. People assume that cats can take care of themselves. Not all cats can fend for themselves. What if they have a toothache and spend their entire lives in pain? One person could trap them, take them to the vet, clean their teeth, pull the bad teeth, give them an antibiotic shot, spay/neuter them, give them a rabies shot, and the next day they can be released and it changes their whole life. That is why I do it."[26] With the rise in unemployment and home foreclosures across the United States, some people are abandoning their friendly family cats outdoors in hopes that they will find food or a new home. For Kris, those cats are easy to identify and help.

Kris says that the process of trap-neuter-return can be as simple or as complicated as you want to make it. If you keep it simple, you will benefit many cat lives. "Just get the trap, put it out, and go watch TV. A few hours later, you may have the cat. You bring it inside within the trap, and then take the cat to your veterinarian. It doesn't really take much time to do this. If it is during winter, do not leave them outside unattended in a trap. Put the trap out at night and the cat will be in there pretty quickly to get the food. A few hours out of your day can change the cat's life forever. You could literally save his life by taking two hours out of your day . . . less time than you spend going to Starbucks."[27]

Kris has countless success stories of feral cats who were helped, but explains that there may also be some situations where the most humane thing is to euthanize the cat to alleviate immediate suffering from fatal injuries or illnesses. During her interview, Kris shared one happy story involving a three-legged cat. "A lady trapped a cat and discovered that it had three legs. The leg was likely ripped out by another animal or from an inhumane leg trap. The veterinarian put the cat under sedation, cleaned the wound, and gave a shot of penicillin. Now the cat is a happy boy and has been adopted. He would have been dead and was getting septic from his leg being ripped out. Now he is happy because one person cared enough to help."[28]

Kris encourages anyone interested in helping feral cats, and reducing the cat overpopulation problem in the United States, to get involved, even if it is just helping one cat that crosses your path. She shares this advice on how to get started: first, locate a veterinarian in your community who will provide affordable care to feral cats and will accept a cat in a trap. Find out if the veterinarian will do more than sterilization and a feline leukemia test. If the cat arrives with abscesses, injuries, bad teeth, or ear mites, will help be given? "You may be able to get a cheap neuter, but if you do not fix an injury, what's the point?"[29] Second, purchase or borrow a humane trap. Do not trap the first time you see a cat. Instead, let the cat get used to your yard. You may actually find that the cat is friendly and trapping is unnecessary. Third, get support from others helping feral cats. Call your local animal shelter for a list of animal organizations that may be able to give you advice or support regarding feral cats. These organizations may also have referrals to veterinarians that can help. Fourth, if you do not have the funds to help a feral cat, do not avoid helping the cat. Instead, call an animal organization that knows how to help feral cats and ask for help. If you can locate a cat shelter or cat welfare organization, they will have resources available for you. And lastly, once you sterilize the cat and return it, provide food and water. The food can be inexpensive cat food or even table scraps. Feeding the cats will reduce their need to harm birds or wildlife in your backyard.

For people who see feral cats as nuisances, Kris tries to get them to understand that it is not the cats' fault that they are unsocialized and thrive living outdoors. Either the cat was born outside or someone abandoned it outside. And try to get neighbors involved in the solution of trap-neuter-return so that kittens are not being born into a feral situation. Kris's final words of advice are simple: "Just open your heart a little and think of what little it will cost in time, money, and emotion to help out a cat that simply ended up where they are. We all can do just a little more to help them."[30]

Sunshine Foundation (St. Croix, U.S. Virgin Islands)

Dr. Stacia Jung began her veterinary career on the island of St. Croix in 2004. After working as the staff veterinarian and shelter director for the

St. Croix Animal Welfare Center and starting an affordable, high-volume spay/neuter clinic at the shelter, she knew that more work needed to be done to combat the island's pet overpopulation crisis. In October 2008, she opened her own state-of-the-art veterinary hospital and boarding center called Sugar Mill Veterinary Center, followed by the February 2009 creation of the Sunshine Foundation, a 501(c)(3) nonprofit organization designed to offer affordable, high-volume spay/neuter services.[31]

The mission of the Sunshine Foundation is to end pet overpopulation on the island of St. Croix by making spay/neuter services available to all pets. This service also expands to feral cats through a trap-neuter-return program. Dr. Jung explains, "I truly believe that pet overpopulation is a 'disease' that can be 'cured' through increasing responsible spay/neuter and ending the cycle of irresponsible pet reproduction."[32] As of October 2010, the Sunshine Foundation has spayed and neutered more than 1,000 island pets simply by working one morning each week to tackle the problem. Together with the animal shelter's program, Dr. Jung has performed more than 4,000 spay/neuter procedures in four years, and it is starting to make a real difference on the island. As featured in chapters 7 and 8, this widespread spay/neuter initiative is needed due to the overpopulation issues at the island shelter and limited adoptive homes on the island.

The trap-neuter-return initiative through the Sunshine Foundation is the first program of its kind on St. Croix. With a large number of feral cats on the island, Dr. Jung explains the efforts that are currently under way. "Our Feral Cat-Snip and Feral Cat Café programs have been very successful. Since we started the Sunshine Foundation we have spayed/neutered and returned 272 feral cats. Under our Feral Cat-Snip program each feral cat is blood tested for FELV [feline leukemia], spayed/neutered, ear tipped, and given a vaccination. We loan humane traps out to the community in exchange for a refundable deposit. Via our Feral Cat Café program we are currently working with several hotels, businesses, and schools on St. Croix to assist them with trap-neuter-return and to set up feeding stations where volunteers can manage the care of the feral cats after they have been spayed/neutered and returned to their location."[33]

Dr. Jung knows that the trap-neuter-return initiative is helping. "Feral cats made up approximately 30 percent of the animals that were euthanized at the local animal shelter during my tenure there. And we know from studies conducted by groups like Alley Cat Allies that trap, remove, and euthanize is not an effective means of controlling the pet population.

Removing the trapped cats opens up space for more to move in, and the cycle continues. This is called the 'vacuum' effect. Trap, neuter, and return is the most effective and humane way to deal with feral cats in a community."[34]

To date, Dr. Jung is the only veterinarian on the island of St. Croix who has taken her passion to help animals to the extent of creating a nonprofit animal welfare program, in addition to her private veterinary practice, to benefit not only the island animals but also the island residents. What motivates her to go this extra mile? She says, "Pure passion and a strong belief that we can solve the problem of pet overpopulation in our community. We are already making a big difference! My goal is to see a day where every animal on St. Croix has an opportunity to enjoy a loving home. I will be spaying/neutering until then!"[35]

Barn Cats, Inc. (Lewisville, Texas)

Peggy Atkerson became involved in helping homeless cats in 1987 when her cat, Ludwig, went missing. She visited the local humane society's adoption event looking for Ludwig and saw fifty cats looking for homes; she'd never realized how many homeless cats were in need of help. She was compelled to get involved and started by helping with adoptions through an animal welfare organization. At one point, she was tasked with finding a creative solution for a semifriendly cat that needed help. Peggy ran an advertisement in the local newspaper asking for a barn that could house the cat. When three people responded, Peggy knew that she was on to something. For cats who are difficult to adopt to homes because of socialization or behavior issues, or feral cats in an unsafe location, she created Barn Cats, Inc.[36] in September 2003, where their motto is "Got rat? We have cats!"

Peggy found that many feral cats, or cats that have behavioral issues and do not do well in an indoor environment, will thrive in a barn. She has found that most of the cats thrive in an open environment. Barn Cats, Inc. does not get involved in trapping cats; instead, they assist with safely relocating cats after the cat has been trapped and received the necessary veterinary work. For Peggy, it is important that all the cats arriving through her organization are spayed/neutered, have their rabies and distemper vaccinations, and have been tested for feline leukemia to avoid the spread of the disease to other barn cats.

Peggy has a unique method of marketing a cat for life in a barn: she labels them as nontoxic pest control and working cats. "If you have a rat, snake, or rodent problem, the cats will kill the rat, which then causes the snakes to leave because they lost their food source."[37] For anyone with a barn, maintaining rodent control is a necessity. So why not invite a feral or indoor-challenged cat to work in your barn? It's a win-win for everyone involved.

Having a barn cat program is also an excellent solution to disgruntled neighbors who do not want feral cats in their neighborhood. Not all people will be willing to help protect feral cats in their neighborhood and may have them rounded up and destroyed. So Peggy's solution of creating a barn cat program helps to safely relocate those cats, while also providing a service to the barn owner. Peggy explains that warehouses sometimes need good mousers, and relocating a cat to those locations is much better than putting out poison. She cautions that only adult cats should be placed in a barn cat program. If the cat is too small, it could become a target of hawks or owls. Also, white or light-colored cats may reflect in the moonlight and draw in a coyote. To solve that problem, Peggy encourages the barn owner to have a donkey, a llama, and/or a Great Pyrenees dog to help ward off coyotes, and she has connections to rescue groups to help with those efforts. For Peggy, the bottom line is moving these outdoor cats to a location where they are appreciated.

Peggy's main rule in helping feral cats is this: "Do not feed a feral cat unless you are going to spay or neuter them. If you feed them, they will continue to breed. And do not just neuter either the females or males; neuter them all, because an unsterilized male or female will attract other unsterilized cats to the area."[38]

If you want to get involved in trap-neuter-return and live in a small community with few resources, Peggy explains that you may need to transport feral cats for spaying and neutering, or for relocation to safer areas. If you can volunteer or connect with an existing group that has a trap-neuter-return program, it will help greatly because they will have resources and assistance in place. Peggy also recommends becoming an advocate for improved legislation impacting feral cats. She explains, "In Dallas, they now have a law where you can register a colony of feral cats. If a cat with a tipped ear arrives at a shelter, the shelter will return the cat to where it came from because it is part of a registered colony."[39] These laws prevent the automatic euthanasia of a feral cat in a shelter. So if you are not in a position to assist with trap-neuter-return efforts or the creation of a barn cat program, considering advocating for statewide or local legislation to protect feral cats.

If you want to start a barn cat program, Peggy advises obtaining 501(c)(3) nonprofit status to help legitimize your work and bring in tax-deductible donations to cover costs. Obtain cages and carriers to transport the cats and begin to spread the word to locate barns. This can be done through the Internet or word of mouth. Consider posting information fliers at Tractor Supply, feed stores, and large animal veterinary clinics. For Peggy's organization, "the smartest thing we ever did was to send out press releases to small-town newspapers, because they often have space to print information. There are not as many small newspapers due to financial concerns, so it is getting more difficult to use that venue. So also consider using social media to spread the word. We recently created a Facebook page to help locate barns and relocate cats to safer areas. On the Internet, if people search barn cats, we almost always come up first. And there are barn cat organizations around the country. Obtaining positive media stories is also a bonus."[40]

When relocating a cat to a barn, Peggy advises keeping the cat in a large cage in the barn for two weeks. Give the cat a chance to acclimate within the safety of a cage before being let out. Be sure to have the barn cat owner sign paperwork indicating that they will take care of the caging and return it, while also agreeing to provide food and water for the cat and medical care as needed. Peggy advises new barn cat owners that if they set up a schedule to feed the cats canned food, the cats will show up at that time to be fed. It is a good way to keep track of the cats. If food is simply put out throughout the day, it is more difficult to keep track of the cats. For those re-homing a cat to a barn, Peggy advises to not worry about performing an adoption follow-up. It may be difficult to see the cat because they are naturally nocturnal, but know that the cat is there doing its job. "Just rest assured that you did a wonderful thing for that particular cat."[41]

You Can Do More

- Donate to help organizations that care for feral cats. Monetary donations will help to cover spay/neuter and other veterinary expenses, or donate items on the organization's wish list.
- Donate to support spay/neuter clinics maintaining affordable rates.

- Sign up for action alerts with Alley Cat Allies at www.alleycat.org and stay informed on issues that affect feral cats in your state or community. Alley Cat Allies has materials on their website to help educate you and your community about feral cats.
- Support legislation and policies locally, statewide, and nationally to protect feral cats.
- If you see feral or stray cats in your neighborhood, borrow a live trap from a shelter or feral cat organization and be trained on how to safely and humanely trap, neuter, and return the cat.
- Volunteer for an organization that helps feral cats. You can search for these organizations through Petfinder.com or go to the Alley Cat Allies website to locate volunteer opportunities. Volunteer work may include assisting with trap-neuter-return, feeding, cleaning cages, transporting, and fostering cats or kittens from feral colonies that can be socialized for adoption.
- Ask your local animal shelter to start a trap-neuter-return program so that fewer feral cats and kittens are brought to the shelter to face euthanasia.
- Adopt from an organization that helps feral cats, because they often encounter friendly cats that need indoor homes.
- Find employment to help feral cats, such as with a veterinary clinic that provides spay/neuter services to feral cats, with an animal shelter that is seeking a feral cat coordinator, for an animal organization that helps feral cats, or for a national organization such as Alley Cat Allies.

CHAPTER 10

Animal Emergency Preparedness: Disaster Response, Search and Rescue

Animal emergency preparedness is something that everyone can join in on, from creating an emergency plan for your pet(s) to joining the efforts of responders who wade through flood waters, destroyed buildings, and other disasters to rescue animals and safely house them until their families are located. Disasters come in all forms, from man-made to natural. Man-made disasters may involve fires, chemical spills, industrial accidents, puppy mills, and animal hoarding situations, whereas natural disasters involve hurricanes, flooding, fires, and earthquakes.

The face of animal disaster response changed in 2005 when three category 5 hurricanes slammed into the United States' Gulf Coast. The most prominent was Hurricane Katrina, which struck the Gulf Coast in the early morning hours of August 29, 2005. The horrors of Hurricane Katrina were played out in national news reports, and the plight of the animals received national attention. One month later, Hurricane Rita struck the same region, dealing a devastating blow to an already-ravaged Gulf Coast. As a result of Katrina, Rita, and subsequently Wilma, Americans learned through tragedy that animals (family pets and livestock) must be included in disaster plans. For those of us who love our animals, we would no less leave our pet behind in a disaster than we would leave our child. Yet during Katrina, government responders would not allow people to evacuate with their pets, and disaster shelters did not allow pets. Watching people standing on their rooftops with their dog or cat was something that most people will never forget. When I give presentations on the human-animal bond, I speak of a man from Slidell, Louisiana, who stood on a chair for three days clutching his beloved seventeen-year-old cat named Miss Kitty.[1] He was airlifted to safety without Miss Kitty and hospitalized;

a week later Miss Kitty was rescued by volunteers with Noah's Wish and was reunited with her owner in the hospital. The man passed away three months later having never left the hospital. However, Miss Kitty's rescuer brought her to visit him during those three months. When the man passed away, Miss Kitty's rescuer adopted her and transported her and three other Katrina-displaced pets to her farm in British Columbia.[2] The human-animal bond was strongly displayed during and after the time when Katrina made landfall. Countless people refused to evacuate without their pet, or took heroic efforts to save their pet, and many of those people perished in order to save their companion. Those deaths could have been avoided by simply changing how we think about animals, especially in disasters.

The animal emergency response to Katrina was immense but disorganized. I saw the disorganization when I assisted the efforts in Jackson, Mississippi, at the state fairgrounds where hundreds of animals were located.[3] For all of the chaos and tragedy that occurred during and after Katrina, the positive benefit was that Katrina exposed flaws in national preparedness programs that brought about a change in the federal government's mind-set regarding animal inclusion during disaster rescue efforts. As a result, President George W. Bush signed the Pet Evacuation and Transportation Standards (PETS) Act in 2006.[4] When a city or state submits their disaster preparedness plan to qualify for Federal Emergency Management Agency (FEMA) funding, the PETS Act now requires that emergency preparedness authorities include how they will accommodate households with pets or service animals when presenting these plans to FEMA. States also began to form State Animal Response Teams (SARTs). SARTs are interagency state organizations dedicated to preparing, planning, responding, and recovering during animal emergencies in the United States. SARTs are public-private partnerships, joining government agencies with the private concerns around the common goal of addressing animal issues during disasters. SART programs train participants to facilitate a safe, environmentally sound, and efficient response to animal emergencies on the local, county, state, and federal level. The teams are organized under the auspices of state and local emergency management, utilizing the principles of the Incident Command System (ICS).[5]

After Katrina, American Humane Association convened a summit of national animal protection organizations that participated in the disaster response to work out issues encountered during Katrina and plan for better collaboration for the next large-scale disaster. From these meetings, the National Animal Rescue and Sheltering Coalition (NARSC) was born through a coalition of these original members: American Humane Association, American Society for the Prevention of Cruelty to Animals, Best Friends Animal Sanctuary, Code 3, International Fund for Animal Welfare, National Animal Control Association, Society for Animal Welfare Administrators, The Humane Society of the United States, and United Animal Nations/Emergency Animal Rescue Services. In 2009 The Humane Society of the United States left the group. In 2010, the Red Cross and the National Alliance of State Animal and Agriculture Emergency Programs joined NARSC. What was learned was that disaster response organizations assisting animals can and should work together, should conform to the National Management System/Incident Command System, and together can be a valuable available resource for local, state, and federal partners.

Since the chaos of the 2005 hurricane season, NARSC has been actively working to standardize training criteria across the various organizations so that responders for animals are similarly trained, qualified, and credentialed; to standardize forms used in the field so that sheltering, tracking, and re-homing of animals is seamless; and to prepare for upcoming hurricane seasons and other natural disasters. NARSC has a working partnership with the U.S. Department of Agriculture and Department of Homeland Security. Outreach has been conducted to the Red Cross about the existence of NARSC as a disaster response partner. NARSC has also created a "Q card," or qualification card, for responders to carry to quickly show their credentials in walking dogs in an emergency shelter, working in the field, managing an animal emergency shelter, and working with human first responder teams in the field on search and rescue efforts. Through the creation of NARSC, the disorganization after Hurricane Katrina has been averted.

Although a hurricane with the threat level of Katrina has not made landfall since 2005, in 2010 much of Haiti was destroyed by an earthquake, and American forces descended on the island nation to help not only the people but also the affected animals. The Animal Relief Coalition for Haiti (ARCH) was created to bring animal protection organizations together to provide aid to the animals on the island. ARCH was founded by the World Society for the Protection of Animals[6] and the International Fund for Animal Welfare[7] and has twenty international partners working together in an ongoing effort to help provide medical care to the animals and avoid the spread of disease. Efforts to help the animals were coordinated with the local government and international response teams. This collaborative effort demonstrated how responders from various organizations work together seamlessly to protect and help animals in disasters.

While many state and local disaster preparedness teams are trained to assist animals, there are national organizations that provide response services to local jurisdictions, as well as training for citizen volunteers. Some of those national organizations include American Humane Association's Red Star Animal Emergency Services®,[8] American Society for the Prevention of Cruelty to Animals,[9] American Veterinary Medical Association,[10] Best Friends Animal Society,[11] Code 3 Associates,[12] International Fund for Animal Welfare,[13] Noah's Wish,[14] The Humane Society of the United States,[15] United Animal Nations,[16] and the World Society for the Protection of Animals.[17] These organizations rely on training volunteers in communities throughout the country so that if a response is needed, local people are ready to quickly respond. With every disaster, trained volunteers are needed to help with search and rescue, as well as operating temporary shelters.

So what is it like to be a disaster responder? My friends Tracy Reis and Diane Robinson, with American Humane Association's Red Star Emergency Services, make a powerful team and share their stories of what it is like to be a career animal emergency responder. American Humane Association is fortunate to be the only national responder that has an eighty-two-foot tractor-trailer rescue rig that travels to certain disaster locations. The rig can sleep twelve responders and also contains all of the search and rescue equipment as well as an on-site emergency veterinary clinic.

Tracy Reis is the program manager for American Humane Association's Emergency Services program and has been working to help animals since the age of fifteen, when she was hired as a kennel worker for her local humane society shelter. What enmeshed her at that young age in helping to rescue animals was a situation where she assisted a police officer in seizing two young pit bull puppies that were being neglected. One puppy was emaciated and unconscious, and when Tracy picked her up, wrapped her in a blanket, and carefully lifted her out to safety, the puppy opened her eyes, wagged her tail, then passed away in her arms. From that point, helping and rescuing animals has been Tracy's life work. In her interview for this book, Tracy shared with me a profound statement that I think many people may not realize: "Through the years I realized that, potentially, every day is a disaster in the life of a shelter worker or animal control officer."[18]

Diane Robinson became involved in animal disaster response in 2005 through her participation in the Douglas County (Colorado) Search and Rescue team and being encouraged to take a basic animal emergency services training by American Humane's vice president of emergency services. At the time, Diane was employed as a teacher. After taking the class, she began to reflect on her life and wanted to do more for animals. Six months later, a position opened for an instructor and curriculum writer with American Humane's Emergency Services program, and Diane was a perfect fit for the job.

Tracy has been involved in more than twenty animal disaster response missions, and Diane is approaching twenty. One particular response to a puppy mill stays in Tracy's memory. "In September of 2007, during our annual conference, we received a request by the state of Maine to assist in a large-scale sheltering operation. They had seized a commercial breeding property shortly before that and had around 200 dogs that needed care. They were still sheltering the dogs at the owner's property temporarily. Not only was this the first puppy-mill seizure/sheltering operation that I had been involved in, it was also the longest deployment for me to date—28 days. No puppy mill or hoarding seizure would be complete with the 'miracle of birth,' and that certainly happened here, but what was more impactful to me was watching the very young puppies grow and develop in the month I was there. A group of four puppies really stands out in my mind. They were American bulldogs and were about seven weeks old when I arrived. Within the first week I was there, we decided to get them outside in the grass and let them play. I had no idea how long it had been since they had been out to run and romp as puppies should. Within minutes of putting them in the grass, it became sadly clear to me. At first, the tripping and falling over was amusing and made me smile, but then the truth that they had *never* been allowed to be outside, on the grass, and had spent the last seven weeks on the cold cement of the kennel, crashed down on me. It was so disturbing to me to see such young puppies have very little desire to run and play. We had to teach them to be puppies, so in the weeks to come, every day, we took them out to play. We had toys, bones, and other fun things for them to chase. They, of course, had never seen toys of any kind before either, so that was an adjustment. Eventually they came completely out of their shells and finally were able to develop into normal puppies. All four of these big puppies ended up being a part of the prison training program, in which they lived at the prison with inmates and were trained in basic obedience and housebreaking before they were adopted into their forever homes. I had the pleasure of visiting them, at the prison, before I left to come home."[19]

Diane has a memorable story from every response, but it was her first response that made the greatest impact. Within a week of starting her position at American Humane she was deployed to a flooding disaster in Miami, Oklahoma. Her first assignment was to join the search boat teams and canvass neighborhoods for stranded animals. Diane discovered a colony of feral cats clinging to trees and on the roofs of houses. The cats were terrified and preferred jumping in the water and swimming to another safe location rather than being handled and rescued by a human. But in that effort, several domesticated cats were rescued. While working in the temporary shelter, Diane came across two small puppies that were being raised by their feral mother. Neither had been socialized with humans, and they were terrified of their surroundings. Diane and another responder were assigned to work with the two puppies in hopes of socializing them for adoption. One was named Brother and the other named Fuzz. Diane explains, "Both were frozen in fear. They didn't know what was happening to them but slowly started to relax. Back in the shelter Fuzz would wander around me on his leash, put his paws on my back and whimper, then come around to the front of me and look up at me. He repeated this, only touching me from behind, then slowly would come closer in front until finally he would touch me in front too. Any attempt to touch him would have him shy back until finally he would sniff the back of my hand."[20]

After a few days, Brother was responding positively to being handled and was walking well on a leash, but Fuzz still cowered in his crate in fear. However, when Diane approached his crate, Fuzz would jump up and wiggle his body. Fuzz was becoming receptive to Diane's attention. Brother started being socialized by other responders, but Diane was the only person able to comfort Fuzz. After three days, Fuzz could only be touched by other people if Diane was nearby. Knowing that she was scheduled to return home the next day, Diane worried whether Fuzz would warm up to other people or regress to his original state of fear. "So the day we were leaving the last two of us went to the shelter to pick up the American Humane Association vehicles for the drive back to Denver. For the longest time I couldn't bring myself to go into the shelter. It was my first time, and I was very emotional. Finally I walked in and looked over where the little feral brothers were caged. New people were feeding the animals, but all they cared about was that they were being fed, except Fuzz. He was sitting in the corner of his cage with his head down while all the others barked and jumped around waiting to be fed. All of a sudden he looked up and over at me. He jumped up, wiggling his whole body so fast and hard that the people feeding nearby looked over at him, then followed his gaze to where I stood. I don't know when I started crying, but I realized I was when Jean [the director of the local animal shelter] walked up beside me, looked at him, back at me, and calmly said, 'So are you taking him?' I don't know that I spoke the words before she was scurrying off to take care of the necessary paperwork and the supplies I would need to get him back home. I walked over, scooped him up, and was immediately covered with kisses. That is still the greeting I get from him today whether I am away from him for five minutes or five days. I have a picture of him in my arms in the emergency shelter I keep as a reminder of the difference a little time and patience can make in the lives of the animals we rescue and shelter. Whenever I get tired or stressed or wonder if I'm really making a difference, I look at that picture or cuddle up with the loving little dog who trusted then chose me."[21]

Tracy and Diane have responded to man-made disasters, such as a Pennsylvania cat hoarding response, as well as natural disasters, including several large-scale hurricanes. The largest response they ever worked on was during Hurricane Gustav in 2008, where their team worked a "mega shelter" in Shreveport, Louisiana, for 1,200 evacuated animals. Tracy was also one of a few Americans who responded in the aftermath of the 2010 Haiti earthquake. Tracy recalls flying in to Port-au-Prince and having a bird's-eye view of the devastation, the military ships waiting in the harbor, and rows of tanks covering the runways at the airport. For eight days, Tracy lived at the United Nations compound and worked in what became a war zone in the aftermath of the earthquake. Her days started from 5 to 6 o'clock in the morning when the Blackhawk helicopters and C-130s revved up their engines for the day.

Tracy explains what the work was like in the aftermath. "Our main mission was to do 'well checks' on any animal brought to us. Each animal was given a quick once-over to check for any major illnesses or injuries.

We gave injections to several of the dogs—a powerful wormer that also aids in the healing of multiple skin issues, such as mange. Depending on the condition of the dogs, several were also given a general antibiotic injection. As a booster, all dogs were also given a vitamin B shot. This particular injection burns as it is given; it was very apparent by the negative reaction of every dog. The cats, kittens, and younger puppies were checked over and given an oral wormer. In the days I was there, we also gave injections to several pigs. In seventeen years of working with animals, I can say that these were certainly the most difficult to handle. The companion animals here were only comfortable being handled by their owners. And even that was questionable at times. Every day, we traveled to different areas in and around the city, and every village welcomed us and seemed to be very grateful that we were there to assist. Even residents of the areas that had not received any assistance for the people were appreciative of the help we offered to the animals. Along with the animals in every village came the children. They would crowd around us as we were examining the animals and just watch. In our 'uniforms' and boots, we may have appeared like soldiers to them, but they were very excited to have us there. One boy stood close to me the entire visit one day and seemed to find comfort there, even though his family was close by. I was amazed at the resilience of the children we met. There are very close family bonds in Haiti, and the basic needs of the children seemed to be met, although given the circumstances, I know there are still needs. Their bright faces and playful nature made them seem blissfully unaware of the true tragedy that had unfolded around them. Our days wrapped up the same every day: in before dark, cold shower, debrief, and dinner."[22]

Tracy returned home to Denver after eight days with a renewed sense of what is important after being exposed to the tragedies in Haiti, for people and animals. Her sentiments struck a chord with me, and hopefully will with you, too. "I've always been grateful for the things in my life. I can say with all honesty that I came back with a renewed sense of what's important to me. As Americans, we rush through our days complaining about traffic, about how slow service is at Starbucks, about how we can't afford the latest and greatest gadget. Seeing the Haitian mother washing clothes in a stream that's polluted by waste, then filling her water buckets up to take that water back for her family to drink, or hearing the story of a man who walks eight miles one way to go to work in a factory, for pennies, made me realize how spoiled many of us Americans really are. I always carry at least one lesson back with me from every deployment, and going to Haiti was no exception. The difference is that I'm willing to share this one: When you go home tonight, look around at all you have. Give your spouse or partner an extra hug and kiss. Spend a few more minutes with your kids; kiss and hug them tightly. Give your pets a couple of extra treats and notice how they live life in the moment. You never know when your time together will end. Let all of the people in your life know how much they mean to you. You only get one turn in this life; make the most of every minute you have."[23]

One thing is certain: being a responder is not a glamorous job. Diane encourages people to get involved for the right reason of helping animals, and not to go out and be a hero. The job entails long, emotional hours (twelve hours or more per day in general), challenging weather conditions at times, being dirty most of the time, limited food and water, and rustic sleeping and showering facilities. For Diane, "If you are aren't volunteering because you want to selflessly give for the good of the people and animals in the community, then it may not be the right thing to do."[24] Depending on your training and expertise, you may be assigned to help fractious dogs or clean the toilets. Tracy explains that while search and rescue efforts may be the "sexier" forms of helping, it is the sheltering work that is the most difficult and most rewarding. Trained responders are needed to help feed the animals, clean cages, sweep the floors, wash bowls, walk the dogs, and calm cats, rabbits, and other small animals. If you are on search and rescue duty, Diane explains, "you are boating through cornfields and city streets looking for animals. It's driving around debris-strewn streets and searching through homes with the mud, furniture, refrigerators knocked over, the contents decomposing. You may spend hours walking around, searching for animals and dropping food and water so they can eat and drink."[25] There is also administrative and technical work to be done before deploying, including tracking weather reports during hurricane season, communicating with state and local government agencies, and coordinating responders. Every position is critical in ensuring a smooth and safe response, for people and the animals.

Why have Tracy and Diane dedicated their careers to animal emergency response? For Tracy, "the best part is the hardest part. Rescuing animals from either Mother Nature or man-made disasters is exhausting both emotionally and physically, but you are rescuing them and oftentimes giving them a second chance on life. I have the best job on the planet."[26]

For Diane, she knows that she is making a difference in the life of each animal in helping to reunite them with their family, while also helping communities recover after a disaster. And although there are animals who cannot be saved, and sometimes stop fighting to live and die as soon as they are rescued and in safe arms, for Diane the eyes of the animals are the window to pain and fear. "It's a sad and scary place their eyes take you to when they arrive, and startling when after only a short time a small spark of life and hope begins to show up."[27]

If you are interested in being trained to become a volunteer or career responder, Tracy and Diane recommend taking courses offered by a training organization, such as American Humane Association's Red Star trainings. Knowing how to work in an animal shelter is far different than operating a temporary disaster shelter. FEMA also offers classes. Participate in a ride-along with your local animal control officer or volunteer at your local animal shelter to learn more about working with animals.

As with any activity, there are dos and don'ts to consider before becoming involved in animal emergency service responses. Tracy and Diane advise against self-deploying to a disaster location; volunteer only with a local or national organization, and deploy when you are invited. Tracy explains, "This was a huge 'lesson learned' that came out of Hurricane Katrina. Uninvited, rouge volunteers stormed into the state of Louisiana with wonderful intentions, but because they were not part of the bigger operation, many animals were taken out of homes without permission, housed at unknown shelter locations (so owners had no idea where to look for their pets), and worst of all transported out of the state (illegally). Many animals were adopted into other homes, and owners were left to wonder what even happened to their pets. Because of what happened at Hurricane Katrina, the spontaneous volunteers will no longer be able to just enter a state without permission—they need to be credentialed and be part of an invited agency."[28]

Other dos and don'ts include working with a kind and considerate attitude to the people and animals that need help; keeping a positive attitude in spite of aching muscles; giving the animals your best every day regardless of what may happen to them the next day; being gentle with the animals who are scared and just need a little patience and time; and leaving your prejudice and judgments at home and focusing solely on helping the animals. You may respond to areas with different cultures and practices involving animals, or to a situation where a criminal and legal seizure of animals has occurred where you must make efforts to avoid imposing your beliefs and judgment on the issue.

Tracy and Diane advise responders to reach out to their team when emotions and feelings become strong. These deployments can invoke a variety of strong emotions, and rather than keep them inside, talk to your teammates. Diane even goes one step further and educates responders to never look into the eyes of the animals, because the eyes show the fear and pain that can make accomplishing the work difficult. Diane knows, because the last time she looked into the eyes of a frightened animal, he followed her home.

If becoming a responder is not fitting for you, then consider other ways to support those helping animals in disasters. Donate to organizations that deploy to disasters, but make sure that your donation will assist with the direct impact to the animals assisted. Offer to provide foster care for an animal impacted by a disaster or for a shelter animal that needs to give up its cage for a disaster animal. Adopt from a shelter that has rescued disaster animals eligible for adoption. Offer to help in other ways, such as taking a home-cooked meal to responders, or help with laundry. Tracy says that responders love homemade cookies! But most of all, make sure that your family and pets are prepared if a disaster strikes your community.

You Can Do More

- Create a disaster plan for yourself and your pets. When evacuating, always take your pets with you, including food, medical supplies, and proof of vaccinations. If you have larger animals, such as livestock, have a plan in place to keep them safe, sheltered, and fed during a disaster.
- Support your local animal shelter or a national animal protection disaster response team if they are involved in responding to a disaster in your community. Open your home to provide foster care to a disaster-rescued pet or a pet in the shelter whose cage is needed for a disaster pet; donate to help the shelter care for the animals; offer to clean cages or clean laundry; or give monetary donations to help with the veterinary expenses invariably associated with disaster response efforts.
- Attend disaster response training and learn how to help animals in a disaster response in your state or elsewhere in the country. If you have a particular interest or specialized knowledge of a species (such as birds, horses, livestock, etc.), that knowledge can be beneficial during a disaster response.

CHAPTER 11

Attorneys Advocating for Animals

In 1993, only seven states had felony animal cruelty laws, yet today all states but three have felony penalties for being cruel to animals.[1] When I started law school in 1990, the concept of a Student Animal Legal Defense Fund chapter was nonexistent, but today there are chapters at more than 150 law schools in the United States.[2] No animal law courses were taught during my law school tenure; however, today there are just over 120 law schools in the United States and Canada that educate on the complexities of animal law.[3] The first state bar animal law section was created in 1995 with the State Bar of Michigan (of which I am a proud council member), and now there are thirty animal law sections and committees nationwide.[4]

I sometimes drift off in philosophical and legal musings about humans' relationships to animals. Who gave humans authority over animals? Who thought up the idea of giving humans the legal right to end the lives of companion animals, particularly those housed in overcrowded shelters, yet ending the life of an animal outside of a shelter is often a crime? How do we reconcile that killing a chicken and eating it is legally protected in the United States, but killing and eating a cat is against the law? Who thought of the concept of animal testing while providing legal protection in animal cruelty statutes to those engaging in animal testing? What is the difference between testing a potentially harmful drug on an animal and a neighbor poisoning your dog? One is legally protected and the other is likely a felony. And why not test on humans for human drugs and illnesses? Why were animals selected rather than, for argument's sake, prison inmates? I often hear from people wondering why death-row prison inmates are not utilized as test specimens. I wonder how a test performed on a rat will cure human cancer, and would the same test, performed on a human, give us quicker results? Who thought it would be entrepreneurial to train dogs or hens to fight each other for profit? How can some people so callously abandon their pet (especially during the financial crisis) in their foreclosed home or surrender their pet to a shelter simply because they are moving? What goes through the mind of a person as they are torturing and killing an animal? The list of musings is endless and exhausting some days. It is disturbing to think about the thought process that goes into the real-life scenarios listed above. Yet as animal advocates, we need to think about these issues and collectively come up with answers and solutions.

It is these philosophical arguments that divide humans on how we care for animals and, therefore, how we protect them through the law. The hypocrisy is blinding some days, yet instinctively many of us know that humans do not have a right to harm another living creature. It will take humans to create a culture and enforce laws to get those points across and alter how American society feels about animals. And it will take attorneys, trained and passionate about animal law, to enforce those laws for the animals that do not have a voice to speak out.

I have conducted training seminars across the country on how animal cruelty is connected to violence against humans and ways we can protect animals. Sometimes it is before a small local audience, and other times it is at a large national conference of several hundred attendees. I am always humbled to provide these trainings and often wonder why I was chosen to educate. With each presentation, I receive the answer from several audience members who approach me afterward and say, "You are so passionate about your work, and now I feel empowered to go back to my job and change the way we handle cases involving animals."

Feeling the gratitude for being able to educate others then brings me back to reality when I think of how much work remains. If only we could stop the violence and get more people interested in caring for animals. But isn't that the same for how humans relate to each other?

As a former prosecuting attorney, I can say that prosecutors are some of the most hardworking and tenacious professionals I have met. However, I become despondent knowing that many are passively allowing animal protection laws to go unenforced. That thought depresses me more than anything. Why? Because people like you and others in the community can receive all the guidance possible on how to protect animals and report abuse, but if investigations and prosecutions are lax, then what is the point?

There are approximately 40,000 prosecutors in the United States. Through my employment with the National District Attorneys Association and as a former prosecuting attorney in the trenches, I interact with prosecutors all across the country. I have trained them, consulted with them, researched emerging topics and unique methods of prosecution for them, wrote articles to assist them, commiserated with them when they felt burnout, and tried to empower them to change the world one victim at a time. I became a prosecutor in 1995, and since 2003 I have dedicated my career to working with the nation's prosecutors to empower, and hopefully inspire, them to tackle the cases involving animals, children, and other violent crimes that are not pleasant to handle.

It saddens and frustrates me to know how few prosecutors take animal cruelty cases seriously. Most often it is because they have too many cases and need to prioritize, and the penalties for animal cruelty are not as severe as for other crimes; other times I sense that prosecutors are ill equipped to tackle the complexities of an animal cruelty case and simply plea-bargain the case away so that they do not have to publicly show that they are untrained in this area. For prosecutors that prioritize their cases and pursue the most violent offenders first, I have been training them to recognize that offenders who are cruel to animals are often the most egregious offenders of child abuse, domestic violence, and homicide. And we all have heard the stories of how many serial killers started with animals. As I write this chapter in the fall of 2010, there is no trial advocacy training for prosecutors on animal abuse cases and I am working to change that. I do not know how many prosecutors seriously pursue animal abuse cases but would guess that the number is minimal. Many of them have found me, or I have found them, and we interact in a fraternity for the benefit of animals.

Ironically, I find that attorneys outside the work of prosecution who are interested in animal welfare law seem to outnumber the prosecutors interested in enforcing the laws that lie before them. These animal law attorneys represent animals in civil court or other legal venues to protect them from harm or to provide them with legal protection through wills and pet trusts if their owner passes on. Yet it is the prosecutors that have the strongest laws available to them to protect animals and create safer communities; they are the chosen ones charged with enforcing the criminal laws in their state or community.

Sometimes I am not very popular with prosecutors when I ask them to look at their selective prosecution lifestyle. Since I have been in their shoes with a crowded docket and had days where I entered the courtroom with a stack of twenty-five cases all scheduled for trial, I know what it means to "pick your battles"; but I also know that summarily ignoring animal cruelty as unimportant because "it's just an animal" is old-school thinking. This selective attitude, however, is not solely limited to prosecutors and extends to those who are charged to investigate animal cruelty, judges, and even to communities in general. Let me give you an example.

In January 2009, I was invited to the beautiful island of St. Croix to teach at the Silent Witness conference hosted by the St. Croix Animal Welfare Center. I was asked to speak about St. Croix's 2005 new animal cruelty laws, the first such laws for the island, and to speak about ways to effectively utilize the law. In preparing the conference, I was amazed at how well-written and comprehensive the laws were for animals. All animals were protected under the law from abuse and neglect, with no exemptions for hunting, animal farming/husbandry, and research, whereas more states provide exemptions for those practices. The penalties were not that severe, with the maximum penalty set at three years, but I was encouraged by the breadth of the statute.

I learned that the island investigators were not pursuing cases, and therefore little was to be done to prosecute those who were cruel or neglectful to animals. Only one case had been sufficiently investigated and charged by the attorney general's office since the law went into effect. That case was proceeding to trial the week after the conference. It involved the case of Max the dog, whose owner was charged with cruelty and torture. I will not go into details of what happened to Max; suffice it to say that Max was lucky to be alive. But this was the first case being prosecuted in three-and-a-half years since the passage of their comprehensive animal cruelty code. Yet abuse and neglect were frequently reported on the island. I was not the only one who was appalled.

In speaking with staff from the animal shelter, I expected that the shelter would be charged with investigating cruelty cases. As in many American cities, I learned that the shelter had no authority and was required to rely on the police to investigate, gather evidence, and arrest. The shelter was eager to pursue these cases, yet they felt unsupported by the police. As in other jurisdictions, I learned that the police were either uneducated on animal cruelty investigations and evidence collection, unable to investigate due to lack of resources and orders to prioritize violent crimes first, or simply unwilling to enforce laws protecting animals due to personal or cultural beliefs. Pursing justice for animal cruelty cases had come to a grinding halt on the island. Their shiny new law was useless unless attitudes changed, and changed quickly. This is why the conference was arranged—so that all relevant professionals and interested citizens on the island could come together and learn how to move forward.

After speaking with many island citizens and taking calls on a local radio show regarding the collective frustrations, I decided to fire up the audience and get them talking about the real issues. I asked why the animal shelter was not deputized to investigate animal cruelty, or why the police department was not available to assist the animal shelter investigators in pursuing and closing these cases. In a blog posted by one of the attendees, she called me a pyrotechnic firecracker. I received some glaring stares from the local police department when I asked why they were engaging in selective police work and not enforcing the laws they took an oath to uphold. I never did receive a sufficient answer.

The open discussion that I had with seventy-five attendees educated everyone in the room and shined a light on the problems. Two years after the conference, the animal shelter has not been provided the arrest powers that they desire. However, the governor, commissioner of agriculture, and the commissioner of police met and agreed that an animal officer/warden was needed on the island and approved the position. However, funding has not been appropriated as of late 2010. Nonetheless, the conference raised the level of awareness for the plight of animals, and change, albeit slow change, is taking place. Unfortunately, the conference came too late for Max the dog. The first-ever prosecution for animal cruelty that occurred that following week ended in an acquittal. The problem was an incomplete investigation, though plenty of evidence was presented to the jury. The problem could also have been associated with a culture that had not pursued animal cruelty seriously in the past. Luckily, Max did not go back to his prior home. But what about the next Max?

The story of St. Croix is not unusual and is familiar all over this country. This leads me to the next issue in the proper pursuit of justice for animals. Prosecutors and civil attorneys are only as good as the case they are given. I frequently say, "Investigators, front-line professionals, and neighbors are the eyes and ears to each case, and the prosecutor is the mouthpiece. We can only say to the court what you give to us." Animal protection requires not only that cases of cruelty are properly investigated and pursued, but also that citizens who observe cruelty or neglect get involved. If one link in the chain fails, the entire case fails, as we saw in the case of Max. Unfortunately, I observe too many people believing that they should not get involved, so they do not report the situation, or if they report it they do so anonymously, thus tying the hands of the police and prosecutor from properly presenting what was observed.

A multitude of legal areas are available if you want to become involved in protecting and advocating for animals. Resources are available through a variety of websites, including the Animal Legal Defense Funds and the Animal Law Coalition.[5] Criminal prosecutors enforce national, state, or local laws on protecting animals from cruelty or neglect. Civil attorneys can become involved in litigating dangerous dog and dog bite cases; divorce cases involving custody battles over pets; injunctions and restraining orders to prevent harm to animals; including pets in trusts and wills; veterinary malpractice and pet wrongful death cases; police liability cases for harming or killing pets in the line of duty; as well as specialize in specific animal areas. There are also opportunities to obtain employment with national animal protection organizations to work on litigating lawsuits for the protection of animals or engage in lobbying. Lauren Silverman Simon, an attorney working as an animal lobbyist, is featured in chapter 12. There are opportunities to teach others about protecting animals and animal law at schools (middle and high school), universities, law schools, veterinary schools, and training conferences for human welfare professionals and lawyers. Some attorneys write articles for professional and/or legal publications or to the general public to raise awareness about animal protection and animal law. If your city or state bar association has an animal law section or committee, join the ranks and become involved in the issues. The Michigan State Bar Animal Law Section has an Animal Legal Help Line where calls are received from people needing legal help for their pet, and section attorneys offer their assistance. If your city or state bar does not have an animal law section or committee, offer to start one. And in your nonwork time, volunteer your efforts to help animals. If you are interested in a legal career to help animals, getting involved directly with animals at an animal shelter, sanctuary, farm, or other location will give you the hands-on expertise needed to benefit your legal specialty. The means to help animals through the law grows exponentially with each passing year, and there are many ways to get involved. Just take the time to educate yourself and you may soon find that you are helping animals in ways that you never imagined.

Featured in this chapter are three attorneys who I personally know and respect in their pursuit of spreading animal law to its farthest reach: one animal law professor, one civil animal law attorney, and one prosecuting attorney. If you are interested in a law career, planning to attend or are attending law school, or already have your law degree, I hope their stories inspire you to become involved in helping animals. If you are not involved in the law, you can still help by supporting those attorneys and future attorneys to pursue cases where our animal companions need a strong voice.

ATTORNEYS WHO ARE MAKING A DIFFERENCE FOR ANIMALS

Associate Professor Joan Schaffner (George Washington University Law School, Washington, D.C.)

Professor Joan Schaffner teaches animal law, civil procedure, sexuality and the law, and remedies at George Washington University Law School in Washington, D.C. Not only is Joan a gifted educator who empowers her students to become entrenched in animal law, but she has opened her home to countless felines who needed a safe haven before finding their forever home. Joan was the chair of the American Bar Association Tort Trial and Insurance Practice Section's (ABA TIPS) Animal Law Committee (2009–2010) and is a published author/editor of animal law books such as *The Lawyer's Guide to Dangerous Dog Issues*,[6] *Litigating Animal Law Disputes: The Complete Guide for Lawyers*,[7] co-edited with Julie Fershtman (also featured in this chapter), and *An Introduction to Animals and the Law*.[8]

Joan did not start her teaching career by focusing on animal law. Her introduction to the possibility began in the fall of 2003 on a pro bono project with her students in collaboration with Professor (and now District of Columbia councilwoman) Mary Cheh to review the district's animal cruelty laws. For one year they reviewed the animal protection laws of the district, as well as those of other states, and prepared a report detailing the status of animals in the district and the laws of the district, and suggested improvements for the laws. Mary Cheh and Joan arranged a summit with national animal protection organizations to discuss the situation concerning animals in the district and reached out to others focusing on animal law nationally. Through this project, Joan realized that the focus of her work needed to be on animal law and protection. The students also became engaged in the process and created the law school's first Student Animal Legal Defense Fund (SALDF) chapter. As a result of this newly found interest in animal law, Joan created an animal law program at the law school and added a second seminar on animal law to the curriculum that she now teaches.

The result of the group's work also benefited the district because their report on the state of animal welfare laws resulted in legislation written by Mary Cheh, Joan, and her students and ultimately introduced by councilwoman Mary Cheh. The legislation was a comprehensive omnibus bill addressing numerous areas where animals needed better protection. In 2007, I along with Joan and others testified in support of this bill before the District of Columbia Council. And through Joan's tenacity, an amended version of the bill was signed into law in 2008.

Law students can delve into the world of animal law in a variety of ways. The Animal Legal Defense Fund[9] is a great resource for anyone interested in animal law issues or career opportunities. As previously mentioned, many law schools have SALDF chapters where students can become involved in animal law issues. If a law school does not have an SALDF chapter, the Animal Legal Defense Fund website has information on how to start a chapter.

Joan explains that there are other ways to get involved. "There are the National Animal Law Competitions sponsored by the Center for Animal Law Studies at Lewis & Clark and held at Harvard every February. These competitions include moot court, closing argument and legislative lobbying, and drafting competitions over the weekend. It is a great way to learn about interesting topics in animal law, develop important legal skills, and meet some of the greats in the animal law area as well as colleagues throughout the country. ABA TIPS has an Animal Law Committee that is very active and provides a great resource for student members. Moreover, many local bar associations have animal law committees or sections as well. These organizations provide a great way to make contacts with practicing attorneys, attend speaker series, etc. Finally, many humane organizations hire students as interns to work on projects, as do private firms who handle animal law cases pro bono."[10]

If you are interested in animal law and are already a practicing attorney or paralegal, Joan explains various ways that you can get involved in animal law. First, use the Internet to locate resources and materials on animal law specialties, like the Animal Legal and Historical Center, to locate animal protection organizations with legal departments such as the Animal Legal Defense Fund, and to join blogs that discuss animal law. Second, check your state or city bar association to see if an animal law committee exists and join. If an animal law committee does not exist, consider creating one. Also join the ABA TIPS Animal Law Committee to connect with other like-minded attorneys and learn how you can grow your practice to help animals. Joan explains that some law firms allow attorneys to handle animal law cases on a pro bono basis. If you work for a law firm that encourages pro bono work, offer to handle animal law cases, such as dangerous dog cases, pet custody disputes, protective orders for pets, or wills and trusts for pets.

If you are not working in the legal profession, Joan explains that there are ways you can get involved in animal protection laws. "(1) Public education: get the word out in your area about the abuses of animals and help raise awareness through the local media and other public education campaigns. Public awareness of the issues provides an opportunity for lawyers and policymakers to enact legislation that will benefit animals. (2) Go vegan and encourage others to do the same. This is critical to offsetting the huge economic interests that benefit from the abuses of animals to make their products. (3) Provide monetary support to organizations doing good legal work on behalf of animals. (4) Lobby your local and national representatives on laws designed to protect animals. You can find out about proposed bills through the various humane organizations that address legal issues important to animals. These groups send alerts to members about legislation being proposed and ask for citizens to help lobby their representatives to get the laws enacted."[11] Joan is dedicating her efforts to train the next generation of lawyers to become engaged in protecting animals through the law, and doing so is the most fulfilling work she could perform.

Julie Fershtman (Foster Swift Collins & Smith, P.C., Farmington Hills, Michigan)

Julie Fershtman became a lawyer in 1986, and for the first seven years of her career was unaware that animal law existed. Julie has a long history with and love of horses and eventually discovered a specialty in equine law. Equine law involves the practice of law involving horses and serves clients such as "breeding farms, race tracks, insurers, syndications, partnerships, trainers, riding instructors, commercial haulers, boarding stables, horse owners, associations, veterinarians, and others."[12]

Julie explains, "I would spend entire weekends at law libraries and gather as much information as I could about horse-related law. I found law review articles, ALR annotations, trade articles, treatises — just about everything I could find that was catalogued with 'horses' and 'law.' I read, and I began to find trends and areas of interest. From that point in 1993, I began writing frequently for as many publications as I could find who were interested in publishing my equine law column. At the time, no other lawyer in the country was undertaking the efforts that I was."[13]

Julie is a shareholder with the Michigan firm Foster Swift Collins & Smith, P.C., in its Farmington Hills, Michigan, office. She finds that her focus on equine law has been beneficial not only for her career, but for her clients. "As an equine law practitioner, I have found that clients greatly appreciate the specialized knowledge of their businesses and needs; they spend little time explaining what they do, and I believe I am in a better position to serve them more efficiently and cost-effectively."[14]

Julie cautions that it is not easy to open an exclusively "animal law" practice. "Because of this, I always caution aspiring animal law practitioners to plan carefully and think through your objectives, both long-term and short-term. What are your monthly living expenses and business expenses? What do you need your practice to net so that your income will cover these expenses, and then some? Consequently, most lawyers I know who practice animal law — myself included! — must combine their animal-related practices with other areas of practice. Lawyers who practice animal law as their sole area of practice focus sometimes say they make ends meet through creative (but ethically appropriate) fee arrangements, highly selective acceptance of cases, low overhead (sometimes having no staff), and a willingness to work for a significantly reduced fee when the situation warrants."[15]

However, attorneys can find several opportunities to practice animal-related law. Julie advises to first learn what animal expertise you can offer. Referrals from other lawyers can be helpful for building a practice of animal law cases. You can seek them by meeting other lawyers or people well positioned to send you business. You can consider attending bar association meetings, speaking at law functions, advertising in legal publications, writing about animal law in legal publications, and joining an animal law committee if your bar association offers one (or try to form an animal law committee if your state or local bar association currently does not). Julie believes that marketing your expertise can help grow a practice, and she accomplishes this through hundreds of articles and three books on equine law. But she cautions to be patient, because it can take years before clients knock on your door.

When you begin to receive calls from clients interested in your animal law expertise, it may feel like a dream come true, and your practice is taking off. However, Julie has found that prospective clients with animal law matters are very frequently unable to afford a retainer for legal services. "Often they have quite complicated legal matters—such as proceedings involving injunctive relief, specific performance, or declaratory judgment actions—that require extensive research, briefing, and trips to the courthouse. Though I personally want to help these people, I am forced to send them elsewhere."[16]

Ethical issues and conflicts are a primary concern for any attorney, and Julie explains how she has encountered ethical conflicts that require her to decline representation. "Both parties to the same dispute may call the same lawyer, and the lawyer engaging in detailed communications under these circumstances might unsuspectingly be forced to turn away both parties due to ethics. At times, I am convinced that parties actually do this to 'conflict me out' so that I will be ethically forbidden from representing the other side—who wants the lawyer with special expertise and industry knowledge to help your opponent fight against you? Though this happens rarely and is completely inappropriate, I still know that it occurs and prevents me from receiving more work in my area of practice."[17]

In spite of some barriers to establishing a successful animal law practice, Julie finds her work in equine law to be rewarding. One particular case stands out in her mind that has made the long hours and difficult work worthwhile.

"My client bought a breathtakingly beautiful and well-bred quarter horse colt from a seller in Florida. The colt, at the time of purchase, was suspected of being a 'cryptorchid' (having only one descended testicle). If the colt did, in fact, turn out to be a cryptorchid, he would be wholly ineligible for breeding in the future and could not be shown in breed shows as a stallion. My client and the seller knew when they negotiated the sale on their own

that it would take about a year after the sale for the colt to mature enough
to determine whether the retained testicle would 'drop.' As a result, my
client—without lawyer involvement, unfortunately—drafted a sale contract
that allowed her a year to see whether the testicle would drop. If so, she
would owe the seller a substantial additional sum. If not, she owed nothing
more. Several months into ownership of the colt, but before passage of the
year, my client took him to a board-certified equine theriogenologist who
found that the retained testicle had practically a zero chance of dropping
because it was undersized and stuck deep in the inguinal canal. My client,
without consent of the seller, authorized the veterinarian to geld the colt so
that he could continue his show career and for other humane reasons. The
seller sued to collect the additional money, claiming that the surgery violated the contract's terms and thwarted the seller's chances of collecting the
extra money. Using expert testimony, we carefully developed my client's
defenses. Then, when discovery ended, we filed a motion to dismiss that
argued the colt would never drop, and the plaintiff could not prove otherwise. We won. I am sure the Florida judge never forgot that one, either."[18]

As with any situation, there are specific dos and don'ts when becoming an animal law attorney. Julie shares these thoughts on how to develop
a respectable animal law practice: "(1) Don't take on cases and matters
where you will not be fairly compensated, unless you agree early on to
accept it pro bono or for a reduced fee and you can afford to do so.[19] (2)
Be very cautious before accepting cases where the fee will far exceed the
amount at stake—even if the client insists that he or she is willing to pay
your fee or that a 'principle' justifies paying your disproportionate fee.[20]
This can result in the client being disgruntled. (3) Don't be discouraged
when fellow lawyers and judges occasionally trivialize your animal law
practice. As we know well, animal law can broadly encompasses numerous areas of the law such as trusts and estates, tax law, administrative law,
commercial/UCC [uniform commercial code] issues, intensive tort issues,
municipal law, serious criminal issues, contracts, and much more. These
are hardly trivial or simple matters—these can actually be very complex
and challenging.[21] (4) Be consistently civil and cordial to opposing parties and counsel. Not only is this the proper way to practice, but opposing
counsel could, down the line, refer business to you.[22] (5) Do take time
to answer inquiries if your schedule allows and if it is ethical to do so.
Whether you realize it or not, you are a representative of the animal law
practitioner community. Make us look good.[23] (6) Do maintain and use

a list of referral lawyers. You will occasionally need to refer business, and a handy reference will allow you to share names quickly to help the prospective client find needed assistance.[24] (7) Use retainer letters. (8) Do find time for pro bono work that involves animal-related law. People and organizations really could use your help and will be very grateful for whatever assistance you can provide. And your efforts, regardless of how small they may be, will help improve the image of lawyers."[25]

Like Joan, Julie is reaching out to young lawyers to share her interest in equine law. She has mentored other lawyers, receives inquiries every month from law students interested in equine law, and she always responds to provide them her insights. "Some lawyers say my willingness to help is unwise because I am setting up competitors. I disagree and strongly believe that a greater number of animal law practitioners is a win-win for everyone. The public clearly benefits from having more lawyers who are knowledgeable of and interested in animal law. Also, I think lawyers enjoy combining personal interests with their professional work; the lawyer who can find even a few animal-related legal matters a year is likely a happier lawyer."[26] For Julie, her love of animals and equine law is something she wants to share with others.

To learn more about her work and to obtain detailed information on how to become an equine law practitioner, visit her website at www .equinelaw.net.

Diane Balkin (Denver District Attorney's Office, Denver, Colorado)

What can I say about Diane Balkin other than she is my hero? For all of the frustrations I feel about the lack of attention on animal cruelty prosecutions, Diane shines a bright light on those cases and is tackling animal cruelty head on as a chief deputy district attorney in the Denver District Attorney's Office.

As with many people involved in protecting animals, Diane's love of animals started at an early age, including the need to shield them from harm. Since becoming a prosecutor in 1979, Diane has handled dozens of animal cruelty and neglect cases. She explains that one particular case launched her specialization in investigating, prosecuting, and training others in crimes against animals. The case involved a Denver disc jockey working for a local hard rock radio station. Diane explains, "He orchestrated an on-air contest in February 2000 that invited listeners to bring a prairie dog to the station to see if it could run across the interstate highway without being hit. When no listeners had an available prairie dog, one offered to bring in a chicken. The disc jockey, Steven 'Willie B' Meade, had the listener bring in the chicken, and Mead had an intern take the chicken to the second floor balcony and toss it off to see if it could fly. He announced it over the air to all of his listeners. When the hen survived the first event, Meade had the intern take the hen to the third floor balcony and once again, on air, directed the intern to heave the chicken over the balcony to the frozen ground. Thankfully several listeners were appalled at the stunt, and one mother and her teenage son were able to rescue the chicken and take it to a veterinarian. The chicken survived with minor injuries. I read about the incident and asked the elected district attorney (now Governor Bill Ritter) if I could handle the case. No one else wanted to take the case. After all, it was just a chicken, the chicken did not die, and the suspect never touched the chicken. I felt at the time that Mr. Meade richly deserved to be held accountable, as he had orchestrated the entire incident. I was very concerned that he was a role model for impressionable children, teenagers, and young adults and by his 'stunt' was delivering a message of gratuitous violence. The case proceeded to trial by jury, and Meade was convicted."[27] And lucky for the chicken named Angel, she was placed in a sanctuary to live out her life in safety.

As with any profession, there are daily joys and frustrations. One primary frustration for Diane involves animal cruelty cases that are poorly investigated, which invariably creates legal challenges for even the most talented prosecutor. "It is a sad reality that I am often faced with refusing charges simply because the case is not provable. I know the perpetrator committed the crime and an animal was harmed or killed and the offender won't be held accountable. Along these lines, it is a challenge to educate and energize some animal control officers and some police officers about the unique proof problems related to crimes involving animals."[28] In spite of these frustrations, Diane experiences many rewards for being the strong voice for these voiceless beings. "To be able to hold an individual accountable for harming or killing a living creature is an accomplishment. I am able to measure this type of an accomplishment on multiple levels—I am able to help the animal and help the public. It is important to stress that these cases embrace animal and human welfare."[29]

Diane has benefited numerous animals by legally advocating for them to be safe from abuse, or ensuring them justice after their death. With so many memorable stories in her repertoire, one particular case stands out in her mind. "In one case, the defendant had a basenji named Spike that he had adopted some twelve years earlier. Spike was becoming deaf, blind, and perhaps incontinent. The defendant became increasingly frustrated with Spike and began to withhold even the most basic care. One day the defendant purchased a BB rifle for his six-year-old son. On the son's birthday he shot Spike in the face with the BB rifle in front of his son. He then chased the dog off his property and told the son, 'If Spike comes back I will shoot him with a real gun. The bullet hole will be small where it goes in and large when it comes out.' The photographs of Spike were so sad. More importantly, the shooting and abandonment of the lifelong pet had a profound impact on the six-year-old son. The dog was older than the child. Spike was found wandering aimlessly, was treated for emaciation and other health-related problems. The 'after' photographs were stunning and uplifting. I was so thankful that I was able to personally meet Spike."[30] Spike was adopted and lived an additional two years. The defendant was convicted and was sentenced to one year in jail.

To be an effective and successful animal cruelty prosecutor, Diane believes in these few simple rules: (1) Establish relationships with agencies involved in public safety, animal welfare, and human welfare. It is important to be proactive in bringing these professionals to the table and reaching out to other experts such as veterinarians and wildlife experts. (2) Take the time to train professionals in several key areas, including animal abuse investigations and prosecution; the co-occurrence between cruelty to animals and violence to humans; and veterinary forensic issues. It is also essential to reach out to the community to talk to people about how to identify and report animal cruelty. (3) Be available to answer questions and give advice to professionals in the field and citizens in the community. (4) Realize that there are times when you will not have sufficient evidence to file criminal animal abuse charges. Diane shares, "these cases may break your heart, but don't let them break your spirit. There is always another animal down the road that will need you and your expertise."[31] And (5) make the focus of these cases about human welfare and public safety and not solely animal welfare. By taking that approach, you will gain more acceptance from the community and the judicial system, and you will be more likely to have a successful result.

What is Diane's advice to law students, attorneys, or people interested in becoming an animal cruelty prosecutor? "The best advice I would give an up-and-coming attorney is to first become proficient in all aspects of criminal law. My success with crimes involving animals is deeply rooted in the experience I had in trying all types of crimes with all sorts of legal twists. I then highly recommend becoming involved with experts in the many professions related to public safety, and human and animal welfare, including (but not limited to) veterinary professionals; veterinary forensic sciences; animal welfare and shelter groups; domestic violence groups; law enforcement (including animal control); teachers; treatment evaluators and providers; academicians; etc. It is also helpful to attend local animal-related conferences and to later offer to speak at said conferences."[32]

For concerned citizens who want to see animals given their day in court, Diane recommends becoming involved with animal protection groups in your community and supporting them through fund-raising events or volunteering your time for the animals. Also be aware of animal-related legislation in your state and support efforts that provide greater legal protections to animals. And lastly, Diane urges everyone to be proactive on the part of animals and get involved. For me, I take comfort in knowing that animals suffering abuse or neglect at the hands of a human in Denver will receive the best legal representation in the criminal justice system because Diane is their advocate.

Regardless of your position in life, you can play an important part in protecting animals, whether it is educating someone on how to properly care for their pet, saving or adopting an animal in need, making a donation to those who spend their lives protecting animals, or reporting cruelty and neglect. Being an engaged participant in your neighborhood and community and speaking up for animals in harmful situations is one of the best ways you can become an animal advocate. The conversation must continue so that together we can raise awareness to protect everyone, including animals, from harm. Together, with each little action, we all can make a difference.

You Can Do More

- For attorneys:
  - Join your state or city bar association's animal law section or committee and become involved in the activities of the committee, including providing legal assistance to people who need help. If your state or

city bar association does not have an animal law section or committee, offer to start one.

- Reach out to attorneys that are practicing animal law and talk to them about their practice. If you are interested in a subspecialty in animal law, connecting with attorneys in those subspecialties will help you determine if that is the appropriate career path.
- Peruse the Internet and learn what you can about animal law and the various subspecialties. Join e-mail groups and blogs and join in on the conversation.
- Once you decide to take on animal law cases, share this information with other attorneys so that they can refer cases to you, and inform your community regarding your animal legal services.
- Attend community events or write articles in local publications (both professional and general) about animal law.

- For law students:
  - Join your law school's Student Animal Legal Defense Fund or other animal law organization. If your law school does not have an animal law group, connect with a professor who is animal-friendly (maybe an environmental law professor) and ask if s/he will sponsor an SALDF chapter or animal law organization. Then spread the word throughout your law school and you will discover many like-minded colleagues.
  - Take animal law courses offered by your law school. If none are offered, seek out conferences that talk about animal law issues (many are featured in chapter 2) or contact your state or city bar association to see if they have lectures on animal law. Also, ask your law school dean to consider offering an animal law course.
  - Obtain an internship with an organization or law firm that handles animal law litigation, advocacy, or legislative issues. Many national animal protection organizations offer internships to law students wishing to learn more about animal law and legislation.

- For concerned citizens:
  - Contact an animal law specialist to create a will and/or trust to care for your pets should you become disabled or pass away. Ensuring the care of your pets when you are unable to care for them is a wonderful way to protect your pets and avoid their entering a shelter.
  - If you become embroiled in a legal dispute involving your pet, search for and hire an animal law attorney who is specialized to protect your animal.

- When you suspect abuse or neglect of an animal, do something! Report what you saw to the authorities and provide your name so that you can testify as a witness if needed.
- If you see someone behaving cruelly toward an animal or not providing appropriate care, do something to educate the person and offer to help them. Sometimes the kind words of a caring neighbor can go a long way to providing a better life for an animal.

CHAPTER 12

Lobbying for Animals

The term *lobbyist* evokes interesting reactions from people: some view a lobbyist as a passionate advocate, while others think back to national news reports of those involved in questionable activities to promote a specific agenda. For several years, I was a lobbyist for American Humane Association, running the organization's Washington, D.C.–based office, and saw the business of lobbying from the inside. Some people believe that to change laws and policies for the better protection of animals you must be employed as a lobbyist. However, I quickly learned that while lobbyists may know how to strategize on an issue for optimal success and have relationships with legislative staff, it is the people who vote politicians into office that have equal, if not greater, power to lobby for change.

As you have read throughout this book, there are many ways to become an animal advocate, whether through employment, volunteering, or simply engaging in acts of kindness toward an animal in need. But there is no doubt that those who are working every day to lobby and advocate for better laws and policies for animals are changing the way Americans think about and treat animals. I have been fortunate to be one of those people speaking for our voiceless companions, and to work side-by-side with others doing the same.

When I was employed with American Humane, I quickly learned about other national animal protection organizations, their strengths, and their weaknesses. I came to respect that every national organization plays a key role in advocacy efforts and has its own contribution toward a common end goal. The Humane Society of the United States (HSUS) has shown itself to be a leader in the animal lobbying movement in recent years. HSUS was established in 1954 with the goal of seeking the humane treatment of all animals. With more than five hundred employees nationwide, and HSUS state directors in thirty states, HSUS has become a powerful voice for the protection of animals. Lauren Silverman Simon, one of HSUS's federal lobbyists with whom I have had the pleasure to collaborate, is featured in this chapter and provides her advice on how to become more involved in animal advocacy.

Advocacy and lobbying do not require that you become employed as such in order to make a difference. Those employed as lobbyists need the assistance of local advocates to help with causes. Holly Thoms, a friend, fellow volunteer advocate, and president of Voiceless-MI, a volunteer nonprofit organization, gives her input in this chapter on how you can become an animal advocate from the place of volunteerism.

What is the difference between advocacy and lobbying? Advocacy is defined as the active support of an idea or a cause, whereas lobbying is defined as a form of advocacy designed to influence legislators and other officials. Lobbying is a subset of the overall concept of advocacy. It is important to understand that anyone can engage in lobbying activities regardless of your career or place in life. If you have ever contacted your national, state, or local legislator to express your opinion on an issue, then you have engaged in lobbying. Whenever I informed people that I was previously employed as a lobbyist, the reactions were always interesting, because most people believed that only a few elite and specialized people were capable of lobbying. Being an expert in a particular area for purposes of lobbying is certainly helpful, and my expertise on certain issues, particularly pound seizure, has gained me access to legislators. But if you are passionate about an issue or cause, take the time to become educated about the issue, and set a strategic plan on how to influence your legislator, then you are doing the work of a lobbyist. Whether you call yourself a lobbyist or an advocate, my goal is to encourage you to take your advocacy to the next level and begin to influence those who create and change laws that affect animals.

Lobbying is broken down into three different categories: direct lobbying, grassroots lobbying, and grasstops lobbying. Direct lobbying involves making direct contact with a legislator or official to discuss a particular issue or legislative bill for the purpose of educating and influencing their position. This contact can be made in person, by telephone, or by correspondence (regular mail, e-mail, or online action alerts). Direct lobbying is powerful because as a voter, you are one of many who decide who will represent you at the national, state, and local levels. It is your vote and your support that decide whether the politician maintains a position of power. On the other hand, grassroots lobbying involves mobilizing communities and voters to learn about an issue affecting their state or community and asking them to collectively become involved in contacting their legislator. I found that one of the easiest and fastest methods to mobilize grassroots advocates is through e-mail messages, online petitions, and online action alerts. Action alerts, generally written by lobbyists or staff employed by an animal protection organization, outline an issue, why the issue is important, and what needs to be done. The alert usually contains a prewritten letter to your legislator to persuade them to support, or oppose, a legislative effort. Anyone with a computer and a list of people supportive of a cause can write an e-mail message that contains an action alert. Grasstops lobbying involves reaching out to experts on a particular issue and engaging them to contact legislators. Connecting with experts to provide their professional opinion on an animal protection issue can be very influential with legislators who need to learn the nuances and all sides of each issue. Having an expert in the field discuss a legislative bill with a legislator, or provide legislative testimony, is a very powerful tool. I have found that all three methods of lobbying must be engaged to achieve success on an issue.

With any social movement, influencing legislators at all levels of government is an integral step that can be best accomplished by engaging people in the community. As a lobbyist covering the federal government and all fifty states, I could not be everywhere at every moment. However, engaging communities to participate in grassroots advocacy was critical, in my view, to successful passage of laws to protect animals. Even organizations that have lobbyists and staff in various states rely on the combined effort of passionate advocates who will help spread the message. This is where you can become an important part of an advocacy movement in your state or community. Offering your assistance to meet with state or local legislators, while receiving guidance on strategy from the lobbyist in charge of the issue, is a winning combination. Because you have the right to cast your vote in elections, your voice is a powerful ally to promote change. Linking that power to the expertise of a lobbyist and/or a national animal protection organization provides the momentum to achieve change.

While some legislators may not directly tell you their position on a particular bill, you can get a sense of their support for animal protection legislation by checking out legislative scorecard websites, such as the HSUS Scorecard website[1] and the Animal Welfare Institute's Compassion Index.[2] Some state animal protection organizations provide scorecards on state legislators, such as the Massachusetts SPCA and the Animal Protection Voters New Mexico. Researching past voting practices of legislators on animal issues is a good way to get started on advocating for change. Lauren Silverman Simon (a professional lobbyist) and Holly Thoms (a volunteer lobbyist and advocate) provide their thoughts on what more you can do to get involved to lobby for animals.

LOBBYISTS WHO ARE MAKING A DIFFERENCE FOR ANIMALS

Lauren Silverman Simon (The Humane Society of the United States, Washington, D.C.)

The Humane Society of the United States (HSUS) is the largest animal protection organization in the United States, with an estimated 11 million supporters. In 2009, the HSUS was involved in the enactment of more than 120 animal protection laws.[3] Lauren Silverman Simon is an attorney who works as a federal lobbyist for HSUS in its Washington, D.C., office. She began advocating for animals in sixth grade when she won an award for giving a speech about cruelty to animals in circuses and rodeos. In college and law school—both at the University of Maryland—she joined animal protection groups and cofounded the Maryland Student Animal Legal Defense Fund, an organization that provided Lauren her first opportunities to testify before the Maryland legislature in support of animal protection bills. She also participated in internships with HSUS in its Government Affairs Department as well as with Meyer & Glitzenstein (now Meyer Glitzenstein & Crystal), a D.C. law firm specializing in animal law litigation. Lauren believes that her law school education has helped in her professional advocacy work because it taught her speaking, writing, debating, and research skills to win for the animals, as well as how to write legislation, analyze laws, and build a case for success.

Lauren, who became a lobbyist for HSUS in 2005, specializes in federal legislative work to protect animals, including efforts to end the use of chimpanzees in invasive research, to protect horses from slaughter, and to prevent the theft of pets for research. Lauren spends her days working with legislators and their staffs, content-expert colleagues within HSUS, other animal protection organizations, outside professional experts, and citizens providing grassroots advocacy support. For many people who love animals, being employed to speak for animals would be a dream job; and for Lauren it is, even though big successes can be slow to materialize. Lauren explains, "There is nothing better than knowing that you've made a positive and lasting difference for animals, and usually such a success comes after much time and energy spent working on the same issue. The legislative process can be slow and difficult—and it can be frustrating to deal with opposition to changes in the law that make complete sense and protect animals at the same time—however, major policy reforms are happening for animals. Even just in the last ten years, these changes to protect animals have been tremendous. I think Owen Feltham articulated it best when he explained: 'The greatest results in life are usually attained by simple means and the exercise of ordinary qualities. These may for the most part be summed in these two: common-sense and perseverance.'"[4]

I share Lauren's sentiments that prevailing for animals can be a slow process with frustrating obstacles to overcome, but those moments of success provide immense joy that fuels perseverance to stay focused on the next issue. In her lobbying efforts to protect the chimpanzees in research and end their exploitation, Lauren explains how an undercover investigation empowered her advocacy voice. "The HSUS conducted a nine-month undercover investigation of the federally funded New Iberia Research Center (NIRC) in Louisiana, revealing the routine and unlawful mistreatment of hundreds of chimpanzees and other primates going on behind closed doors. This investigation was the most comprehensive ever at any major primate research facility; it resulted in a 108-page complaint to the USDA, alleging a minimum of 338 possible violations of the federal Animal Welfare Act. The videotape evidence showed severe distress of primates in isolation (engaging in self-mutilation by tearing gaping wounds into their arms and legs), routine procedures such as the use of powerful and painful dart guns and frightening squeeze cages for sedation causing acute psychological distress to chimpanzees and monkeys, and infant monkeys screaming as they were forcibly removed from their mothers so that tubes could be forced down their throats. As difficult as this footage was to obtain—and as hard as it is to watch—it has been a critical tool in gaining the support of members of Congress and their staff for the Great Ape Protection Act—legislation to end the use of chimpanzees in invasive research and retire approximately 500 chimpanzees to sanctuary.

Public release of this footage has prompted a huge spike in the number of cosponsors. The countless hours of misery endured by these animals have been documented, and this documentation has enabled us to bring their suffering to the halls of Congress—to educate legislators and congressional staff about this issue and the need to pass this crucial legislation."[5]

If you are interested in engaging in lobbying to promote the passage of animal protection legislation, Lauren shares these ten points that will provide you with the foundation to being a successful lobbyist:

1. Show respect for congressional staff—and listen carefully to concerns they have about bills that you support.
2. Make sure to always first point out good things that a member of Congress has done to help animals (cosponsorships, votes, score in the Humane Scorecard, letters written or signed on to)—a "thank you" should always come before an "ask."
3. Build rapport with legislators and their staff and develop relationships with key people who have influence over animal issues.
4. Be clear about what you want congressional staff or a member of Congress to do and welcome their suggestions for bill/issue strategy.
5. Take notes, not just during meetings but also during phone conversations.
6. If you do not know the answer to a question, never lie to or mislead congressional staff—do your homework and get back to them in a reasonable period of time.
7. Always follow up with congressional staff after a meeting—thank anyone and everyone for their time.
8. Get your views across, professionally and with class. Remember you are speaking on behalf of the animals who cannot speak for themselves, so everything you say—and how you say it—is important.
9. Always stay focused on your end goal.
10. Be prepared. There is no substitute for being prepared.[6]

One question that frequently arises about animal advocacy is "How do I get started?" Lauren recommends volunteering with an animal protection organization to become knowledgeable about animals; from that viewpoint you may begin to see what legal protections are missing in your community or state for animals. Meet with your legislator (local, state, and federal) to share where you stand on an issue. Testify as a citizen lobbyist in support of an animal protection bill at the local or state level of government or form a grassroots group to support the passage of an animal protection bill. Begin to network with and talk to people in animal advocacy if you are interested in working as a lobbyist. By attending events in support of animal protection issues, you will meet people who can provide guidance. Lastly, Lauren recommends, "Always be an advocate for animals in all that you do—what you eat, what you wear, how you vote, what you buy, etc. So much that we do in our everyday lives can either help animals or contribute to their suffering. Your actions are your message to the public—encourage others to help animals in their everyday activities as well."[7]

I echo Lauren's comments on how to become involved in advocating and lobbying for animals. If you are interested in delving into this world, it is important to "walk the talk" and to do your best to live your life in the support of protecting animals. Lauren exemplifies someone who has dedicated her life to bettering the lives of all animals, and she hopes that her path to becoming a lobbyist will empower others to join in the movement.

Holly Thoms (Voiceless-MI)

Holly Thoms is the president of Voiceless-MI,[8] a nonprofit organization formed to help animals throughout the state of Michigan as well as to be a strong voice in advocating for the protection of animals. While Holly is not employed in animal protection, she spends many hours each day helping animals, particularly shelter animals. I have seen Holly in action when she helped with the 2003 effort to end pound seizure in our shelter in Ingham County, Michigan. When she joined Friends of Ingham County Animal Shelter in 2002, an organization that I cofounded, she did not realize that one day she would lead that organization and would subsequently organize another nonprofit to help Michigan's animals. In 2009–2010, her advocacy efforts rose to a new level and she became directly involved in lobbying for two bills that I created with my staff at American Humane Association: bills to end pound seizure and to end gas chamber euthanasia of shelter animals.

So how did Holly become a volunteer animal advocate? She started by volunteering at the county animal shelter because the shelter did not have enough jail inmates to clean cages or feed the animals, and this shortage was resulting in euthanasia of the animals. So Holly rolled up her sleeves

and began helping the shelter animals. In this process, she learned that
the shelter engaged in pound seizure, a practice that she could not com-
prehend occurring at an animal shelter. She shares, "Aren't they there to
protect the animals? I wasn't even convinced at first this wasn't just an
outlandish story. But I found out very soon that it was in fact the truth.
Some of the very animals I kissed on the head the day before and prayed
to find adoptive homes disappeared. And the shelter wasn't so forthcom-
ing with the information of where they went. That was when I stayed up
at night thinking about the faces and thinking about what I could do to
help change things at our local county shelter."[9] Holly decided to join with
other volunteers to end pound seizure, which resulted in successful passage of an ordinance to ban the Class B dealer from the shelter.

Although her advocacy began at the local level, Holly now advocates
as a volunteer at the state level to help protect shelter animals. With the
2009–2010 Michigan bills to end pound seizure and gas chamber euthanasia, Holly has worked with me to mobilize grassroots advocates across
the state to not only support the bills but also to get active and contact
their legislators. Holly was my pipeline to the e-mail animal groups in
Michigan to keep people updated on the bills and to mobilize the troops
on the next steps. Holly herself attended legislative hearings, called her
legislators to discuss the bills and learn their position, posted information
on her organization's website, and took time off from work to speak with
the chairman of the Senate Agriculture Committee, and other committee
members, to push for hearings.

Holly shares these words of advice based on her own experience as
a volunteer lobbyist. First, be willing to step out of your comfort zone.
"The first time I had to go talk to a senator, I thought I was going to have
a heart attack before I reached their office. I thought I was way out of
my league. It turns out I made a valuable contact and received a lot of
valuable information. It could have been a missed opportunity if I had
not stepped outside of my comfort zone."[10] Second, be respectful to your
legislator. Although your legislator may not agree with your position
on one animal issue, they may support you on another issue later. Holly
explains, "Animal issues can become very emotional, and you cannot let
your emotions get the best of you in public. There is always someone
waiting to call us 'crazy animal fanatics'; don't ever give them a reason
to say that."[11] Third, speak only the facts. Never present any information,
verbally or in writing, that is not supported by facts. If you are using in-

formation to lobby, you need to back it up. Fourth, know your cause. Be prepared to answer any question about the issue and back up your answers with facts. "If you are talking about banning gas chambers in Michigan, you better know how many gas chambers in Michigan are left."[12] Fifth, keep an e-mail list of like-minded people you know and meet. This helps if you need to send out e-mail alerts in a quick manner and to get people mobilized to take action on a petition or action alert, attend a meeting, or make a phone call to a legislator. Sixth, be careful what you put in writing, especially in e-mail messages. "The Internet is a great tool, but it can be used against you. Anything you put out there can come back to haunt you."[13] Seventh, ask questions. "If there is something you don't understand about a process or terminology, ask someone that is 'in the know' or get online and Google it. We are all on a learning curve here. I remember not knowing how a bill became law and found out most people do not know either."[14] And lastly, do not listen to the naysayers, even those who are animal advocates. "There are always going to be keyboard warriors on the sidelines that are negative and telling you what you are doing wrong. I would encourage you to listen to people you would consider mentors. It is another thing when people are downright nasty. You will notice many of them sit behind their keyboard typing out what should have been done while they actually did nothing to help the cause. Ignore the negativity and move on."[15]

Holly has experienced the slow process of making change for animals. Having worked with me extensively for two years toward the passage of Michigan's bills to end pound seizure and gas chamber euthanasia, she knows not to give up. She shares, "A lot of these fights can become timely battles that last not months, but in fact years. So be prepared to go for the long haul once you jump in. Pray for a short battle, but be prepared for a long one."[16]

What does it take to become a volunteer lobbyist? First and foremost, Holly explains that you must be willing to stand up for what you believe is right, even when others are telling you that you are wrong. If you only partially believe in something, it will show. "The best person to advocate for an issue is one that truly believes in what they are saying and is educated about that issue. A true believer can get people to listen and learn about their cause."[17] Holly has found that effective advocates are outgoing and people-oriented. She explains, "Once you get a person's or potential advocate's attention, the best weapon in your arsenal is communication. It is up to you to communicate to them why they need to take action. It is up to you to communicate to the legislators why it is crucial to make change. It is always a plus to be good at public speaking, but not completely necessary. But you need to have good 'one-on-one' skills."[18] It is also important to be a self-starter. "Most of the time there won't be someone standing around telling you what to do next. It will be up to you the majority of the time to make the next step without prodding from anyone. It will be up to you to make action happen. It may be something as simple as making sure you send out e-mails to your 'warm market' (family/friends) to get them to sign a petition. But it may be looking up meeting times and places in the Capitol so that you can be at the meeting to listen to your legislators talk about your issue in public. Be sure to do the research yourself and you will then be sure that the information you have and are disseminating is correct."[19] Lastly, be prepared to compromise. With any legislative bill, there will be opposition that believes as strongly in their position as you do in yours. "Be ready to take smaller steps toward your goal. It does not have to be 'all or nothing,' because if that is all you are willing to accept, many times you will be accepting nothing."[20]

While there are great joys in passing legislation to protect animals, there are also frustrations that invariably ride along. The greatest frustration I encountered was with legislative committees that scheduled few opportunities for legislative hearings and, thus, fewer opportunities for legislation to become law. Legislators may only be "in session" a few days a week and may take off a month in the summer as well as a month or more before election time, even if they are not up for re-election. Before the 2010 midterm elections, it was frustrating when the Michigan legislature closed shop for six weeks before the election to work on campaigns. After the November election, deer hunting season arrived, then Thanksgiving, then the close of the two-year legislative session in early December. They also had most of August off for summer recess. So in the final half of the year, the number of days in session was minimal. It was frustrating because two bills that I had spent years working on, which had passed the House, still required a Senate hearing. But the bills were dying because the legislators were simply not in business. From the midterm elections in November to the close of the legislative session in December, the committee assigned these two bills had only one hearing day. Although the legislators may have a good reason for scheduling so few session days, it is frustrating to those of us who have worked on a bill for years and have come so close to having the bill become law. It is frustrating for me to know that legislative committees, the first stop for bills, are allowed to end a session with dozens of unheard bills on their calendars.

Frustration also comes from opposing organizations that cling to outdated practices that do not benefit animals, especially when those organizations' lobbyists seem unwilling to discuss the merits of the issues, thus stalling progress toward compromise. I enjoy a healthy debate on issues involving the protection of animals; but when an opposing lobbyist simply behaves in an abusive manner, refuses to talk, while actively working to ruin animal protection bills, that can bring the process to a grinding halt. A good lobbyist will always discuss and defend his or her position and will not shy away from debate or confrontational conversations.

Despite the frustrations and the slow progress in passing bills to protect animals, each federal or state bill that is enacted into law for the benefit of animals rejuvenates the people involved to keep working toward the next issue. Whether you are employed as a lobbyist, or become involved as a volunteer advocate, we must work together to effectuate change. After all, the animals are voiceless and need us to speak up to protect them from harm.

You Can Do More

- Sign up for action alerts with an animal protection organization. National organizations send out action alerts on legislative issues that they follow, such as American Anti-Vivisection Society, American Humane Association, American Society for the Prevention of Cruelty to Animals, Animal Law Coalition, Animal Legal Defense Fund, International Fund for Animal Welfare, People for the Ethical Treatment of Animals, and The Humane Society of the United States. Many state and local animal protection groups also send out action alerts. Receiving and taking action on these alerts is a good way to learn the issues and get involved.
- If a particular legislative issue interests you, reach out to local, state, or national organizations working on the issue and offer your help. Learn about the issue. Offering to meet with your legislator, especially if the legislator is in a leadership role or part of the committee hearing the bill, will greatly help.

- Attend Lobby Days that may be scheduled at your state capitol building. HSUS sponsors several state Lobby Days, usually held each February. This is a good opportunity to learn how to lobby and learn about particular animal protection bills affecting your state.
- If you are knowledgeable about a particular legislative issue impacting your community or state, testify as a citizen advocate. In many local and state venues, you can sign up at the beginning of a legislative hearing to provide your views, sometimes for three minutes. Lending your voice is crucial to demonstrating why legislation protecting animals is important in communities.
- Mobilize a grassroots effort in your community to support a legislative bill.
- If legislation is needed in your community or statewide, reach out to animal protection organizations about drafting a bill and locating a legislator to file the bill. You may find other like-minded advocates who can help with this effort.
- Create a website or social networking page that contains information about a legislative bill. The more people are educated regarding the facts behind a bill, the most support it will receive.
- If you are interested in being employed as an animal lobbyist, connect with people currently employed as lobbyists on animal protection issues. Ask them to mentor or provide assistance so that you can learn how to become an effective animal lobbyist.

CHAPTER 13

Using Your Words to Benefit Animals

In the past decade, media news has become more involved in publicizing stories about animals. On June 1, 1996,[1] the cable station Animal Planet was launched by the Discovery Channel and now features more than thirty shows dedicated to celebrating animals, including popular ones like *Animal Cops, Confessions: Animal Hoarding, Last Chance Highway*, and *It's Me or the Dog*. The National Geographic Channel also features shows about wildlife and exotic animals, most of which we would never see without these feature programs. With each passing year, Americans become more fixated on the world of animals through the media. Even animal-based radio programs are growing, such as Animal Radio[2] and Animal Magnet Pet Radio.[3] The Internet, YouTube, blogs, social media sites, books, and magazines all provide an expanding media source for every species of animal and every possible animal topic. Regardless of whether you like to dabble in the fine arts of writing, blogging, Facebooking, or Tweeting about animals, there is a place for animal advocates to share their voice about animals through media.

This chapter features three "media hounds" who promote the protection of animals and celebrate the special relationships people have with animals. Each has their own platform for promoting awareness and speaking for those furry and feathered members of society that need a strong voice.

MEDIA PERSONALITIES MAKING A DIFFERENCE FOR ANIMALS

Steve Dale, Radio Show Host

I met Steve Dale in 2008 when he joined the board of directors for American Humane Association. Steve Dale is a dynamic, multifaceted

media and animal personality in Chicago whose résumé on animal issues reads like a book of its own.[4] He is a journalist with a pet column
syndicated by Tribune Media Services, contributing editor to *USA Weekend*, and host of syndicated radio shows *Steve Dale's Pet World and Pet
Minute*. He's worked at two Chicago 50,000-watt radio stations and is a
columnist for *Cat Fancy,* and he's made dozens of appearances on TV
shows, national and local. Steve is a certified dog and cat behaviorist. He
is also on the board of directors of the Winn Feline Foundation, CATalyst
Council, and Tree House Humane Society in Chicago, and speaks out,
whether popular or not, on issues related to animal welfare.

Steve has been entrenched in media since high school and attributes
his love of animals to his dad. He has worked in a variety of media jobs,
including reporting for *USA Today*, *People* magazine, and the *Chicago
Tribune*. Steve explains, "Without consciously thinking about it, no matter where I landed I suppose I brought my interest in animals with me."[5]
Regardless of the assignment, his writings veered toward the animals.
"More than once, my wonderful editor at *People* would read my file and
comment that I barely mentioned the movie star's hot boyfriend but instead devoted ten paragraphs to her dog. She wasn't complaining, really;
she also noticed that stars enjoyed being asked about their pets, and as a
result they revealed more as they began to trust me. When you covered
showbiz around Chicago, you covered Oprah Winfrey. And for a few
years, whenever Oprah was at a public event, odds are I would be there
also. I was the first to regularly report on her dogs."[6]

In 1995, Steve accepted an offer to write a nationally syndicated newspaper column about pets. Worried that he would be typecast into writing
exclusively about animals, he now joyfully reports that his worries came
true, but that writing about animals has been a positive career move. In focusing his work on animal issues, Steve found that people wanted to learn
about animal behavior and were craving information on how to resolve
pet behavioral issues. This realization occurred in conjunction with his
adopting Chaser, a ten-month-old rescue dog who suffered from separation anxiety; at that time there were no veterinary behaviorists or certified
dog behavior consultants available to help Chaser. Steve saw this as an
opportunity to focus his work on helping people and their pets. Knowing
he is helping animals and educating families to understand certain behaviors keeps him motivated each day. "Making a difference by effecting
social or legislative changes is important, but touching individual families

makes me feel good and was actually my goal all those years ago. People say I help pets. No, pets are a part of the family. I help families."[7]

The notoriety of Steve's public career has benefited animals in many ways, and he has actively used his public platform to advocate for animals. One of the first opportunities he saw to educate others on animal issues and take a position as a journalist, which was not the norm at the time, involved a movement in Chicago to ban Rottweilers and pit bull dogs, because the public officials who supported this idea said they are "dangerous animals." A Chicago alderman was leading this proposal, and Steve began to educate her on breed-specific legislation (BSL) and why it is not an answer to prevent dangerous dogs or dog attacks. Steve explains, "I cajoled her to appear on the radio with me. She agreed, and my listeners did an amazing job without resorting to insults, using facts and common sense. You could tell by watching her expression in the studio, she became enlightened. Following my last commercial break, the alderman said my listeners convinced her that BSL is not a solution and tasked me live on the air to create a 'Blue Ribbon Task Force' to find a better solution. I did create a task force, though I never received a blue ribbon. We simply stiffened the animal control act and included all dogs—regardless of breed or mix."[8] Most recently, Steve's show on WLS Radio helped to launch and pass legislation in Illinois to enhance penalties for dogfighting activities occurring near day care centers, playgrounds, or schools. In congratulating Cook County sheriff Tom Dart on the air for exposing a dogfighting ring occurring at a day care outside of Chicago, Steve remarked that in spite of the felony penalties for dogfighting, the situation seemed more egregious and was desensitizing children to violence. Based on his comments, Sheriff Dart encouraged Steve to do something about his concerns. Steve contacted Ledy VanKavage, an attorney for Best Friends Animal Society, and she and her staff created legislation to enhance the penalty for dogfighting around children that was signed into law in August 2010, the first of its kind in the United States. Steve proudly knows, "Without my WLS Radio platform, this couldn't have happened."[9]

Steve actively uses his media platform to raise awareness about animals. After Hurricane Katrina he learned that the largest animal shelter in Louisiana, the Louisiana SPCA, had been destroyed, so he organized the "Mardi Growl" benefit to raise money for a new shelter. In ten days, and with the assistance of the Chicago Veterinary Medical Association, nearly 500 people and 50 dogs attended the benefit. Veterinarians and dog trainers around

Chicago also collected donations. In the end, $40,000 was raised to benefit the Louisiana SPCA and the veterinary medical assistance teams who responded after the disaster. Through his radio show on WGN, Steve helped to organize DOG/Chicago to develop dog-friendly areas throughout the city. He also initiated a campaign in 2000 to change the practice of Chicago cab drivers who refused to transport people with service or assistance dogs. Through his public platform, Steve changed the policy to one in which taxis display "Chicago Welcomes Service Dogs" tags.

Steve takes his responsibility as a media personality seriously and believes it is his responsibility to help animals through his platform. "Dogs and cats can't broadcast or blog about their plights or concerns. I understand why animal issues are sometimes not seen or heard in the media. After all, there are wars, there is terrorism, and murders take place daily in America, not to mention the latest news with Paris Hilton and Lindsay Lohan. But pets are my beat. I am not the only one who can make a difference simply by using platforms. The problem is there are fewer platforms for 'pet experts' than ever. Newspapers that once took my column have cut back on the syndicated material they accept, and some are out of business altogether. There aren't many professional radio or TV performers who host pet shows."[10]

But with the growth of social media sites, Steve encourages anyone who loves animals to get involved by speaking out, working with others, and utilizing the power of social media. The more people who become involved in publicly speaking about and advocating for animals, the better life will be for the animals. As for Steve, he says, "I suppose if it all ends tomorrow—I can say I mattered. And that is gratifying."[11]

DUSTY RAINBOLT, WRITER

Dusty Rainbolt is all things feline. She is the vice president of the Cat Writers' Association, contributing writer to *Cat Fancy* magazine, monthly columnist for Tufts University newsletter *Catnip*, writer for various pet-related websites, and the author of six books on cats, including *Kittens for Dummies*. She is also a behaviorist consultant and enjoys helping people work through cat behavioral issues.[12]

Dusty knows cats and how to promote them positively. She began her journalism career at the age of thirty-three. She became involved in animal advocacy when she opened her home to foster a pregnant cat and the subsequent litter of kittens. When Dusty kept two of those kittens, she combined her passion for cats with her writing skills and found herself writing about animals. She explains, "My first article about animal advocacy was a feature on the local animal control manager. It was written to bring personality to a person who is usually labeled 'the bad guy' who puts animals to sleep. When I interviewed him and he started talking about the euthanasia process, tears ran down his face. It was obviously difficult for him to talk about and to perform. I wrote that article to change the image of the shelter and about owner responsibility to reduce euthanasia in shelters. I got so much response from people in the rescue community. Every chance from that point, I wrote articles about animals."[13] From that article, to securing a position at a newspaper, to writing more and more about animals, and cats in particular, this has now become Dusty's career.

There is a misperception in society about cats; some people view them negatively and may shy away from them due to inaccurate labels that they are aloof or bring bad luck. Dusty writes about cats to change people's minds and portray them as deeply feeling, sentient beings. Dusty also feels compelled to write about difficult issues—the darker side of animal protection. "I wrote an article called 'Hope Rises' in *Cat Fancy* magazine about a foster cat I took in that no one else wanted. He had been beaten nearly to death by his young owner's dad. He was just an amazing, sweet, and wonderful cat in spite of what he suffered. After I wrote that article and became involved with you, Allie, I learned about the need to protect animals from domestic violence and safely house them when other family members enter a shelter. I worked with our local shelter, and now when victims of domestic violence go to the police department with their pet, the shelter picks up the pet for safekeeping, and that stops the batterer from further harm. Lucky for Phoenix, he was safe and was adopted right before Christmas of 2008."[14] Dusty's article won the Hartz Milk Replacement for Kittens Award at the annual Cat Writers' Association conference in 2010 for the best single article on the topic of rescuing kittens.

Dusty encourages anyone who is interested in writing, whether for fun or for a career, and loves animals to get involved in writing about animals. She suggests offering to write articles and stories for shelter newsletters to get started. There are numerous topics to write about, from how people can get involved in helping animals, to raising awareness about issues like Phoenix the cat, to writing features on shelter animals needing homes, to addressing the horrendous overpopulation problem.

The Cat Writers' Association accepts associate members who have written in nonprofessional venues, as well as members who have published professionally. Joining the association is what helped Dusty grow her writing career. She even encouraged me to join and was my sponsor into professional membership with the association in 2010.

Caring for and writing about Phoenix developed Dusty's awareness, and she now feels compelled to raise awareness of cruelty to animals and what people can do to help. "I feel really blessed to combine my two passions: cat rescue and cat writing. I take a lot of the difficult cases like Phoenix, and while helping the cat, I write about the situation to raise awareness. Even with the tragedies that occur, maybe I can help another animal down the road through my writing and raising awareness."[15]

MANDY MOORE, ONLINE AUTHOR

While promoting animals through the media on a national scale is vitally important, there are other ways you can help animals in your community if you enjoy writing and communicating your thoughts about animals. Mandy Moore is just starting her career in journalism with a determination to focus on raising awareness about animals. After receiving her degree from Penn State in professional writing and communications in 2008, she now feels that her childhood voice to protect animals will be respected. She currently writes for the *Harrisburg Cat Rescue Examiner*,[16] an online outlet raising awareness about a variety of cat-related topics.

Mandy became involved in writing about animals after first rescuing several cats. While living with her parents, Mandy heard faint meows coming from a woodpile. She discovered three little orange tabbies with their eyes barely open. They were only a few days old. After a quick education from a local veterinarian, Mandy took on the task of being the surrogate mother and bottle-feeding the three kittens. She loved all three and kept them.

Through Mandy's love of animals and writing, she now takes her passion to reach out to local animal shelters and offer her writing services if they have a cause or event that needs public awareness. "The biggest impact I've made so far, I believe, is to highlight all of the low-cost spay/neuter clinics in the area, the dates they are performing surgeries, and their locations."[17] Mandy admits that she has been disappointed by the public's reaction to media stories about animals. "They may read a story and say, 'that's horrible!' But then they move on without thinking twice or asking themselves, 'What can I do to make a difference?' The biggest thing I ask people to do is to read and pass on information. I am always sharing links on Facebook and other social media websites. I also publicly speak out against breeding, and if a friend of mine is trying to find a stray animal a home, I do everything to make sure they are successful."[18]

Mandy describes one of her favorite articles about a nursing home that paired elderly people with elderly cats. "I thought this was a brilliant idea. The cats are great companions to lonely seniors and vice versa. I really believe all nursing homes should advocate this program. Nursing homes house many individuals. If thirty seniors were to participate in the program, that's thirty cats saved from living out the rest of their lives in a shelter with an extremely high risk of being euthanized."[19] Mandy is putting her dream to action and is working on launching a campaign to introduce her idea to nursing homes in her community and working with local shelters to participate as well. "It will take a lot of time, effort, and convincing to get shelters to agree to relocate the cats for free and to also provide supplies necessary to care for the animals, as well as convincing senior centers that it would be beneficial to their patients, but I'm up for the challenge."[20]

Mandy's goal is to use her writing abilities to get people involved and empowered to solve the many issues that plague animals. "People can always get involved by offering their time by volunteering. It gets their foot in the door for greater opportunities to help in the future. They can also participate in fund-raisers by offering themselves to bake goods, hand out fliers and raffle tickets, and run booths." Mandy believes that the best way to become an animal advocate is to use your voice. "Word of mouth is everything. Write e-mails, tell friends and family members, and establish relationships with your local pet supply stores."[21]

Without media outlets, the Internet, and social networking sites, coming together for the benefit of animals and sharing information and knowledge on how to protect animals would be difficult. Social movements are now growing in strength because of these platforms (which is something Americans witnessed in the 2008 presidential election). Even if you do not believe you are a writer, if you have a presence on any social networking sites such as Facebook, Twitter, or MySpace and you love animals, post information about protecting animals, newsworthy stories about animals that need help, and community events to benefit animals.

YOU CAN DO MORE

- Read and purchase publications that promote the well-being of animals. If there is a financial demand for books, magazines, and articles about animals, then media businesses may hire more writers to promote animal issues.
- Contact publishers, editors, and reporters who report positively on animal issues and thank them. If you show support for these stories, they may dedicate a weekly column to animal protection topics.
- Join animal-related blogs and social networking sites to learn more about what is happening in the world of animal protection and also to show support. There are too many animal blogs to list here, but an Internet search of "animal blogs," "animal protection blogs," "animal welfare blogs," "animal rights blogs," or specific animal topic blogs will get you started.
- If you love to write about cats and dogs, check out the Cat Writers' Association and Dog Writers Association of America and consider becoming a member.
- Offer to write for your local animal shelter or animal adoption organization newsletter, or to write website stories of animals that are available for adoption. A heartfelt, well-written story about an animal in need can make a difference in how quickly that animal finds a new home.
- Create a blog or social networking site where you can write about animals, special breeds, or animal topics that interest you, or simply celebrate the joy of animals.
- Create a social networking site dedicated to celebrating and protecting animals.
- Join Facebook's "You Can Do More for Animals" page, which I created to bring people together to find solutions to benefit animals.

CHAPTER 14

Communicating With and Healing Animals

Writing this chapter was saved for last, after all the other chapters had been written and rewritten. I wrote this chapter because, to me, it is one of the most important aspects of helping animals, yet is often not considered. And I saved this incredible topic as a treat for myself after months of researching and writing this book. After animals have been rescued from inhumane conditions, or re-homed from a shelter, living in a place of safety and love is certainly a good start, but is it enough to help them heal? With so many animals needing our help, healing can be pushed to the bottom of the list in the flurry of activity to help "just one more" and is often not considered. Most times, we do not know what the animal went through to get to safety; we are unsure whether abuse or neglect occurred, or the extent of the harm; and we may misunderstand the emotional trauma that the animal experienced. After animals experience trauma, the loss of their beloved home or owner, or abandonment outdoors, are they able to instantly forget and move on? Will the pet suffer physical ailments as a result? In working with shelter animals over the past decade, I have found that many pets are resilient and simply need a loving person. However, other pets may suffer behavioral and medical issues because they need to work through the trauma or grief; they may need a helping hand from someone who is gifted at healing and communicating with animals.

Have you ever wondered what your pet would say if he or she could talk? Have you ever come across an animal that was visibly upset, scared, or fearful, and you wondered what happened or how you could help? For animals that have been abused, neglected, or suffered the loss of their owner or home, I want to enter their minds and hearts to find out what they are thinking and feeling. If only they could speak our language, or vice versa, we could do a better job in healing their past. Did they feel pain and suffer like a person would? When losing their family and home, do they feel sadness, grief, and depression?

Science has proven that animals do have feelings similar to humans' and have their own thought processes. For years, people believed that animals were unable to think in a meaningful way, unable to suffer the way people do, unable to love or worry. According to Jeffrey Kluger, a senior writer with *Time* magazine, "Humans are the only animals that use tools, we used to say. But what about the birds and apes that we now know do as well? Humans are the only ones who are empathetic and generous, then. But what about the monkeys that practice charity and the elephants that mourn their dead? Humans are the only ones who experience joy and a knowledge of the future. But what about the U.K. study just last month [July 2010] showing that pigs raised in comfortable environments exhibit optimism, moving expectantly toward a new sound instead of retreating warily from it? And as for humans as the only beasts with language? Kanzi [a 29-year-old bonobo raised with language at the Great Ape Trust] himself could tell you that's not true."[1]

Betsy, a Border collie dog in Vienna, Austria, is also giving new meaning to the intelligence and thought process of animals. "'Betsy' can put names to objects faster than a great ape, and her vocabulary is at 340 words and counting. Her smarts showed up early: At ten weeks she could sit on command and was soon picking up on names of items and rushing to retrieve them—ball, rope, paper, box, keys, and dozens more. She now knows at least 15 people by name, and in scientific tests she's proven skilled at linking photographs with the objects they represent."[2] Increasing efforts to study the thoughts and feelings of animals are giving legitimacy to the argument that we should not inflict pain or suffering on any animal that we would not want inflicted upon ourselves.

Anyone who has enjoyed the company of an animal, particularly a family pet, has witnessed exhibitions of happiness, jealousy, protectiveness, and possibly sadness and grief. So after we have brought an animal to safety and placed it into a loving environment, what else can we do to heal the heart and mind of the animal? This chapter may challenge your beliefs, but hopefully it will open your mind to considering that there are gifted people in the world who can take communicating with and healing animals to another level by delving deeply into what the animal is thinking and feeling. This chapter will feature two different methods to help animals: those that heal animals through communication, and those that provide healing treatments. In my experience, communicating with and healing animals can be some of the most rewarding work to benefit animals.

COMMUNICATING WITH ANIMALS

Animal communicators have sometimes been called animal psychics or animal whisperers. A psychic can perceive information not through normal senses and may obtain information about the future or the past. An animal communicator, or animal whisperer, communicates directly with an animal by tapping into intuitive energies, symbols, and feelings to translate through telepathy what an animal is trying to communicate. Telepathy involves transferring information from one being to another in a way not involving the five traditional senses. Some people may say that it is impossible for people to communicate with animals and turn an animal's thoughts and feelings into words. However, I have witnessed how a communicator can unlock the mind of an animal and answer our questions regarding behavioral or other issues. Most people agree that people come into this world with special gifts: the gift of musicality, like Michael Jackson; the gift of humanitarianism like Mother Teresa; the gift of entrepreneurialism like Donald Trump; and the gift of innovation like Bill Gates. Likewise, people come to this world with gifts of communicating on multiple levels.

Christina Montana, Animal Whisperer

I met Christina Montana in 2004 through my volunteer work at King Street Cats in Virginia. Christina would come to the cat orphanage and help kitties that struggled to adjust to their changed circumstances or were suffering from unexplained medical conditions. I had never encountered anyone who could communicate with animals before meeting Christina, but quickly became a believer when I saw Christina communicating with a gray-tan tortoiseshell kitty named Scooter. Scooter came to King Street Cats in April 2004 when she was about ten years old. For months, she was outwardly unhappy about losing her home and living with other cats. We were having trouble finding an adoptive home for Scooter because she would lash out at people and the other cats, and we knew that she was simply miserable. I watched as Christina sat with Scooter, sometimes talking out loud, but often just sitting with her. It was noticeable that Scooter was listening to Christina, who was explaining that Scooter needed to alter her behavior; otherwise, she would forever be living at the orphanage with other kitties. From that point on, Scooter no longer struck out at people without warning, and her skirmishes with other cats were significantly less. It allowed us to then place her in a wonderful home where she lived happy and thriving until her passing in April 2011.

Christina became aware of her gift of animal communication in 2003 when she attended a workshop given by Penelope Smith on animal communication at the Omega Institute in New York. "Before attending, I always felt close to animals but had never really pursued that aspect. I had a recurring dream for years of a white miniature horse who would exchange thoughts with me. Ten years later, I attended a class on animal communication."[3] Christina described how during the class, a large chocolate-brown llama stood in front of the group of students, who were asked to mentally send him questions. The llama's owner was present and available to help verify the answers people were receiving. Christina describes her interaction with the llama: "I had my eyes open and was in the front row. I thought to myself, 'He's just absolutely gorgeous.' Suddenly, he turned his head and looked directly at me. I thought, 'He heard me.' He walked over to me, stopped in front of me, bent down, and kissed me twice on the lips. When he was walking over, I had felt a wave of warm, embracing energy precede him that translated as 'thank you' for appreciating him. He then stood back and serenaded me. That was my first communication session, and I was hooked. That taught me everything that I needed to know how to do it. It's all heart-centered."[4]

Christina explains that the animals send her pictures, emotions and physical sensations she can feel, sounds, and sometimes phrases she can understand. One of her first clients was a King Charles cavalier spaniel who was old and nearing the end of life. The family wanted him to feel comfortable and asked for Christina's help. Christina received the sensation of coldness and realized that the dog was cold. She sent him a mental image of a sweater, and the dog sent back a sense of excitement. The family bought the dog little sweaters and moved his bed into their bedroom so that he would be warmer.

Christina helps many animals to modify negative behavior. "If I am modifying behavior, we will do a movie together and act out how they need to act. We will act it out three times in our mind, talk about other things, and then come back to the issue where I will send the animal a picture asking them what they need to do, and they send me back a video of the new film of new behavior. If the issue is deep seated (based in a past life), then I have to do a shamanic journey."

Christina is trained in shamanic journeys, which involves healing through the assistance of spiritual helpers such as guides and angels. She describes how a shamanic journey is conducted for an animal. "A shamanic journey is done in a trance state, to the beat of a drum, where you go to parallel worlds. There are three shamanic worlds: lower, middle, and upper. For animals, I usually do a lower-world journey. When I come out into that world, it is always the same landscape that I am in, but the animal and guides will vary. I state my intention and the problem and ask for help in finding a solution. A shamanic journey is a way to shift behavior, and you may be shown a story. I helped a golden retriever named Molly who was afraid of fireworks and loud noises and suffered from terrible separation anxiety in the present. A shamanic journey revealed for Molly that as a young dog she had died in the blitz in London. Her family had left her at home, and this is why she had separation anxiety. The journey involved going back to the time that it happened. We changed the story by making her a puppy and providing her a little hole for her to crawl out of the wreckage and be reunited with her family. We replayed that past history so Molly survived. Afterward, I take that new version of the story and carry it back to her current physical body. For Molly, there was a dramatic shift. She exhibited less anxiety and started acting like a puppy, and she was twelve years old at the time."[5]

Christina had no issues coming out of the "animal communication closet" and finds that nowadays people are open to the subject. Only recently has she publicized her shamanic abilities because initially she believed people would be skeptical. How does she handle people who do not believe in her abilities? Christina explains, "I am not contacted by people who don't believe. I do a check-in with the people and the pet to see if they are serious about getting their pet help and will follow recommendations. If I am asked, I say that I'm an animal whisperer and I work with animal owners to help them solve behavior issues or other problems so that they have a happy or better relationship together. Most clients are women and are usually responsive. I don't try to convince people who are skeptics."[6]

Christina enjoys an active practice as an "animal whisperer."[7] She works directly with individual clients and their animals as well as volunteers to help shelter animals at the Fredericksburg SPCA shelter in Virginia. When volunteering at the shelter, she finds many of the animals want to communicate, so she puts up a filter so that it is not too overwhelming. By doing this, she can maintain her energy and help the animals one at a time. What do the shelter animals tell Christina? Roady was a shelter dog who wanted to ride around in trucks, sit on couches, and be buddies with someone. Christina conveyed that information to the shelter staff, and now Roady is in a good home and he rides around in a truck. Some shelter pets are discouraged, and Christina helps to boost their spirits. Lucy was a hound mix that had been returned to the shelter twice. Lucy was unresponsive, docile, and not interacting with anyone. Christina knew she had been traumatized by all of the changes because her eyes were blank. After conducting two healing journeys for Lucy, the spark came back to her eyes, her tail began to wag, and she was then adopted to a wonderful home.

Most animals want to talk once they know that Christina can decipher their thoughts and feelings. "I always ask their permission. Most seem eager to talk, and I see improvement even after just one session. They feel relieved to get things off their chest. There is always a shift. Their faces change and their eyes are brighter. When you release the trauma, the face changes and becomes more relaxed."[8]

If you are interested in communicating with your pet, Christina recommends taking a workshop on animal communication and practicing meditation to find a way to slow down and step out of the fast pace of life so that you can connect with your animals at their vibrational level. Removing yourself from the hectic pace of life will help to calm your mind so that you can receive messages from your pets. Our pets and other animals want to communicate with us; we just need to put ourselves in a place where we can hear them.

Diane Roadcap, Animal Communicator

Diane Roadcap is also a gifted animal communicator. I have witnessed her compelling work with animals and how they communicate their thoughts and feelings to her. She shares how she first became aware of her gift to connect with animals. "Animal communication started for me as an inner knowing when I was a young child. The first memory I have is when I was four years old, accompanying my parents on a twenty-minute trip to the city's landfill. I grew up in Luray, Virginia, and trash service was not offered at the time so townsfolk were accustomed to taking their trash there. Not safe for a child, I was strictly instructed to stay in the car. Once we arrived, my attention went to a closed cardboard box about twenty-five yards away amidst debris. As my parents proceeded to dump the trash, I was determined to see what was in that box. Despite broken glass, unpleasant smells, and poor footing, I was able to bring home an underfed, barely weaned male puppy, too malnourished to move or even make a sound. A year later, Blackie would save my life. Playing in front of my home on the dirt driveway, I was enjoying a slight breeze blowing through my shoulder-length blonde hair. I loved playing with dolls, climbing trees, and playing near the earth. I remember seeing me and my brother's toys strewn to my left. As I began to reach my hand down to the right with the intention of smoothing out the brown, dusty soil that was our driveway, I could not see the copperhead ready to strike, but I heard an unseen female voice loudly warn, 'DANGER.' At lightning speed, Blackie came between us, pushed me back, bit the snake, and stood his ground until I was able to run and find my parents. Blackie, a mix of Doberman, Lab, and terrier, would be my dog for a wonderful eight years."[9]

It was her dog, Blackie, who helped Diane maintain and develop her natural talent of communicating with animals. Diane and Blackie would go for long walks in the countryside and dialogue along the way. As Diane grew up, she began to see colors, lights, and symbols and sense smells and physical sensations that would mirror the condition of the animal. As she matured and her spiritual practice grew, she would ask for help on how to help animals and their owners. She discovered many loving beings that help when asked.

One particular event solidified that Diane had a gift that could be shared to benefit others. In 1995, Diane was enjoying a girls' weekend away at a bed and breakfast despite tumultuous weather. Late one evening, Diane heard someone screaming that a nearby house was on fire. Diane explains, "After putting on my slippers, the three of us ran to the burning house. I saw a young man with a glow around him carrying out some ducks in a large crate. There was no time to pause and talk. I also saw a woman to the right, from whom I intuited that the homeowners were not aware of the blaze." The man with the glow was a spirit, because she later learned that the crate housing the ducks was too large to be removed from the burning home in its assembled position. As the fire blazed, an elderly woman came out of the house crying that her dogs were still inside. Diane asked

Three Feathers, one of her Native American spirit guides, for help. She then telepathically told the dogs to come to the front of the house. The dogs obeyed and came to the front of the house, where Diane carried them to safety. Diane heard the dogs say thank you. This event changed Diane's life and put her on the path to dedicating her life to helping animals.

Diane still lives in Virginia and has a nationwide practice of helping people and their pets.[10] She helps any and all animals that want to communicate, including pets at animal shelters, rescue leagues, veterinary clinics, farms, ranches, pets in homes, and even animals on the sides of roadways who have been hit and need to pass over. Diane finds communicating with animals to be a special gift, but helping an animal pass over is a sacred experience. She has communicated with cats, dogs, birds, mice, wombats, lizards, snakes, turtles, horses, sheep, cows, goats, hens, roosters, dolphins, seagulls, and sea crabs. Diane hopes to expand her work to wildlife and zoo animals to learn what they bring to the planet and what humans can do to help them.

Diane has been featured on radio programs and helps callers with questions about their pets. "One caller had a six-foot-long python diagnosed with cancer of the intestinal tract. The snake's owner was getting ready to put the python down, as advised. Well, the radio commentators were joking around, not understanding how serious this business is. The large reptile showed me that he did not have cancer, but rather had been cut in the intestines by a live mouse he had been fed, and was now bleeding internally with extreme pain. The loving reptile owner had this confirmed with a second veterinary opinion, and learned that pet reptiles are better served with frozen and prepared dead mice. That was my first time speaking to a large reptile, and I was a little scared. But he was so friendly and accepting of me that we quickly got to the source of his pain."[11]

Clients may seek Diane's services once or twice, or may become lifelong clients with periodic wellness checks on their pet, like I do. "Animals want to communicate, almost immediately. All animals want to be heard. Even if an animal's personality is afraid of strangers, I can still reach and speak to their inner self. I convey health, preferences, and psychological concerns to their human guardians, so these issues can improve by actions by their owners, veterinarians, and homeopathic sources."[12]

So how does she handle nonbelievers? Diane once told me that she will give a human client a "zinger," something communicated to her that no one else would know. Sometimes a client will later discover that something Diane conveyed months or years earlier has come true. Diane explains, "I was seeing a husband and wife for their pet. The husband wanted nothing to do with me, nor did he want to miss out, so he kept coming in and out of the room during the session. I was getting distracted, so I explained that he would either need to stay in or go out, so I could focus better. He went into the garage and slammed the door behind him. Once the pet's needs were covered, I told the wife that her husband had a heart condition. She said that could not be, because he ran ten to twelve miles a day. A couple of days later, the husband and wife were working in the yard when he said he needed to go lie down. He was feeling pain going down his shoulder and arm. The wife remembered my warning and took him to the ER, where they found he was having a heart attack. He later told his wife to thank me."[13]

Like Christina, Diane encourages others to communicate with animals. While you may not have fine-tuned the gift as Diane has, she believes that everyone is born with the gift to communicate with animals. It takes work and practice to learn, but anyone can do it. Diane recommends reading books, listening to training CDs, or taking a class to learn more about animal communication. She is also available to help.

Diane shares these words to help us all do better for the animals in our lives. "Our animal friends are here to assist us. They know our own physical, psychological, and relationship needs better than we may know ourselves. Slow down and let them help you just by enjoying them. Take good care of their food, exercise, and health needs the best you can and you will never be sorry. Stop and listen."[14]

HEALING ANIMALS

I became a Usui Reiki Master in 2008, and subsequently a Master Teacher in 2011, through the Reiki Center of Greater Washington[15] and my amazing Master Teacher, David Gleekel. I subsequently became certified as a Master Instructor in Integrated Energy Therapy (IET®) in 2011, including certification in pet IET. I was introduced to healing energy in 2006 when a Reiki practitioner was able to remove a long-standing dull pain in my left shoulder in a matter of fifteen minutes. I had an energy attachment that was toxic, and removing the attachment alleviated the pain. I instantly became a believer. Since being certified in Reiki and IET, I have enjoyed providing energy healing to shelter animals and my own cats.[16]

Reiki is a Japanese healing method that allows for emotional and physical healing. Reiki energy is channeled through your hands to distribute the energy to people or animals, as well as to sense imbalances through the hands. Simply by placing hands on or above an animal (or person), a trained Reiki practitioner can feel imbalances and send healing. Anyone can practice Reiki healing by attending a training session where you receive Reiki attunements and learn how to become sensitive to the energy. The energy can also be transmitted distantly without being near the subject. Although I may not know exactly how the healing energy is helping each animal, I do receive clear signals from the animals that they want healing. The animals come to the energy if they need it, often by moving directly into my hands. And I have found that animals are sensitive to healing energy and only need a few minutes of healing, whereas a person may need an hour-long session, or more. Animals are naturally attuned to this energy and often seek it. Although I have found some animals are hesitant around the energy and may shy away, many crave the energy and understand that it is helpful. With Reiki healing, the recipient must agree to receive healing. If an animal moves away from the energy, they are not ready to receive it. But if an animal moves into my hands or comes near me to receive the energy from a distance, then that is their way of giving permission.

IET is another healing energy developed by Steven Thayer. "IET uses the violet angelic energy ray, as brought to us through the nine Healing Angels of the Energy Field, to work directly with your 12-Strand Spiritual DNA. IET supports you in safely and gently releasing limiting energy patterns of your past, empowering and balancing your life in the present."[17] IET is different from Reiki in that the healing energy derives from a different source, an angelic source, and is distributed to an animal (or person) through nine cellular memory areas on the body that relate to specific issues. For example, the kidneys represent the emotional issue of fear. Removing the blockage of fear and integrating safety in its place allows for any physical manifestations in the kidneys to resolve. By removing emotional issues from these areas, healing on a physical, emotional, mental, and spiritual level can occur.

I have performed Reiki and IET on more than a hundred shelter cats, as well as some pets of friends. I have been amazed at how the animals accept the energy and use the energy for whatever healing they need. It is wonderful to watch a frightened animal, or grieving pet, start to blossom during and after receiving healing energy. As I write this chapter, I have two cats, Minxy and Lucy, from the island of St. Croix in foster care at my house. Lucy, a four-year-old unique snowshoe cream/blue lynx point Siamese, arrived with a past history of being abused when she was younger, and she is timid around new people. She also lost her home due to a divorce, along with Minxy and another cat named Desi, and flew as cargo in an airplane from St. Croix to Virginia to be re-homed. Lucy was dealing with trauma from the past as well as trauma from losing her home and having a lengthy airplane flight. Lucy spent the first twenty-four hours under a La-Z-Boy chair in my foster care room. I would sit quietly in the room, activate Reiki energy in my hands, and simply hold my hands out to spread the energy throughout the room. Minxy, an outgoing black Manx cat, accepted the energy immediately and would weave in and out of my hands. The next day, Lucy greeted me at the door and wanted me to pet her, so I felt that the energy was helping. It was obvious that she felt more secure. Although she was timid and flinched around sudden movements or noises, I continued to open my hands to her for her to accept the energy.

I also provide healing energy to my cats on a daily basis. My flame point Siamese, Sammy, is around thirteen years old (or maybe older) and has started to encounter some kidney decline. At night, I will lie on the couch and Sammy immediately lies on top of me. I place my hands on his back, near his kidneys, to send healing. That area of his body feels hot, which is a signal to me that his kidneys are struggling. While most pets may only want a few minutes of the energy, Sammy will soak it in for almost an hour.

Healing energy can do no harm and can only benefit an animal. Those trained in Reiki or other healing modalities, such as Healing Touch for Animals®,[18] are transmitting energy to help animals that need to heal. In 2010, I was excited to learn of the Shelter Animal Reiki Association (SARA), which was formed to help train others in providing Reiki healing energy to shelter animals. "The mission of the Shelter Animal Reiki Association (SARA) is to improve the lives of animals by promoting the use of Reiki in animal shelters, sanctuaries and rescues worldwide through education, training, specialized research and the advancement of Reiki programs that meet the highest standards of integrity and professionalism."[19] Cofounder Kathleen Prasad agreed to be interviewed for this chapter and to share how others can get involved in helping to heal animals, particularly those in animal shelters. And I am now proud to be a SARA practitioner member.

Kathleen Prasad, Cofounder of Shelter Animal Reiki Association (SARA)

Kathleen describes how she became involved in Reiki and establishing SARA. "I have always had an animal as my best friend. A natural empath, I have been able to intuit the moods and feelings of the animals around me as early as three years old. As a child I was nicknamed 'Jiminy Cricket' for my compassion and conscience toward the world around me. I remember my dad bringing home injured animals for help and assistance when I was little. As an adult in my early twenties, I adopted a puppy from an animal shelter that had a high euthanasia rate. This puppy, Dakota, turned out to be my first 'Reiki animal' and also my greatest animal teacher to date! Soon after I learned Reiki in 1998, I began volunteering to walk dogs and do Reiki for them at a local shelter. As a language arts/social studies teacher at that time in a public middle school in San Francisco, I had been amazed and inspired many times by the ability of animals to reach even my most unmotivated students. Reiki seemed a natural way for me to be able to give just a little back for all the animals did for us humans! And so my path with Reiki and animals continued to unfold. I still teach, but since 2002 my teaching career has been dedicated to animal Reiki."[20]

Kathleen started her company, Animal Reiki Source, in 2004 and has developed Reiki training curriculums for animals. She has trained more than 2,000 people around the world, in person, and through teleclasses or correspondence and has published three books: *The Animal Reiki Handbook*, *Tails from the Source*, and *Animal Reiki Tails*. To help expand her practice to benefit shelter animals, she cofounded SARA with Leah D'Ambrosio in 2008. SARA now has twenty-eight animal organizations, twenty-five teachers, and twenty-four practitioners as members, and growing. SARA is also open to the public at the supporter level of membership. The monetary support we receive from our members has enabled us to reach out to shelters and sanctuaries across the United States. Kathleen explains, "For me, Reiki is simply about practicing techniques and strategies that help develop our compassionate intention in a way that supports our animals' health and wellness. A simple way of describing it is 'energy healing,' but it is something I believe all of us who love animals are already doing on some level. When we connect from the heart and share compassion and love with an animal, this is the essence of Reiki. And in this compassionate space, healing happens."[21]

Kathleen has worked with hundreds of animals over the years while supporting other Reiki practitioners and SARA students. She shares one memorable story of how Reiki helped a shelter animal. "One of my favorite memories of Reiki healing is that of a shelter dog who had been so severely traumatized that he shook uncontrollably at all times and walked with his belly low to the ground in fear. This kind of a dog is very difficult to adopt out because of his appearance to potential adopters. I took him to a quiet room and offered the Reiki treatment to him from a few feet away, but within a moment or two he crawled right up into my lap. He continued to shake for about fifteen minutes while I offered him Reiki. Then suddenly he had a particularly big shaking episode—as if he were letting it all out. Then he stopped shaking, looked at me, sighed, and lowered his head and went to sleep. He did not shake again, and when I returned him to his kennel after the treatment he was walking (albeit shyly) standing up straight like a normal dog. It was truly a miracle! He was adopted shortly afterward. Not every animal is able to heal so quickly in just one Reiki treatment, but it is pretty awesome when it happens. Being able to help animals relax and release fear and trauma goes a long way toward making them more adoptable."[22]

Animal shelters have been receptive to having Reiki practitioners assist the animals with a better quality of life, and to help them resolve issues to become more adoptable. Kathleen explains how Reiki's primary side effect is deep relaxation; therefore, it is beneficial in a shelter setting where animals may show signs of distress. This is why Kathleen is so passionate about training shelter staff and volunteers in Reiki so that animals benefit. Her goal is to finalize standards on providing Reiki to shelter animals so that whether you are a Reiki practitioner in England or the United States, the same process and philosophy is used. The SARA website lists their Code of Ethics and Guiding Principles.[23]

Anyone can become a Reiki practitioner to benefit animals. Many Reiki training facilities and classes are offered across the country. SARA also offers classes that are specific to providing Reiki to animals. Kathleen encourages that once you receive your basic Reiki training, you should read *The Animal Reiki Handbook* to provide additional information on helping animals with Reiki. Kathleen cautions, "The most important part of working with animals and energy is to remember that animals always lead the way. As energetically sensitive and wise as they are, they really are our teachers in this. This journey of healing with our animals is not so much that we are 'giving' and they are 'getting' as it is a circle of offering and receptivity where both animals and people can deepen their relationship with each other and heal in wonderful ways!"[24]

If you are intrigued by healing energy to help animals, take an introductory training course in Reiki or other healing energy modality. For Kathleen, "Reiki is a wonderful way to build trust and a new beginning with animals who have difficult pasts. Because physical touch is not necessary, it's also a way to begin to connect with animals who have experienced such severe trauma that they are unable to be touched. Many times, animals, when offered Reiki from several feet away in this gentle, passive way will actually come forward and ask for physical contact when they are ready. It is an amazing moment when they do so! Reiki is a way for us to be present with our animals in their truth—the good, the bad, the happy, the sad—whatever it may be. With Reiki we can be fully with them through it all and support positivity and rebalancing on all levels: physical, emotional, mental, and spiritual. It is up to the animal to heal, but with Reiki we can support them as they do so. When we learn to be open and receptive, to *not* push, and instead allow animals who have been traumatized to decide when they are ready to come forward toward us to connect—this is when we can see the miracles unfold! Reiki can bring healing possibilities to any animal, no matter what his or her past may be."[25]

Innovative Veterinary Healing Methods

I could not complete this section on healing animals without discussing innovative veterinary methods to keep pets healthy and provide healing from physical, mental, and emotional issues. Since 2005, I have been fascinated by natural healing methods. Through my research, I found veterinarians specializing in holistic practices such as homeopathy, Chinese herbal medicine, acupuncture, and dietary changes to promote healing. The plight of one cat impressed upon me the benefits of homeopathy and a holistic approach. The cat's name was Smudgie, and she was an exotic-looking calico cat. Her story was told in chapter 3. Briefly, Smudgie began to suffer from seizures, though no medical reason could be pinpointed. After a few months of the antiseizure medication, Smudgie was having trouble walking, was wobbly on her feet, and would fall over, and her once-sassy attitude turned into obvious frustration. Frustrated with the medication, I took Smudgie to see a holistic veterinarian at South Paws

Veterinary Clinic in Fairfax, Virginia. The veterinarian spent three hours with Smudgie and me and asked very detailed questions about Smudgie's lifestyle, behavior, and attitude. I will never forget him asking, "If Smudgie had a job, what would she do?" I immediately blurted out, "Broadway singer, like Barbra Streisand. Powerful and dynamic when in front of her admirers, but shy and insecure otherwise." The veterinarian came to the conclusion that Smudgie was grieving over the loss of Serendipity. She was internally grieving, like crying, where she was shaking from the inside out. He explained how she was stuck in the grieving process; she was like a car going up a steep hill, gunning the engine, and then running out of energy and being stuck while still gunning the engine. He explained that through homeopathy, he would prescribe a remedy that would force her to grieve; force her to get over the hill. After a few months, and one large grand mal seizure in the interim (which he said was a wonderful sign of healing), Smudgie stopped seizing, was weaned off the antiseizure medication, and now lives seizure- and medication-free. Witnessing Smudgie transform from a once-sassy cat to no spark of life and a declining will to live back to her original Smudgie-ness was truly a miracle. While not all veterinarians support alternative medicine treatments, I became a firm believer thereafter in alternative medicine modalities to treat animals that were otherwise untreatable with conventional medicine.

Currently, my cats treat with a conventional veterinarian as well as a homeopathic veterinarian, if needed. My flame point, Sammy, as previously discussed, is encountering some kidney decline and my goal is to maintain his good health for as long as possible while also working to hold off, or even reverse, the kidney decline. He has been treated by a homeopathic veterinarian, Dr. Andrea Tasi, who has instituted dietary changes for Sammy and my other cats. I have been amazed at the improved health of my chronologically "elder" cats, who at the ages of twelve and thirteen now play like kittens and their fur feels healthy. Dr. Tasi agreed to be interviewed for this chapter to discuss how she has changed the way she helps animals through homeopathy and dietary choices.

Dr. Tasi is a traditionally educated veterinarian, having completed her education at the University of Pennsylvania School of Veterinary Medicine in 1988. She then practiced conventional veterinary medicine in Oak Park, Illinois; Philadelphia, Pennsylvania; and now in northern Virginia. She subsequently became a feline-only practitioner in 1991. Dr. Tasi gives back to the animal community by donating her time to spay/neuter clinics for trap-neuter-return programs, as well as providing pro bono homeopathic medicine for a dedicated cat rescue person. She also provides educational seminars on the benefits of homeopathy, proper cat nutrition, and behavioral issues.

In 2008, Dr. Tasi opened "Just Cats, Naturally,"[26] a house-call, homeopathic practice for cats. Dr. Tasi altered her practice in 2005 when she began to question her role as a veterinarian in a conventional practice. She explains, "It seemed that more and more cats were coming to me with chronic diseases that I could not help much, or certainly not cure. These problems included things like lower urinary tract (bladder) disease, inflammatory bowel disease resulting in chronic vomiting and/or chronic diarrhea, diabetes, obesity, chronic ear and skin problems, feline asthma, etc. I could put these cats on prescription drugs or diets to help reduce their symptoms but I could not actually return them to a state of health. The drugs themselves could be expensive, often had deleterious side effects, were difficult to administer, and frankly, often didn't do that much to help the patient. I also began to really question the rationale and safety of many vaccinations used routinely in veterinary practice. I began to believe that many of the drugs, vaccines, and highly processed pet foods were *adding* to my patients' health problems, *not* making them better. I began to learn a little bit about other systems of medicine, with an interest in a more holistic approach. I read about and spoke to practitioners of Traditional Chinese Medicine (which includes Chinese herbal medicine, Chinese nutritional therapy, and acupuncture), chiropractic medicine, Western herbal medicine, and finally, classical (Hahnemannian) homeopathy. Homeopathy was the best fit for me, both intellectually and practically, as classical homeopathy uses small doses of gentle, tasteless medicine, usually given at long intervals, which seemed to be perfect for cats who hate to take medicine. I also was intrigued with homeopathy's basic tenet that medicine should help the body return to a state of health, in which ongoing medication would not be necessary."[27]

While a discussion of homeopathy for animals could encompass an entire book of its own, Dr. Tasi provides this basic explanation of how it works to help animals. "Homeopathy uses natural substances to stimulate the body's own natural defenses and healing capacity based on the principle of 'like cures like.' Homeopathic medicines have all been thoroughly studied as to their unique effects on body, emotions, and mind. The medicine chosen for a patient must be based on that patient as a whole individual and works by causing the body's own reactive processes to gently and gradually overcome the disease."[28] Homeopathy is not an Eastern modality, as it was developed in Germany around 1760.

Dr. Tasi's homeopathic practice involves a combined effort in treating the lifestyle of each cat, including nutrition, supplements, and ensuring that her patients are mentally and emotionally well. "Nutrition is a huge part of my job, as most cats that come to me are on highly processed dry or canned diets that contain ingredients that can be harmful to cats' health. I try to get all my patients on to grain-free, meat-based diets. This may include good quality, grain-free canned food, or better yet, balanced raw or cooked fresh meat–based diets. I often see huge improvements in health with diet changes alone."[29] I can attest that Dr. Tasi's recommendations on food choice do work. While there is controversy within the veterinary community about raw food diets, I can say that raw food has helped my cat, Sammy. Dr. Tasi educates her clients on providing the most natural environment for cats, which includes meeting each cat's physical needs (through food) but also emotional and mental needs (by providing a stimulating environment, especially for indoor cats). My tuxedo cat, Oscar, now enjoys it when I bring inside a tree stick or fallen leaf, which then provides him with hours, if not days, of entertainment.

While some conventional veterinary practitioners may dismiss homeopathy as nonsense, often due to lack of understanding of its history, principles, and the science behind it, Dr. Tasi has seen homeopathy restore cats to good health. Bailey, a two-year-old cat, began treating with Dr. Tasi in April 2010 after suffering from three months of ongoing, painful, and frequent straining to urinate, including persistent bloody urine. His conventional veterinarians tried everything available to help Bailey, but the symptoms continued. The family spent thousands of dollars on diagnostic tests, veterinary visits, medications, and dietary changes, while Bailey remained locked in a bathroom to prevent him from urinating throughout the home. Dr. Tasi explains how homeopathy helped Bailey. "I prescribed one dose of a homeopathic medicine that fit his symptoms best and put him on a diet of nonprescription grain-free canned food and some balanced raw diet. Within three days of taking the remedy, his symptoms began to wane, and by one week after the remedy he was back to normal in all respects and has remained so since, now six months completely symptom free, with no need for further medicine. This case illustrates homeopathy at its very best, when it almost seems like 'magic.'

Not every case can be expected to resolve with one dose of one remedy, but when it happens, it demonstrates the incredible power homeopathy has to help the body heal itself."[30]

With cases like Bailey, Dr. Tasi is a firm believer that most chronic diseases can be treated more effectively with homeopathy than with conventional medicine. Homeopathy has the ability to actually "cure" some diseases that are considered incurable by conventional medicine. "Conventional medicine considers allergies, asthma, inflammatory bowel disease, chronic bladder problems, and many other chronic feline diseases as incurable, treating them by controlling symptoms with the ongoing use of drugs. I have had cases of all of these diseases resolve completely with homeopathic treatment: the patient becomes better and stays better and needs no ongoing drug therapy. I do not mean to imply that I can cure all these problems in every case, but that I have accomplished it in some cases, whereas when I was in conventional practice I never cured a single one of these diseases. Of all the problems I have faced, I have had the best track record with chronic lower urinary tract problems (sometimes called FLUTD or FIC), as nearly every case I have treated has gone on to resolve completely and not have recurrences, some now symptom free over several years of follow-up."[31]

Dr. Tasi recognizes that homeopathy is not effective in all cases. For example, cats that have undergone longstanding conventional drug and surgical treatments, or taken significant doses of cortisone-type drugs, may not respond significantly to homeopathic treatment. Moreover, advanced or irreversible physical changes, like cancerous tumors, are not generally considered curable. "I do not expect to cure cancer patients, but I have, at times, helped them be more comfortable and perhaps live a bit longer and better."[32] Dr. Tasi knows that when homeopathy cannot help in those situations, other treatments may help to prolong life or provide for more comfort. My cat Sammy only partially responded to homeopathy with some success in reducing symptoms from his declining kidneys. In November 2010, Dr. Tasi recommended treating Sammy with Chinese herbal medicine, especially to control his vomiting, while continuing with a mostly raw food diet. After a few weeks on the Chinese herbs, I noticed that the vomiting has lessened and his appetite is ravenous; after a few months, his blood test results on his kidney function actually improved slightly. Both are good signs. Veterinarians who practice holistically endeavor to treat the whole pet, to actually get to the root problem and end up with healthier and happier patients.

While the number of veterinary practitioners of homeopathy, Chinese medicine, and acupuncture is growing, Dr. Tasi believes that it will take clients of conventional veterinary clinics asking for these services to get more veterinarians trained in these modalities, as well as veterinarians becoming dissatisfied with the status quo of conventional medicine. To learn more, Dr. Tasi recommends Dr. Don Hamilton's book called *Homeopathic Care for Cats and Dogs: Small Doses for Small Animals.* It was this book that "cinched it" for Dr. Tasi to move her practice into homeopathy. "Those of us who practice homeopathy are, I believe, obligated to do the very best work we can, as that will lead to simple word-of-mouth dissemination of the fact that homeopathy can heal. Most of my new clients find me because I treated a friend or family member's cat. If suddenly hundreds of people wanted homeopathic care for their pets, the real limitation would be that there are simply not that many veterinarians trained and practicing homeopathy."[33]

If you are interested in learning more about these integrative treatments for animals, these organizations provide information and opportunities to find practitioners:

- American Holistic Veterinary Association[34] "explores and supports alternative and complementary approaches to veterinary healthcare, and is dedicated to integrating all aspects of animal wellness in a socially and environmentally responsible manner." The website provides a search engine to locate a holistic veterinary practitioner.
- The Academy of Veterinary Homeopathy provides a list of homeopathic veterinarians and explains homeopathy and how it can help animal patients, as "Almost any problem that can be treated by traditional western medicine (allopathy) can be treated by homeopathy. Examples of chronic diseases that respond to homeopathy include skin allergies, ear infections, asthma, diabetes, inflammatory bowel disease, epilepsy, thyroid disease and a host of other conditions. Veterinarians who practice classical homeopathy according to academy standards have found that many otherwise chronically ill patients can be restored to health. They have also found that homeopathy can rapidly and gently treat a diverse array of acute conditions from traumatic injuries to infections and poisonings. Homeopathy is a holistic discipline and the principles of good health such as diet, exercise, and removal of stresses are also part of the process of restoring health.

Veterinarians who practice homeopathy have found it to be a gentle, safe, and effective medical system which offers a true cure to many patients."[35]

- The International Veterinary Acupuncture Society[36] and its affiliate the American Academy of Veterinary Acupuncture[37] also provide a listing of practitioners.
- The Chi Institute: Traditional Chinese Veterinary Medicine[38] is the leading organization training veterinary practitioners in the art and science of acupuncture and Chinese herbal medicine for animals.

As discussed by Dr. Tasi, proper nutrition is key to promoting the health and well-being of her clients. In the past few years, I have learned the benefits of proper nutrition for my cats. In recent years, specialized pet food stores have been appearing throughout the United States, offering a variety of food choices that are healthy for pets. In my community in northern Virginia, there are many of these stores. One particular store is Pet Sage,[39] which prides itself on providing only quality, natural pet products while being a leader in the holistic health of animals. Mainstream pet food stores, like Petco and PetSmart, are also beginning to offer some of these natural food products for pets, thus showing the increase in demand from pet families, and the growing knowledge that "you are what you eat" also applies to animals.

I do not want to be viewed as criticizing certain pet food suppliers. However, I can attest, as can Dr. Tasi, that pet food based on natural ingredients (not animal by-products or ingredients that you cannot pronounce) and prepared naturally can make a significant difference in the life of a pet, especially a pet that has been maltreated and needs to regain its health. Always check the ingredients in pet food, and a good rule to follow is if you would eat the first three ingredients listed and at least one is a high-quality meat, then buy it for your pet.

For animals that are removed from abusive or neglectful situations, or are traumatized over the loss of their family, there are ways that we can help them after getting them to safety. Recognizing that animals are whole beings, just like us, we can begin to address their physical, mental, and emotional well-being to ensure that they are healed and healthy. While our love can provide immeasurable benefit to an animal, offering healing through the methods discussed in this chapter can noticeably benefit an animal and ensure a long, happy, and healthy life.

CHAPTER 15

Keeping People and Pets Together:
Everyone Can Help

In all of my work over the years to help companion animals, from prosecuting their abusers, to protecting them from harm, to healing and loving them and helping them to find new homes, the most heartwarming aspect has been keeping people and pets together. Watching the human-animal connection unfold is a beautiful sight and an amazing relationship filled with unconditional love and acceptance. Animals can bring out the best in us, something that humans struggle to do for other humans.

When I think of why people donate to companion animal causes, volunteer at shelters, or adopt an animal, it is all focused on joining people with pets. We want shelter animals to find homes because we want them to have a family; we volunteer to help animals because we want them to know the kindness of a human; and we adopt an animal because we want to share human love with them, and receive their unconditional love in return. Plainly put, it is all about the human-animal connection. Programs are developing all across the country to honor this connection. A few amazing programs recognizing and supporting the human-animal connection will be featured in this chapter to show how you can get involved from a different angle of helping animals. In the spirit of *You Can Do More*, three of the programs mentioned in this chapter joined together in early 2011 to provide greater access to safe housing for people and their pets: the Sheltering Animals & Families Together, the Safe Havens Program, and Pets of the Homeless.

HUMAN-ANIMAL INTERACTION PROGRAMS

Sheltering Animals & Families Together (SAF-T), previously the Pets and Women's Shelters (PAWS)® Program

While working as a new assistant prosecuting attorney handling numerous family violence cases on my court docket, I encountered one case that challenged what I thought I knew about people and eventually changed my view of the human-animal connection. The case involved a woman who had been beaten by her husband. As we stood in a crowded courthouse hallway, she explained how she had returned home to her abuser in order to protect her pets. He had already killed one dog, and she could not live through another pet being harmed. She needed me to dismiss the case against her husband. I was naïve and new to prosecution, and after the O.J. Simpson case I was working under new policies to pursue all domestic violence cases, with or without the victim's cooperation. I asked her if she would testify if I could gain her entry to the local family violence shelter with her pets. What I did not know was that the shelter did not accept family pets when families were fleeing abusive homes. It was frankly not even a consideration. After speaking with the local shelter about taking this woman and her pets, and receiving an unwelcoming and sarcastic laugh on the other end of the phone, I was angry. To me, the solution was easy: set up simplistic kennels or in-room housing for family pets. Instinctively, I knew that the violence that harms families is the same violence that harms family pets. Why did the shelter not see that?

She walked out of court hand-in-hand with her abuser that day. I never saw her again, which worried me because I usually saw many of the same families return with new allegations of violence. I can only hope that the violence stopped or she left safely with her pets. But the case gnawed at me; I felt helpless, like she must have felt. But I was just a new prosecutor in a midsized office in Michigan. What could I do?

Well, that fire to change how family violence shelters view pets went underground for many years, but never died. When I moved to the Washington, D.C., area to work for the National District Attorneys Association, the fire came back and I finally felt like I could do something to change perceptions of family pets caught in the crossfire of violence. As I trained child protection workers, prosecutors, and law enforcement professionals on child abuse issues, I started to incorporate this concept of pet-friendly violence shelters to the audiences. People seemed to like the concept, but

I was not seeing much action to change how we handle families fleeing violence. When I joined American Humane Association in 2007, one of the first things I did was pitch this concept. I was quickly given the green light to pursue it.

I had the guidelines sketched out for several years on how a family violence shelter could house pets on site. So I spent nine months birthing a manual that outlined from start to finish how to house pets with their families at family violence shelters. In February 2007, the Pets and Women's Shelters (PAWS) Program[1] was born, after more than a decade of stewing in the back of my mind. It became the first and only national initiative to safely house domestic violence survivors with their pets.

The concept is basic, thus making it easy to implement: (1) Place the family pets inside the residential room with their family. This costs little or no money to get started. However, there may be issues to consider such as allergies among the staff and other residents. (2) Transform a room inside the shelter to be an indoor kennel. For the cost of purchasing animal crates or cages, this indoor kennel can be set up within a matter of days. Or (3) build an outdoor kennel. This method is perfect for shelter staff who worry about client or staff allergies, or expect to have a large number of animals at a time. The outdoor kennel can be as simple as refurbishing a prebuilt shed to house animals in cages, to building fenced dog runs and play areas, to erecting a building to mimic an animal shelter. This scenario can be a little more expensive, costing from a few thousand dollars to several million dollars. My goal was to provide simple and inexpensive models so that family violence shelters would embrace the concept and not shy away out of fear of lack of money or staff time.

When PAWS was launched, I knew of only four shelters in the country that were housing pets on site. As of October 2010, sixty shelters are housing pets, with another ten in the process of implementing. With approximately 2,500 family violence shelters in the country, this is not enough to keep families and their pets safe.

The focal point of the PAWS Program was twofold: Provide families fleeing abusive homes the opportunity to take their pets with them so that pets left behind would not become victims of abuse to coerce their families to return; and embrace the human-animal connection by recognizing that when a family leaves an abusive home, sometimes with just the clothing on their back, having the comfort and unconditional love of a family pet can help heal the trauma and move the family more quickly toward getting back on their feet. Leaving pets behind in abusive homes can not only cause trauma to the family, especially children, but can prevent a family from staying in safety if they attempt to return to retrieve their pets or care for them.

In just a short time period, hundreds of families with pets found safety at a PAWS shelter across the United States. Here is one story from the Kingman Aid for Abused People PAWS shelter in Kingman, Arizona: "The victim entered our shelter after being accepted into the program with her pregnant champion-line brindle boxer. The abuser threatened to kill the dog if she ever left him; thus she stayed in the relationship too long. When the dog became pregnant, the abuse escalated and the victim felt trapped. A neighbor told her to call the local shelter and had heard we accepted animals. We placed the victim and dog in their own room, knowing that the dog would be delivering any day. And she did so that night. The local vet that assists with our agency came in to help with the delivery and continued follow-up care throughout the course of their stay. The victim, mommy dog, and six puppies continue to do well; however, they have moved out into their own place free from violence."[2] And this story about a dog named Sparkplug came in from the Mitchell County SafePlace PAWS shelter in Spruce Pine, North Carolina: "Susan endured many years with her husband. Beatings were natural and par for the course, and hospitalizations were commonplace. Along with the abuse came constant threats to harm or kill her beloved dog Sparkplug if she did anything to protect herself. Most all of Susan's family had abandoned her because she 'must like it if she stays.' So as the years passed, Sparkplug was Susan's only source of love and acceptance. She felt she must protect him at all cost. Then during a camping trip to the Cherokee Indian Reservation, Susan's husband brutally beat her. He was arrested and convicted on federal domestic violence and is currently serving six years in federal prison. Susan has told me she could have never made it through all those years and all that violence had she not had Sparkplug to love her, and she knew she had to go on living no matter how much she wanted to give up, because Sparkplug was counting on her. Today, Susan and Sparkplug live in their own home and SafePlace continues to support them. We are proud to be able provide a place for all those like Susan and Sparkplug to find safety and comfort. To this day Sparkplug remains the 'best client I ever had.'"[3]

I am proud that the PAWS Program has been embraced by the family violence shelter community, yet more needs to be done. It is heartbreaking to receive a call from a victim looking for a PAWS shelter, when the nearest one is four states away. Two of the main obstacles to creating a PAWS shelter in every community is changing the mind-set of those in the domestic violence sheltering business and having funds available to assist with small start-up grants. Getting advocates to contact their local family violence shelter and encourage the implementation of PAWS will keep families, their pets, and communities safer. Although American Humane discontinued the PAWS Program in September 2010, I am still working with family violence shelters to incorporate housing for pets on-site under the name Sheltering Animals & Families Together.[4] At the end of this chapter are recommendations for how you can get involved to help animals in the crossfire of family violence.

Safe Havens® Program

The Safe Havens Program name has been defined in a variety of different ways, but is mostly a concept that involves off-site housing of pets of domestic violence—for example, safely housing the pets at a partner animal shelter or adoption partner organization, veterinary clinic, boarding facility, or in a foster home. In 2000, Dr. Frank Ascione (a colleague and friend of mine) wrote *Safe Havens for Pets: Guidelines for Programs Sheltering Pets for Women Who Are Battered*,[5] a manual of more than 300 pages containing information, best practices, and policies for starting and maintaining a Safe Havens Program. A Safe Havens Program is a good start for a shelter that is not ready to implement an on-site housing program for pets.

Ahimsa House is a nonprofit organization in Atlanta, Georgia, whose sole focus is to help pets in homes of domestic violence get to safety. Ahimsa House hosts on its website a listing of Safe Havens Programs across the country. Although 900 family violence shelters have indicated that they provide some sort of referral or assistance to families with pets, as of late 2010 Ahimsa House has confirmed that only 171 shelters in the United States have a plan in place to provide housing for pets.[6]

There are many ways you can help to support a Safe Havens Program, such as opening your home to provide foster care to pets escaping domestic violence situations, supporting a Safe Havens Program in your community through donations of money or supplies, asking your local family violence shelter to create a Safe Havens Program, and offering to help implement it.

Helping Pets and People in Crisis: A Program of the Mayor's Alliance for New York City Animals

Jenny Coffey is like you and me, a person who loves animals and wants to make a difference. I met Jenny a few years ago through my creation of the PAWS Program. Jenny is a social worker in New York City. In the aftermath of September 11, she was assigned to help families who lost people in the World Trade towers attack. In one particular case, she worked with a man who falsified that his son was killed so that he could gain financially. After that, she became dismayed as a social worker and decided to become employed with the community health department. She then became involved in work on animal hoarding cases. To date, she has assisted with more than 100 animal hoarding cases (her work with hoarders is featured in chapter 8). Now she works with the Mayor's Alliance for Animal Welfare[7] and oversees the Helping Pets and People in Crisis Program. Her focus is managing people with pets in situations of domestic violence, homelessness, illness, or even serving jail sentences with the end goal of reuniting people with their pets and reducing the number of pets entering New York City shelters. She works with people to provide short-term care and long-term safety for their pets. The program has helped more than 250 animals in less than three years.

Jenny explains, "Sometimes people give up their pets because they are unaware of services available and they just need a little extra help from someone who can navigate public services."[8] Jenny described her work with a woman who was entering a homeless shelter and had a dog named Crystal. The woman was discovered outside Madison Square Garden struggling to keep control of all of her belongings, including Crystal. A colleague working with a cat adoption event noticed the woman and offered help from the program. Initially not trusting these strangers, the woman left, but only after being given outfits for herself and food for the dog. Eventually the woman returned and became comfortable leaving Crystal with the program staff while she sought help for her homelessness. Eventually, Crystal entered the foster care program while the woman entered a homeless outreach program. She was able to visit with Crystal a few times each month. The goal was to get the woman into her own housing so that she could be reunited with Crystal. That goal was realized after one year.

Jenny explains that, sadly, sometimes the best situation is to separate a pet from their owner—at least temporarily while the person gets help.

In one case, Jenny was assisting a man who had been sentenced to prison and had an unspayed cat. The cat was emaciated and in poor health. Normally the cat would have been taken to animal control and held for a week. Instead, Jenny bypassed the system and went to the jail, where the man signed over ownership of the cat. The cat went to a foster home, was spayed, regained her health, and was eventually re-homed. Jenny says that about half of the clients end up surrendering their pet for adoption because obstacles are too cumbersome. And in situations of family violence, the pets are held temporarily but not returned if the family returns to the abusive environment.

The program is successful with the volunteer assistance of nearly 100 foster homes. The alliance is helping animals avoid entering the shelter while also assisting with temporary placement until pets are reunited with their families. This is successfully accomplished with the assistance of volunteer foster homes and more than 100 different adoption partner organizations.

Jenny says there are many ways to get involved in helping vulnerable people keep their pets. First, if you are in a profession where you work with people, begin to think about pets and ask your clients how you can help. "Always think beyond just helping the person," says Jenny.[9] This may involve including pets in the planning process for getting help for the client. This is particularly true if you work (or volunteer) at a homeless shelter, soup kitchen, or family violence shelter. Second, open your heart and home to foster animals that are in transition and waiting to be reunited with their families. Contact your local human welfare agency and offer your help. Third, donate to organizations that are working to keep people and their pets together. Fourth, volunteer to transport animals to foster homes or other safe locations. And last, become an advocate to keep people and pets together. If your community does not have a SAF-T Program, Safe Havens Program, or program like Helping Pets and People in Crisis, then advocate to your community officials to begin these programs. Change often begins with one person speaking out. Be that person.

Pet Peace of Mind

I learned about Pet Peace of Mind in early 2010 and have been enamored with the program ever since. It is an innovative program to help hospice patients keep their pets with them through the end of life. Patients in hospice care often suffer from loneliness because family and friends may not be available or the patient may not want visitors. However, the patient's pet can alleviate the loneliness and provide a better quality of life. The program also works on locating new homes for these pets while their owner is still alive, so that the pet does not end up in a shelter after the owner passes on; this provides peace of mind that their pet will have a home. It is an amazing program because many people who have pets worry about what will happen to their pet if they are no longer around. Pet Peace of Mind is working to spread across the country to ease that concern.

Pet Peace of Mind, a program of Banfield Charitable Trusts, is modeled after a successful program created by Delana Taylor-McNac, a veterinarian and chaplain. The program was established to create a network of hospice centers that can be trained and can receive funding to provide in-home volunteer pet care services to clients. In a moving video on Pet Peace of Mind's blog, Delana explained how the program was created.[10] Delana spoke of an elderly couple who had been married sixty years. The husband was in hospice care when a dachshund dog showed up on their doorstep. They took in the dog and named him Stretch. Shortly thereafter, the wife began to decline and was placed in an assisted living facility with her husband, but Stretch was not allowed and went to live out of state with a son. Delana described how she visited the man on his last evening and saw him sitting in the dark with the television on; he was talking to someone and making motions as if to pet a dog. Delana explained, "I will never forget that. That was such a powerful thing to me. And I think we could have made a difference. He died that night. I think we could have changed the way that he died if we had intervened."[11]

Delana is now the program manager for Pet Peace of Mind. Since its inception in May 2009, it has grown to twenty hospice centers in seventeen states, with eleven more in training as of October 2010. Within the first two weeks of the launch, 110 hospice centers voiced interest in joining, but funding was not available.

Pet Peace of Mind is not simply a program that feeds and cares for pets of hospice patients; instead, it is an extension of hospice services. It is an important program that celebrates the human-animal bond because it allows people in hospice care to still have the love and support of their pet, which in some cases gives the owner a stronger will to live and lengthens their time with their pet.

Pets of the Homeless

According to the National Coalition on Homelessness, there are 3.5 million homeless people in the United States. You may be surprised to learn that up to 10 percent of these people enjoy the companionship of a cat or dog.[12] Although you may initially think that these pets are not in a good living situation, what is important to recognize is that pets can be versatile, and if they are with the person they love, they can live in any environment. Pets of the Homeless[13] is a nonprofit organization designed to provide food and veterinary care to the animals of the homeless. It was started in 2007 by Genevieve Frederick from Carson City, Nevada, who created the concept after visiting New York City and seeing a homeless man begging with a dog at his side. She was not able to shake the image from her mind and began researching pets of homeless people. Like most people, her initial question was why a homeless person would have a pet when they have trouble feeding and caring for themselves. She realized that the bond between a person and their pet provides nonjudgmental acceptance and, for homeless people, warmth and protection. She also learned that homeless people may often give their own food to their pet. But the tragedy was that pets of homeless people do not choose their owners. With the decline in the economy, many previously employed pet owners are now living in their cars, in tents, or on the streets, and some are with their pets.

Since services are available to homeless people, Genevieve launched the program to provide assistance to the pets and link it to the services for people. She first started a pet food drive in her community, and a 55-gallon container was filled with food in the first day. As others learned about the program, it grew and is now a nonprofit organization reaching out all across the country to help homeless people and their pets. With the assistance of donations, grants are now given to veterinarians to visit locations where homeless people congregate and provide care to pets in need, and grants are given to shelters that will open their doors to allow pets to stay with their owner. Collection sites are also recruited to accept donated food, which is then passed on to distributing organizations (such as food banks, soup kitchens, and shelters).

If you are interested in getting involved in helping pets with homeless people, Pets of the Homeless is available to answer questions and provide assistance.[14]

Educating laypeople and professionals on the benefits of human-animal interactions is growing more popular in the United States. For many professions, especially those that assist people, recognizing that animals play an important part in people's lives will help you provide better care to your clients. Whether you are a psychologist, psychiatrist, nurse, medical doctor, hospice worker, child or adult protective services worker, attorney, or shelter or other housing facility worker, learning how to help the animals of your clients is important.

Here are a few of the institutions and organizations that are making a difference in the lives of animals every day by training professionals in human-animal interactions:

- Virginia Commonwealth University's Center for Human-Animal Interaction[15] was started in the School of Medicine in June 2001 and focuses on interdisciplinary education and research to promote human-animal interactions.
- The University of Missouri College of Veterinary Medicine created the Research Center for Human-Animal Interaction[16] and includes programs such as animal-assisted therapy to benefit older adults and encouraging retirement housing systems to allow pets to live with their owners.
- Purdue University School of Veterinary Medicine has the Center for the Human-Animal Bond that was established in 1982 and fosters relationships with other departments to collaborate on human-animal bond and animal welfare issues.[17]
- Tufts University has the Center for Animals and Public Policy, which contains a program on human-animal interactions and animal-facilitated activities.[18]
- University of Denver hosts the Institute for Human-Animal Connection in the Graduate School of Social Work and is expanding the research field in the areas of human-animal interactions and animal cruelty assessments.[19]
- Animals and Society Institute[20] is a nonprofit, independent research and educational organization that advances the status of animals in public policy and promotes the study of human-animal relationships.
- The American Psychological Association recently created a Division on Human-Animal Interactions.[21]

- The International Association of Human-Animal Interaction Organizations seeks to bring researchers together from all over the globe to collaborate and discuss their research and findings promoting the benefits of human-animal interactions.

This is just a partial listing of what is being done to train others on the benefits of human-animal interactions and keeping people and their pets together.

Regardless of your career or place in life, there are many venues in which people are struggling to keep their pets. These situations may include people in a foreclosure crisis; people who lost their job; people who are sick, hospitalized, or in hospice; the homeless; people in assisted living and nursing homes; and families fleeing abusive homes, just to name a few. If we all chipped in and helped out, we could drastically lower the number of family pets being surrendered to shelters. Just a little help can go a long way.

You Can Do More

- Contact your community family violence shelter or agency and ask them if they provide safe housing and safety planning for pets. If they provide on-site or off-site housing for pets, volunteer your time to help. This might entail opening your home to foster a pet, helping to raise money to support the programs, or donating. If your community family violence shelter or agency does not provide safe housing or safety planning for pets, offer to help set up a SAF-T Program or Safe Havens Program or to raise funds to establish a program.
- If you know of an apartment community that does not allow pets, ask them to change their policy so that residents can keep their pets. Too often, property owners simply have "no pet" policies for no specific reason. Encouraging property owners to provide pet-friendly housing, while asking for a pet deposit to cover any pet-related damage, is a good way to keep people and their pets together.
- Find out if your community hospice agency considers the needs of clients with pets. If not, encourage them to connect with Pet Peace of Mind and learn how to become involved.

- If your community has a soup kitchen or homeless shelter, ask if they provide services to pets and, if not, refer them to Pets of the Homeless to receive information on how to get involved. Consider hosting a pet food drive in your community to benefit an existing pet food pantry, or create a pet food pantry to help pets of homeless people as well as pets with families that have homes but are struggling financially.
- If you are interested in a career in human-animal interactions, or have a career that involves the care of people, contact some of the organizations and institutions mentioned in this chapter and learn more of what you can do to help.
- If you work or volunteer to help animals, create programs to help people keep their pets. For example, have a pet food pantry to help with food for families that are financially struggling, offer affordable spay/neuter or vaccinations, or offer to house pets at no cost if a family lost their home and needs a few weeks or months to locate new housing so that they can be reunited with their pet.

CHAPTER 16

Conclusion: Welcome to the Journey!

Over the past several decades, Americans have made cats, dogs, and other companion animals a larger part of their family. It is important for the livelihood of these domesticated animals, as well as for the health and benefit of humans, that we continue to strengthen the human-animal connection. If people are bonded with their pets, they are less likely to abandon them or surrender them to a shelter, even when life becomes challenging. One way we can strengthen this bond is to change how we view companion animals, especially those that have been abandoned or treated with neglect or cruelty. For animals in shelters, we need to change how we view a shelter so that it is not only a beneficial temporary environment for the animal, but also welcoming to people. Why do we need to change how we view shelters? It is because too many people who love animals will not enter a shelter because they find it to be a depressing and sad place where animals may not make it out alive. These people are our lost volunteers, adopters, and donors, because we have not made the shelter a place where they can feel good about making a difference.

In a Facebook poll taken in October 2010, I asked fans of my "You Can Do More for Animals" page[1] to explain why they are hesitant to go to a shelter to volunteer or adopt. These are some of the responses that I received:

- I would love to volunteer at a shelter, but not sure I can handle it. I would obsess over every animal and worry about them, and cry all the time. I wouldn't sleep, I would be a wreck. I do what I can by donating money and sending towels, blankets, etc., to local shelters. I have no problem with adopting from a shelter, but my husband has to go in and choose. I just can't walk through the door. (Posted by Tracy P.)

- People have told me that they can't go there because it's too hard, even to adopt, because they know some of the cats or dogs will be put to sleep. They cannot look them in the eye knowing that they might be euthanized. That's why if rescues can bring cats and dogs to PetSmart and other stores, it is a much better idea. (Posted by Diane H.)

- I think that for one, we have to get beyond the idea that a shelter is "jail" or "prison." For many animals, the shelter is the first place it has ever received food, love and care on a regular basis. If the animal is in a shelter, it is not on the street subject to the elements and cruel humans, it is not in an abusive home and it is alive and being cared for! I realize there are some really bad shelters out there—but progressive shelters provide food, water, veterinary care, shelter, socialization, exercise and LOVE to the animals housed there. I know, because I work at a small, but progressive, shelter. The shelter is just a transition—the animal placed for adoption is on its way to a permanent home. It's really an extraordinary thing to be involved in that transition phase, to know you had a hand in a wonderful pet going from homeless to a loving home. Shelters are portrayed as sad places, but again, if it's a good, progressive shelter, it's truthfully a positive, happy place. I think volunteer recruiters and shelter staff need to be truthful about the sad side (yes, there is a sad side at times) but reinforce the happy side. The joy that we all feel when one of our animals gets adopted into a fantastic home. The animal that came in emaciated, neglected, wounded, sick, frightened . . . now healthy and happy and part of a family. If it's a good shelter, you won't feel sad about not being able to take them all home—you'll know they're on their way to the right home for them. I could say so much more . . . but I'll stop here, and just say, it's time to reexamine beliefs and attitudes about shelters and what we do. (Posted by Gina G.)

- One of the problems is how shelters market themselves—they sell the sadness. Even inspiring songs like Sarah McLachlan's appeal to this methodology. Sadness is a double-edged sword. It's good for raising money, but in my opinion, it also scares people away from shelters. I have shared my shelter experiences with many people on various sites, and the most common thing I hear is "Thank you for everything you do" and "I could never handle the sadness of volunteering at a shelter." I presume the same sentiment would apply to people thinking of getting an animal—that they couldn't go into a shelter because they would want to adopt all of the animals . . . so they don't go, and end up adopting none. Or worse yet, they buy from a store, perpetuating the problem. (Posted by Cully M.)

- Yes, how we market shelters is very important. It's important to see the sad, but also to follow through with the happy ending. Show people HOW their donations help—"because of your donations, we were able to give Simon's wounds proper veterinary care and he has now found the perfect forever home." "Your donations allowed us to provide heartworm treatment for Lucky, and now he is living the high life in his new home." I think people NEED to see the sad side at some point —they need to understand the abuse and neglect that is going on in this nation today. But we need to show them that because they helped—either through financial donations, or donations of time, effort and talent, they gave that animal's sad story a happy ending. We need to know how and why we make a difference. (Posted by Gina G.)

With the fluctuating economy and declining resources available to care for companion animals, it is easy to shrug off the notion of making shelters more pleasing environments for people and pets as impossible in lieu of other expenses. However, if we are truly to make a difference for animals and re-home more pets than are euthanized, then we must find a way. I say "must" because without the assistance of volunteers, adopters, and donors, these beautiful companions have little hope of a happy domesticated life.

Many animal shelters raise funds and awareness regarding the pet overpopulation problem by showing faces of sad animals behind steel barred cages and send out the message that if you do not donate or adopt, that particular pet will be euthanized. Although those are very powerful messages that certainly get people to take action, it has the unintended side effect of labeling shelters as unsafe places that "kill" animals. Sadly, there are shelters in the United States that are not properly caring for the animals in their facilities, either through lack of resources, education, or desire. Some of the lack of care may be a defense mechanism in handling daily intake of animals and not finding enough adoptable homes, thus contributing to daily high numbers of euthanasia. For anyone reading this book, imagine having to go to work each day knowing that it is your job to euthanize beautiful companion animals. You would put up a hardened exterior to survive that occupation. And that is what we see in some animal shelter staff. These workers may appear to be heartless and uncaring, but underneath it all they may have a coping mechanism in place to help them get through the day.

So let's turn the message around and start promoting the good that is done in the world of companion animals. Even if you live in a community with a struggling shelter, take that first step and offer to volunteer to help make the shelter a welcoming place for people and pets, to assist with positive promotion of the pets and the work that is done at the shelter, and to get people excited about visiting the shelter. With each visitor, that person may be your next adopter, donor, or volunteer. Have your local newspaper celebrate adoption or fund-raising successes; reach out to potential donors by talking about the good that can be done with a $20 donation, rather than describing how many animals will die without their help; and portray shelter animals in the best light possible. If we continue to depict shelters as sad places where desperate animals are pleading for their lives, then the kindhearted people who typically adopt animals, volunteer, and donate to animal causes will continue to turn away in hopes that "someone else" will help. With 3 to 4 million shelter pets euthanized in shelters every year, we cannot continue to think that "someone else" will solve the problem. And let's expand this to promoting the human-animal connection and working toward keeping people and pets together, at all costs.

You chose this book for a reason. Maybe the title or cover photo caught your eye, or the message resonated with you. Something in your heart caused you to reach for this book because you want to do more. If you have read to this point, you are being called to action. It would be easy to run through scenarios in your mind that you are too busy to get involved, you work in a career that does not involve animals, your budget does not allow you donate as you would like to, or you just cannot fathom going into a shelter to adopt or volunteer. With any cause where change is occurring, there is always the tipping point where you take a step toward something that may seem uncomfortable, yet in spite of the anxiety you know it is right. For most people, change is scary and uncomfortable. Once you take that step, instinctively you feel more alive and know that you are on the path to making a difference. After all, don't most people in this world want to make a difference? That is one of the most common answers when asked, "What do you want to do with your life?" You have been given countless opportunities in this book to help animals, both inside and outside of shelters. So heed the call that you have been given with this book and take one small step, or take a huge leap, and get involved. The rewards that you will receive in return will be purrs, excitedly wagging tails, nose kisses, and the unconditional look of love from the eyes of a furry companion. Take that step, and you will find more fulfillment than you may ever have known. To know that you have made a difference in the life of an animal is priceless.

Welcome to the journey.

Pound Seizure Fact Sheet

1. **Ending pound seizure will not prevent lifesaving biomedical research. Facilities that still wish to utilize animals would still be able to obtain them. Ending pound seizure also does not impact the research of facilities utilizing alternative nonanimal techniques.**

   Laws that end pound seizure still permit researcher access to genetically diverse and purpose-bred animals from a variety of legal sources, including (1) Class A dealers that breed animals for research,[1] (2) individuals who donate their pets for research or include their family pet in a clinical trial, and (3) research facilities with breeding programs. Ending pound seizure cuts out USDA Class B dealers who act as "middlemen," animal brokers who have been investigated for acquiring "random source animals" from questionable sources and then reselling them, often for hundreds of dollars each, to laboratories and training facilities.

2. **The issue with ending pound seizure relates to disallowing Class B random source animal dealers to obtain shelter cats and dogs for research.**

   In recent years, research and training facilities have moved away from live animal research toward simulated or in vitro research techniques. An even greater number are choosing not to use shelter animals supplied by Class B dealers.[2] According to the Physicians Committee for Responsible Medicine, in 2008 the last U.S. medical school using dogs for medical education ceased this practice. As of 2010, 152 of 159 U.S. medical schools do not use any live animals for education, and 197 of 202 surveyed programs do not use live animals for advanced trauma life support (ATLS) courses.[3] In 2008, following recommendations from the National Research Council of the Academy of Sciences, three national governmental agencies (Environmental Protection Agency, the National Toxicology Program, and the National Institutes of Health) signed a memorandum of understanding to replace the use of animals with in vitro methods for chemical safety testing.[4] In 2009, Congress ordered a study on the use of random source animals in research. In the same year, a report on the Scientific and Humane Issues in the Use of Random Source Dogs and Cats was issued by the National Research Council of the National Academies of Science.[5] After months of testimony and gathering information, the council concluded that random source Class B dealers are not needed for providing random source animals for National Institutes of Health–funded research projects.[6]

3. **USDA has increased inspections of Class B dealers to include quarterly on-site inspections because they are deemed a "high risk" due to concerns about pet theft.**

These inspections include a "trace-back" procedure that has verified that some random source animals were improperly obtained.[7] Illegality and abuse are so rampant among Class B random source animal dealers that the number of USDA-licensed dealers decreased through enforcement from 100 in 1993 to only 9 in 2010.[8] As of 2010, six of the nine dealers are under investigation by the USDA for chronic violations of the Animal Welfare Act; an additional dealer is under a five-year suspension.[9]

A USDA director has confirmed that "We use a risk-based inspection system (RBIS) to target our inspections. RBIS encourages frequent inspections at types of facilities that, in our experience, have more problems and fewer inspections than types of facilities with consistent compliance. Random Source Class B Dealers are considered high risk in RBIS and are inspected at least quarterly. We had 10 licensed Random Source Class B Dealers in FY2008 and conducted 74 inspections."[10] As an example of the nature of the Class B random source animal business, a 2006 HBO documentary called Dealing Dogs exposed similar illegal actions of C. C. Baird, an Arkansas Class B dealer. An undercover investigation by Last Chance for Animals revealed that Baird was brokering stolen animals, and his facility was shut down after subsequent criminal prosecution. Over the five-month investigation, footage revealed that Baird paid "bunchers" (people who collect animals) to steal family pets or fraudulently acquire dogs and cats from "free to good home" ads. Baird faced felony charges relating to money laundering and mail fraud and was charged with hundreds of violations of the Animal Welfare Act.[11] Responding to the need to eliminate such illegal activities of Class B dealers, the USDA authorized a standard operating procedure in 2008 to strengthen inspections.

4. **The USDA currently has insufficient resources to properly regulate Class B dealers.**

The USDA admits it spends too much of its limited resources in an attempt to regulate nine random source Class B dealers who resell dogs and cats for research. In a meeting held in January 2009 at the National Academies of Science, a USDA representative stated that USDA has prioritized its focus on Class B dealers because of allegations and investigations into "improperly obtaining animals," but a loophole in the Animal Welfare Act prevents them from doing the necessary job no matter how much money they have. He stated, "The oversight of random source dealers is the single most important thing USDA does based on public and congressional expectations. Random source dealers have always been an issue over the years, even with declining numbers of dealers and animals involved."[12] Each year, the USDA admits "it is expensive" to regulate nine random source Class B dealers, who are each inspected in person more than four times yearly. In FY2008, there were 4,200 Class A dealers (who breed animals), and 6,300 inspections were conducted. USDA oversees about 10,000 total licensees and registrants that need inspection and oversight.

5. **Ending pound seizure will not put Class B dealers and research facilities out of business.**
Random source Class B dealers and research facilities will still be able to conduct business by legally obtaining dogs and cats from other nonrandom sources. Although ending pound seizure will prevent shelter animals, strays, and other random source animals from being obtained for research, researchers and dealers can still obtain animals from other sources, including other dealers.

6. **The National Animal Control Association[13] and the Association of Shelter Veterinarians[14] oppose the practice of pound seizure, as do all national animal welfare organizations. Moreover, seventeen states and the District of Columbia have passed laws banning the practice.**
These states have banned pound seizure: California, Connecticut, the District of Columbia, Delaware, Hawaii, Illinois, Maine, Maryland, Massachusetts, New Hampshire, New Jersey, New York, Pennsylvania, Rhode Island, South Carolina, Vermont, Virginia, and West Virginia. Minnesota and Oklahoma have laws that mandate pound seizure. That means that if a dealer or research facility goes to a shelter looking for cats and dogs for research, the shelter has no legal authority to deny them access. An additional nine states—Arizona, Colorado, Iowa, Michigan, Ohio, South Dakota, Tennessee, Utah, and Wisconsin—have passed laws leaving the decision on pound seizure to the discretion of individual counties or shelters. The remaining twenty-two states have no law on pound seizure and, therefore, the practice is allowed. Moreover, national organizations that specialize in animal control and animal sheltering (such as American Humane Association,[15] American Society for the Prevention of Cruelty to Animals,[16] and The Humane Society of the United States)

have long opposed the practice of pound seizure as a violation of the purpose of an animal shelter.

7. **Subjecting former family pets to pound seizure and experimentation has been overwhelmingly rejected by the citizens who learn of the practice, because it betrays citizens' trust in shelters.**
Shelter animals taken for research are most often former family pets that are the friendliest and most trusting because they are the easiest to handle during experiments. Taking these former family pets in this way angers communities and violates the growing body of research involving the human-animal bond. It also violates the purpose of an animal shelter to be a safe haven for animals. Given the economic difficulties facing American families, thousands of pets are being surrendered to shelters. Their owners do so hoping that the pets will be adopted by people who can afford pet care. However, many of these pets are now being utilized in experiments unbeknown to their former owners. This is a betrayal of trust even in the best of economic times. Most state laws require that citizens report stray dogs to county or city officials so they might be reunited with their family. Citizens are also encouraged to call in complaints of animal abuse or neglect so that the pets can be brought to the shelter for safekeeping. Yet people will not comply with those laws when they realize a shelter practices pound seizure. In April 2009, American Humane conducted a survey[17] on how people feel about pound seizure. Responses were received from 3,044 individuals, and responses included:

- "Would you bring a lost animal you'd found to a shelter that released unclaimed animals to research?" More than 97 percent of the people survey responded by saying no.
- "If there were a stray dog in your neighborhood, would you be less likely to report it to animal control if you knew it might end up in a research laboratory?" More than 91 percent of those surveyed answered yes.
- "If you knew of an animal that was being abused or neglected, would you be less likely to report it to animal control if you knew it might end up in a research laboratory?" Almost 80 percent of those surveyed said yes.
- "Would you donate money to an animal shelter that voluntarily sold or gave animals to laboratories?" Almost 98 percent of people surveyed said no.

Shelters with high euthanasia rates do not need to rely on pound seizure. There is a growing movement in the United States to reduce shelter euthanasia rates via increasing foster care programs, spay/neuter programs, education, volunteer and rescue services, and general outreach. These efforts have proven to increase adoptions and pet ownership and reduce euthanasia (all of which increase revenue and reduce costs). Lastly, as more research and training facilities move toward simulated and alternative research methods, the need to breed animals for research will also decline.

8. **Shelter cats and dogs that are given to the Class B dealer are not unwanted pets but are healthy and adoptable pets. Moreover, people are not informed that their pet could be sent to research.**

   Due to the recession, many people who love their pets are unable to care for them. People believe that an animal shelter is where you take your pet to find a new home. People may be informed that their pet could be euthanized, but they are frequently not informed that their pet could be used in experimental research. One Michigan dealer has stated, "they may have been a pet at one time, but at the point [a dealer] becomes involved, they are an unwanted, unclaimed animal about to be euthanized."[18] That statement is simply false. This attitude is particularly egregious in our current economic climate, where people are being forced to make difficult decisions, one of which may be to reluctantly relinquish a beloved pet in the hopes it will find a new home.

Humane Euthanasia Fact Sheet

1. **Euthanasia by injection (EBI) is the safest way for humans to euthanize shelter animals.**

   - Carbon monoxide poses a danger to humans because it is colorless, tasteless, odorless, and highly explosive.[1] A gas chamber must be constantly checked and maintained to ensure there are no cracks in the structure or failing seals. When carbon monoxide is released in a confined area, it can cause asphyxiation, kidney damage, or induced coma.
   - The gas chamber can jeopardize the safety of shelter workers. In 2008, an explosion in the Iredell County, North Carolina Animal Services' gas chamber revealed that, contrary to recommendations, the equipment in the vicinity of the chamber was not explosion proof. A shelter worker was in the room at the time, and other personnel were nearby. In 2000, a shelter worker in Tennessee was asphyxiated while operating a faulty gas chamber. And in 1997, a shelter veterinarian in Illinois was severely injured while operating a gas chamber. In contrast, there are no documented reports of any shelter worker being killed from an accidental injection of sodium pentobarbital.[2]
   - The American Veterinary Medical Association (AVMA) 2007 Guidelines on Euthanasia state *"Carbon Monoxide is <u>extremely hazardous for personnel</u> because it is highly toxic and difficult to detect. . . . The advantages of using barbiturates for euthanasia in small animals far outweigh the disadvantages. Intravenous injection of a barbituric acid derivative is the preferred method for euthanasia of dogs, cats, other small animals, and horses."*[3]

2. **EBI is the *most* humane method of euthanizing shelter animals.**

   - *If* successful, the gas chamber can take up to twenty-five minutes to end an animal's life, whereas EBI causes loss of consciousness within three to five seconds and death within five minutes.[4] EBI causes animals to lose consciousness and brain function before their vital organs shut down. In a chamber, however, animals lose consciousness and brain function only *after* their vital organs shut down, causing prolonged suffering and distress.

- EBI is the method preferred by the National Animal Control Association, the American Veterinary Medical Association, the Association of Shelter Veterinarians, American Humane Association, American Society for the Prevention of Cruelty to Animals, and The Humane Society of the United States.
- The American Veterinary Medical Association states that carbon dioxide and carbon monoxide is only suitable for *most* small species.[5] However, old, neonatal, and injured animals are often biologically unable to absorb the gas as readily as larger or healthier animals, which prolongs trauma and stress.[6]
- Birds and neonatal animals are commonly euthanized by using halothane or isoflurane anesthesia gas, followed by an intraperitoneal injection into the abdominal cavity. Birds are commonly euthanized via an oral injection of sodium pentobarbital. Using dioxide on these animals is unnecessary.
- *The animals don't always die in gas chambers*, as documented by the fact that a dog survived the St. Louis, Missouri, animal regulation center's gas chamber in 2003 and a puppy survived the Davie County, North Carolina, animal shelter's gas chamber in 2005.[7]
- Referring to the horrors of carbon monoxide, Doug Fakkema, the nation's animal euthanasia expert,[8] has stated, "[t]he animal is in a warm or hot box, usually with other animals. They don't know what is going on. They get dizzy, and then they panic. Fights can break out, and animals' calls can sometimes be heard."[9]

3. **Many states have passed laws prohibiting carbon dioxide and monoxide for shelter animals.**
   Arizona, Delaware, Illinois, New Jersey, New York, Rhode Island, Wyoming, and Washington prohibit carbon dioxide and monoxide gas for all shelter animals (including ferals and wildlife). California bans carbon monoxide for all conscious animals. Connecticut, Florida, Maine, Maryland, New Mexico, Oregon, Tennessee, and Virginia have prohibited carbon dioxide and monoxide for shelter cats and dogs.[10]

4. **It is dangerous to put aggressive and/or wild animals in the gas chamber. Sedation methods utilized with EBI are safer for shelter staff in cases of highly aggressive and wild animals, and more humane for those animals.**
   It is much safer to sedate and then inject an aggressive animal instead of dragging it frantically into a gas chamber. Many common restraint methods do

not require shelter workers to handle the animal themselves if the animal is deemed dangerous. These include restraint poles, squeeze gates, and syringe poles. Shelter workers can then anesthetize the animal with an intramuscular injection of pre-euthanasia drugs, followed by sodium pentobarbital once the animal is unconscious. If these restraint methods are not available, shelter workers can give aggressive animals sodium pentobarbital by mouth by mixing its powder form (called Fatal Plus) with canned food or by squirting it into the animal's mouth. Once the animal is unconscious, they can administer a lethal dose of the drug.[11]

5. **EBI provides shelter workers the dignity they deserve when facing the difficult reality of euthanizing pets.**

Many shelter workers wish to hold and comfort a frightened animal in its final moments of life. That act may be the only kindness the animal has ever known. In contrast, the gas chamber is both inhumane and demoralizing to the emotional and physical health of human beings and animals.

6. **A 2009 study by American Humane Association shows EBI is less costly than gas to communities.**

American Humane Association commissioned a study on the costs associated between EBI and gas. Using data from an animal sheltering organization in North Carolina, the number of dogs and cats euthanized in 2007 was 5,427. The study shows that the cost to use carbon monoxide gas is $4.98 per animal. The cost to use carbon monoxide poisoning without a tranquilizer is $4.66 per animal. The cost to use EBI, however, was only $2.29 per animal.[12] Cost figures from North Carolina are comparable to other states. Thus, EBI is more cost effective than gas.

7. **Sodium pentobarbital–euthanized carcasses do not present a significant threat to scavenger animals.**

Sodium pentobarbital–euthanized carcasses are placed in landfills across the nation, and the incidents of death among scavenger animals are rare. According to national euthanasia expert Doug Fakkema, "In order to be killed from exposure to sodium pentobarbital, a scavenger would need to absorb a lethal amount of a euthanized carcass. Because sodium pentobarbital is not a poison but an *anesthetic*, a scavenger would need to absorb a significant amount of a large and edible carcass in order to be killed, versus possibly temporarily lethargic, from exposure."

Notes

INTRODUCTION

1. American Pet Products Association 2009/2010 National Pet Owner Survey, www
.americanpetproducts.org/press_industrytrends.asp (accessed 15 Dec. 2010).

2. House Bill 4663, filed 20 March 2009 by Rep. John Espinoza.

CHAPTER 1

1. Idaho, South Dakota, and North Dakota do not have felony animal cruelty laws.

2. Humane Research Council, Wave Three Report (March 2010) www.humanespot
.org (accessed 30 May 2010), p. 4.

3. Humane Research Council, Wave One Report (June 2008) www.humanespot.org
(accessed 30 May 2010), p. 2.

4. Wave Three Report, 4.

5. Wave Three Report, 7–8.

6. Wave Three Report, 8.

7. Wave Three Report, 8.

8. Wave Three Report, 7.

9. Wave Three Report, 8.

10. Wave One Report, 9.

11. Wave One Report, 5.

12. Wave One Report, 11.

13. Wave One Report, 12.

14. Larry S. Katz, "Animal Rights versus Animal Welfare," *Fact Sheet*, Rutgers Cooperative Extension (2003), 1.

15. www.peta.org/about/WhyAnimalRights.asp (accessed 20 June 2010).

16. Animal Bill of Rights http://org2.democracyinaction.org/o/5154/t/3755/petition.
jsp?petition_KEY=82 (access 6 June 2010).

17. Katz, 2.

CHAPTER 2

1. www.humanesociety.org/about/events/tafa/ (accessed 20 June 2010).
2. www.animalsheltering.org/expo/ (accessed 20 June 2010).
3. www.arconference.org/ (accessed 20 June 2010).
4. www.nokillconference.org/ (accessed 20 June 2010).
5. www.nomorehomelesspetsconference.com/ (accessed 20 June 2010).
6. www.aphe.org/ (accessed 20 June 2010).
7. www.usa.gov/Business/Nonprofit_State.shtml (accessed 29 Aug. 2010).
8. www.irs.gov/charities/charitable/index.html (accessed 29 Aug. 2010).
9. www.irs.gov/pub/irs-pdf/f1023.pdf (accessed 29 Aug. 2010).
10. www.irs.gov/charities/charitable/article/0,,id=175418,00.html (accessed 29 Aug. 2010).
11. www.irs.gov/charities/charitable/article/0,,id=123368,00.html (accessed 29 Aug. 2010).
12. www.irs.gov/charities/charitable/article/0,,id=163395,00.html (accessed 29 Aug. 2010).
13. www.irs.gov/charities/article/0,,id=163392,00.html (accessed 29 Aug. 2010).
14. The Humane Touch, http://thehumanetouch.org/ (accessed 14 Dec. 2010).
15. Animal Welfare Approved, www.animalwelfareapproved.org/ (accessed 14 Dec. 2010).
16. Certified Humane, www.certifiedhumane.org/ (accessed 14 Dec. 2010).
17. Leaping Bunny, www.leapingbunny.org (accessed 14 Dec. 2010).
18. Caring Consumer, www.peta.org/living/pages/living_articles/Search-Cruelty-Free -Companies-Products.aspx (accessed 14 Dec. 2010).
19. Healthy Stuff, www.healthystuff.org (accessed 14 Dec. 2010).
20. Born Free USA Compassionate Consumer website, www.compassionate consumer.org/donations/index.php?main_page=page&id=13 (accessed 14 Dec. 2010).
21. "No Animals Were Harmed" is a trademark of American Humane Association, where for 75 years the Film and Television Unit, located in Los Angeles, California, has been protecting animals on film and television sets.

CHAPTER 3

1. Mark Goldstein, "Animal Welfare in San Diego County: The Big Picture," *San Diego Union-Tribune*, 2 October 2010.

CHAPTER 4

1. A. H. Kidd & A. M. Kidd, "Children's Attitudes towards Their Pets," *Psychological Reports*, 57 (1985): 15–31.
2. www.aphe.org/ (accessed 11 July 2010).

3. www.aphe.org (accessed 2 Aug. 2010).

4. http://teachhumane.org/heart/

5. www.humanesociety.org/parents_educators/ (accessed 1 Aug. 2010).

6. www.kindnews.org/ (accessed 2 Aug. 2010).

7. www.humanesociety.org/parents_educators/classroom/ (accessed 1 Aug. 2010).

8. www.aspca.org/aspcakids/ (accessed 1 Aug. 2010).

9. www.latham.org/ (accessed 2 Aug. 2010).

10. www.humanesocietyuniversity.org (accessed 2 Aug. 2010).

11. www.humaneeducation.org/ (accessed 2 Aug. 2010).

12. To purchase, please visit www.aspcaonlinestore.com/index.php?productID=1943 (accessed 2 Aug. 2010).

13. American Humane Shelter Operations Guide: Humane Education www.american humane.org/interaction/professional-resources/humane-education/guide-to-animal-shelter ing.html (accessed 13 March 2011).

14. Interview with Jane Greco Deming (9 July 2010).

15. Interview with Jane Greco Deming (9 July 2010).

16. Interview with Jane Greco Deming (9 July 2010).

17. Interview with Jane Greco Deming (9 July 2010).

18. Interview with Sheryl Pipe (28 July 2010).

19. Interview with Stacey Zeitlin (8 Sept. 2010).

20. Interview with Stacey Zeitlin (8 Sept. 2010).

21. Interview with Stacey Zeitlin (8 Sept. 2010).

22. Interview with Stacey Zeitlin (8 Sept. 2010).

23. www.americanhumane.org/assets/pdfs/interaction/2010-bkaw-curriculum.pdf (accessed 11 July 2010).

24. Interview with Jane Greco Deming (9 July 2010).

25. Debra J. White, "Pennies for Pups: One Child's Mission to Help Homeless Animals," *The Latham Letter,* vol. 31, no. 3 (Summer 2010): 14-15.

26. Interview with Maya Alcala (5 Aug. 2010).

27. Interview with Maya Alcala (5 Aug. 2010).

28. Interview with Sheryl Pipe (28 July 2010).

29. Interview with Stacey Zeitlin (8 Sept. 2010).

30. Interview with Jane Greco Deming (9 July 2010).

31. To purchase, please visit www.freespirit.com/catalog/item_detail.cfm?ITEM_ID =624 (accessed 10 Aug. 2010).

32. To purchase, please visit www.amazon.com/Kids-Making-Difference-Animals-ASPCA/dp/0470410868 (accessed 10 Aug. 2010).

CHAPTER 5

1. California, Connecticut, District of Columbia, Delaware, Hawaii, Illinois, Maine, Maryland, Massachusetts, New Hampshire, New Jersey, New York, Pennsylvania (banned for dogs only), Rhode Island, South Carolina, Vermont, Virginia, West Virginia.

2. Allie Phillips, *How Shelter Pets Are Brokered for Experimentation: Understanding Pound Seizure* (Lanham, MD: Rowman & Littlefield, 2010).

3. Jackson County Volunteers Against Pound Seizure, www.s275870067.onlinehome .us/conan.html (3 Oct. 2009).

4. www.aphis.usda.gov/animal_welfare/downloads/manuals/dealer/randomsource .pdf (accessed 29 Aug. 2010).

5. www.awionline.org/ht/d/sp/i/12974/pid/12974 (accessed 29 Aug. 2010).

6. www.awionline.org/ht/d/sp/i/12974/pid/12974 and www.aphis.usda.gov/animal _welfare/efoia/index.shtml (click on "Inspection Reports and License and Registration Lists" to search for B Dealer inspection records and violations) (accessed 29 Aug. 2010).

7. Allie Phillips, *How Shelter Pets Are Brokered for Experimentation: Understanding Pound Seizure* (Lanham, MD: Rowman & Littlefield, 2010), 43–44.

8. www.lcanimal.org/index.html (accessed 29 Aug. 2010).

9. "Scientific and Humane Issues in the Use of Random Source Dogs and Cats," Institute for Laboratory Animal Research Division on Earth and Life Studies, National Research Council of the National Academies of Science www.nap.edu/catalog/12641.html (The National Academies Press, 29 May 2009).

10. http://grants.nih.gov/grants/olaw/Random_Source_Dog_and_Cat_Report.pdf (accessed 29 Aug. 2010).

11. www.americanhumane.org/animals/stop-animal-abuse/advocacy/campaigns/stop -pound-seizure.html (accessed 29 Aug. 2010).

12. "Scientific and Humane Issues," 68-71.

13. Phillips, *Understanding Pound Seizure*.

14. The shelter in Dillingham, Alaska, would take shelter animals to the local landfill and shoot them. This practice ended in 2010 after an animal control officer, who was unable to continue that practice, abandoned dogs at the shelter; they eventually died from starvation and dehydration. See http://community.adn.com/node/146800.

15. www.humanesociety.org/animal_community/resources/qa/common_questions _on_shelters.html#How_many_animals_enter_animal_shelters_e.

16. On August 24, 2010, National Animal Control Association amended its position statement on "Disposition of Animals—Euthanasia" to state that injection is the only method of choice for euthanizing shelter cats and dogs and that the organization condemns the use of any form of gas, gunshot, electrocution, or blunt force trauma. www.nacanet .org/guidelines.html#euthanasia (accessed 30 Oct. 2010).

17. American Veterinary Medical Association Guidelines in Euthanasia: 11. www .avma.org/issues/animal_welfare/euthanasia.pdf (accessed 28 Dec. 2010).

18. www.sheltervet.org/associations/4853/files/Euthanasia%20position%20statement .pdf (accessed 28 Dec. 2010).

19. www.americanhumane.org/assets/pdfs/about/position-statements/animal-position.pdf.

20. www.aspca.org/about-us/policy-positions/euthanasia.html.

21. www.humanesociety.org/about/policy_statements/statement_euthanasia.html (accessed 28 Dec. 2010).

22. American Veterinary Medical Association Guidelines on Euthanasia: 28. www .avma.org/issues/animal_welfare/euthanasia.pdf (accessed 28 Dec. 2010).

23. American Veterinary Medical Association Guidelines on Euthanasia, p. 30 (2007). AVMA Guidelines also "recommend that inhalant agents not be used alone in animals less than 16 weeks old except to induce loss of consciousness, followed by the use of some other method to kill the animal" (p. 10).

24. Randy Grim, *Miracle Dog: How Quentin Survived the Gas Chamber to Speak for Animals on Death Row*, (Blue Ribbon Books, 2005): 27.

25. Maryann Mott, "Animal Gas Chambers Draw Fire in U.S.," *National Geographic News* (April 11, 2005).

26. Christopher Henry, et al. "Myocardial Injury and Long-Term Mortality Following Moderate to Severe Carbon Monoxide Poisoning," *The Journal of the American Medical Association*, 295:4 (2006).

27. "Sodium Pentobarbital Is Not Considered a Health Hazard to Staff Unless It Is Deliberately Misused or Handled Incorrectly." (American Humane Association, *Operational Guide for Animal Care and Control Agencies: Euthanasia by Injection)*, p. 19, 2005.

28. Steven Rogelberg, et al. "What Shelters Can Do About Euthanasia-Related Stress: An Examination of Recommendations from Those on the Front Line," *Journal of Applied Animal Welfare Science*, 10(4), 332 (2007).

29. Rogelberg, "What Shelters Can Do," 332.

30. Rogelberg, "What Shelters Can Do," 337–41.

31. Help Furry Friends, www.helpfurryfriends.com/ (accessed 28 Dec. 2010).

32. Interview with Maria Lott (29 Sept. 2010).

33. Interview with Maria Lott (29 Sept. 2010).

34. Interview with Maria Lott (29 Sept. 2010).

35. Interview with Neil Wackerle (13 Nov. 2010).

36. Interview with Neil Wackerle (29 Aug. 2010).

37. Interview with Neil Wackerle (29 Aug. 2010).

38. Interview with Neil Wackerle (13 Nov. 2010).

39. Interview with Neil Wackerle (13 Nov. 2010)

CHAPTER 6

1. Interview with Tracy Coppola (20 July 2010).

2. www.nokilladvocacycenter.org/ (accessed 3 Aug. 2010).

3. www.amazon.com/Redemption-Myth-Overpopulation-Revolution-America/dp/0979074312/ref=sr_1_1?ie=UTF8&s=books&qid=1244466993&sr=1-1 (accessed 3 Aug. 2010).

4. www.amazon.com/Irreconcilable-Differences-Battle-Americas-Shelters/dp/1449591132/ref=pd_rhf_shvl_1 (accessed 3 Aug. 2010).

5. Interview with Tracy Coppola (20 July 2010).

6. Interview with Dr. Mark Goldstein (8 Oct. 2010).

7. "How We Did It," www.nevadahumanesociety.org/pdf/HowWeDidIt11-08.pdf (accessed 1 Aug. 2010): 2.

8. How We Did It, 4.

9. How We Did It, 4.

10. How We Did It, 10.

11. www.barncats.org (accessed 4 Aug. 2010).

12. How We Did It, 12.

13. Steven Rogelberg, et al. "What Shelters Can Do About Euthanasia-Related Stress: An Examination of Recommendations from Those on the Front Line," *Journal of Applied Animal Welfare Science,* 10(4), 332 (2007).

14. Interview with Dr. Mark Goldstein (8 Oct. 2010).

15. Interview with Dr. Mark Goldstein (8 Oct. 2010).

16. Interview with Dr. Mark Goldstein (8 Oct. 2010).

17. Interview with Dr. Mark Goldstein (8 Oct. 2010).

18. Interview with Dr. Mark Goldstein (8 Oct. 2010).

19. Interview with Dr. Mark Goldstein (8 Oct. 2010).

20. Shelter website www.petfinder.com/shelters/MI257.html (accessed 22 Nov. 2010).

21. Interview with Terry MacKillop (15 Nov. 2010).

22. Interview with Terry MacKillop (15 Nov. 2010).

23. "Roscommon County Animal Shelter: A Success Story," *Pet Friends Magazine of Northern Michigan* (November 2010), www.petfriendsmagazine.com/ (accessed 21 Nov. 2010).

24. "Roscommon County Animal Shelter: A Success Story."

25. Interview with Terry MacKillop (15 Nov. 2010).

26. Shelter website www.petfinder.com/shelters/MI257.html (accessed 22 Nov. 2010).

27. Interview with Steve Smith (8 Aug. 2010).

28. www.rollingdogranch.org (accessed 14 Oct. 2010).

29. Interview with Steve Smith (8 Aug. 2010).

30. Interview with Steve Smith (8 Aug. 2010).

31. Interview with Steve Smith (8 Aug. 2010).

32. Interview with Steve Smith (8 Aug. 2010).

33. Interview with Steve Smith (8 Aug. 2010).

34. Interview with Steve Smith (8 Aug. 2010).

35. Interview with Tracy Coppola (20 July 2010).

36. Interview with Tracy Coppola (20 July 2010).

37. "Reinforcing Good Behavior: Real-Life Rooms vs. Runs," *American Humane Association Protecting Animals*, 27.3 (Fall 2010): 17.

CHAPTER 7

1. PetSmart Charities Rescue Waggin' website, www.petsmartcharities.org/rescue -waggin/ (accessed 10 Dec. 2010).

2. "PetSmart Charities Rescue Waggin' Program," *American Humane Association's Protecting Animals*, 27.3 (Fall 2010): 4.

3. Interview with Donna Cascarelli (30 July 2010).

4. Interview with Donna Cascarelli (30 July 2010).

5. Interview with Donna Cascarelli (30 July 2010).

6. Interview with Donna Cascarelli (30 July 2010).

7. Interview with Donna Cascarelli (30 July 2010).

8. Interview with Donna Cascarelli (30 July 2010).

9. Rolling Rescue website, www.rollingrescue.info or http://pets.groups.yahoo.com/group/rollingrescue/.

10. Interview with Laurel Barrick (4 Aug. 2010).

11. Interview with Laurel Barrick (4 Aug. 2010).

12. Interview with Laurel Barrick (4 Aug. 2010).

13. Interview with Laurel Barrick (4 Aug. 2010).

14. Interview with Laurel Barrick (4 Aug. 2010).

15. Interview with Laurel Barrick (4 Aug. 2010).

16. Interview with Laurel Barrick (4 Aug. 2010).

17. Rolling Rescue Yahoo Group, http://pets.groups.yahoo.com/group/rollingrescue/.

18. Interview with Laurel Barrick (4 Aug. 2010).

19. Interview with Laurel Barrick (4 Aug. 2010).

20. Going to the Dogs Rescue, www.goingtothedogsrescue.org/ (accessed 28 Dec. 2010).

21. Interview with Melissa Henchen (10 Sept. 2010).

22. Interview with Melissa Henchen (10 Sept. 2010).

23. Interview with Melissa Henchen (10 Sept. 2010).

24. Interview with Melissa Henchen (10 Sept. 2010).

CHAPTER 8

1. Interview with Dr. Randy Lockwood (4 Oct. 2010).

2. Interview with Dr. Randy Lockwood (4 Oct. 2010).

3. Interview with Dr. Randy Lockwood (4 Oct. 2010).

4. Interview with Dr. Randy Lockwood (4 Oct. 2010).

5. Interview with Dr. Randy Lockwood (4 Oct. 2010).

6. Interview with Dr. Randy Lockwood (4 Oct. 2010).

7. Interview with Kathleen Summers (12 Nov. 2010).

8. Interview with Kathleen Summers (12 Nov. 2010).

9. HSUS Pet Store Doublespeak, www.humanesociety.org/issues/puppy_mills/facts/pet_store_doublespeak.html (accessed 30 Oct. 2010).

10. Interview with Kathleen Summers (12 Nov. 2010).

11. A more detailed list of ideas can found at: www.humanesociety.org/issues/puppy_mills/tips/what_you_can_do_stop_puppy_mills.html (accessed 14 Nov. 2010).

12. Interview with Kathleen Summers (12 Nov. 2010).

13. HSUS listing of puppy lemon laws, www.humanesociety.org/assets/pdfs/pets/puppy_mills/puppy_mill_lemon_law_chart.pdf (accessed 18 Nov. 2010).

14. Interview with Kathleen Summers (12 Nov. 2010).

15. HSUS listing of puppy mill laws, www.humanesociety.org/assets/pdfs/legislation/state_puppy_mill_laws.pdf (accessed 15 Nov. 2010).

16. Information about USDA-licensed breeders can be found at: http://www.aphis .usda.gov/animal_welfare/efoia/. Or call one of the following numbers: USDA Headquarters, (301) 734-7833, e-mail ace@aphis.usda.gov; USDA Western Region, (970) 494-7478, ac-west@aphis.usda.gov; and USDA Eastern Region, (919) 855-7100, aceast@aphis.usda.gov.

17. Gary J. Patronek, Lynn Loar, and Jane N. Nathanson, eds. *Animal Hoarding: Structuring Interdisciplinary Responses to Help People, Animals, and Communities at Risk.* www.tufts.edu/vet/hoarding/pubs/AngellReport.pdf (accessed 28 Oct. 2010).

18. www.tufts.edu/vet/hoarding/index.html (accessed 28 Oct. 2010).

19. Patronek, *Animal Hoarding*, 1.

20. 12th International Association of Human-Animal Interaction Organizations Conference Abstract: 59 www.manimalis.se/uploads/4c3d5abbc74e04c3d5abbc9041.pdf (accessed 28 Oct. 2010).

21. www.tufts.edu/vet/hoarding/abthoard.htm#A1 (accessed 28 Oct. 2010).

22. Patronek, *Animal Hoarding*, 21.

23. www.tufts.edu/vet/hoarding/abthoard.htm#A1 (accessed 28 Oct. 2010).

24. Personal interview with Jenny Coffey (25 Oct. 2010).

25. 2009–2010 National Pet Owner's Survey (American Pet Products Association).

26. 2007 U.S. Pet Ownership and Demographics Source Book, AVMA.

27. Information obtained from Cheryl Lang, president of No Paws Left Behind and president/CEO of Integrated Mortgage Solutions in Houston, TX.

28. <http://nopawsleftbehind.org> (accessed 29 Oct. 2010).

29. <http://nopawsleftbehind.org or 281-994-4546.

30. <http://sunshinefoundationstx.org/> (accessed 28 Dec. 2010).

31. Personal interview with Dr. Stacia Jung (11 Oct. 2010).

32. www.aspca.org/fight-animal-cruelty/how-to-recognize-cruelty.html (accessed 22 Oct. 2010).

CHAPTER 9

1. Wendy Anderson, "Who Speaks for the Animals," *American Bar Association Animal Law Committee*, Spring 2007.

2. Alley Cat Allies, www.alleycats.org (accessed 1 Oct. 2010).

3. Karen Chu and Wendy M. Anderson, "U.S. Public Opinion on Humane Treatment of Stray Cats," *Law & Policy Brief* (Bethesda, MD: Alley Cat Allies, September 2007): 1.

4. Chu and Anderson, "Humane Treatment of Stray Cats," 2.

5. Chu and Anderson, "Humane Treatment of Stray Cats," 2.

6. Gary J. Patronek et al., "Risk Factors for Relinquishment of Cats to an Animal Shelter," 209(3) *J. Am. Vet. Med. Assoc.* 582, 582 (1996).

7. Chu and Anderson, "Humane Treatment of Stray Cats," 3, citing to Jennifer L. Wallace and July K. Levy, "Population Characteristics of Feral Cats Admitted to Seven Trap-Neuter-Return Programs in the United States," *J. Feline Med. Surg.* 8(4) (2006): 279, 282; Karen C. Scott et al., "Body Condition of Feral Cats and the Effect of Neutering," *J. Appl. Anim. Welf. Sci.* 5(3) (2002): 203, 210; Brian J. Luria, et al., "Prevalence of Infectious Diseases in Feral Cats in Northern Florida," *J. Feline Med. Surg.* 6(5) (2004): 287, 287.

8. Chu and Anderson, "Humane Treatment of Stray Cats," 4, citing to Juliet Clutton-Brock, *A Natural History of Domesticated Mammals* (Cambridge, United Kingdom: Cambridge University Press, 1999), 131.

9. Anderson, "Who Speaks for the Animals," 2.

10. Alley Cat Allies, Key Scientific Studies on Trap-Neuter Return, www.alleycat.org/NetCommunity/Page.aspx?pid=667 (accessed 19 Oct. 2010).

11. Interview with Kristen Flory (2 Nov. 2010).

12. Interview with Kristen Flory (2 Nov. 2010).

13. Interview with Kristen Flory (2 Nov. 2010).

14. Interview with Kristen Flory (2 Nov. 2010).

15. Interview with Kristen Flory (2 Nov. 2010).

16. Interview with Kristen Brock (13 Oct. 2010).

17. Interview with Kristen Brock (13 Oct. 2010).

18. Interview with Carol Manos (2 Aug. 2010).

19. Vicky's Pet Connection, www.vickyspetconnection.com (accessed 6 Nov. 2010).

20. Interview with Carol Manos (2 Aug. 2010).

21. Interview with Carol Manos (2 Aug. 2010).

22. Carol's Ferals, www.carolsferals.org/rehoming-barn-cats/ (accessed 6 Nov. 2010).

23. Interview with Carol Manos (2 Aug. 2010).

24. Interview with Carol Manos (2 Aug. 2010).

25. Interview with Kris Field (11 July 2010).

26. Interview with Kris Field (11 July 2010).

27. Interview with Kris Field (11 July 2010).

28. Interview with Kris Field (11 July 2010).

29. Interview with Kris Field (11 July 2010).

30. Interview with Kris Field (11 July 2010).

31. The Sunshine Foundation, sunshinefoundationstx.org (accessed 1 Oct. 2010).

32. Interview with Dr. Stacia Jung (11 Oct. 2010).

33. Interview with Dr. Stacia Jung (11 Oct. 2010).

34. Interview with Dr. Stacia Jung (11 Oct. 2010).

35. Interview with Dr. Stacia Jung (11 Oct. 2010).

36. Barn Cats, Inc., www.barncats.org (accessed 1 Oct. 2010).

37. Interview with Peggy Atkerson (24 Sept. 2010).

38. Interview with Peggy Atkerson (24 Sept. 2010).

39. Interview with Peggy Atkerson (24 Sept. 2010).

40. Interview with Peggy Atkerson (24 Sept. 2010).

41. Interview with Peggy Atkerson (24 Sept. 2010).

CHAPTER 10

1. Mike Brunker, "Katrina Survivor and Miss Kitty's Owner Dies," www.msnbc.msn.com/id/10179439/ (accessed 9 Nov. 2010).

2. "Miss Kitty Headed for a New Home in Canada," www.msnbc.msn.com/id/10241592/ (accessed 9 Nov. 2010).

3. To read about my experiences in the aftermath of Hurricane Katrina, visit Michigan Bar Association's Animal Law Section at www.michbar.org/animal/pdfs/winter2006.pdf (accessed 9 Nov. 2010).

4. <http://thomas.loc.gov/cgi-bin/bdquery/z?d109:h.r.03858:> (accessed 9 Nov. 2010).

5. www.sartusa.org (accessed 9 Nov. 2010).

6. www.wspa-international.org/ (accessed 9 Nov. 2010).

7. http://ifaw.org (accessed 9 Nov. 2010).

8. www.americanhumane.org/protecting-animals/programs/animal-emergency-services/ (accessed 9 Nov. 2010).

9. www.aspca.org/about-us/programs-services.html#Disaster (accessed 9 Nov. 2010).

10. www.avma.org/disaster/default.asp (accessed 9 Nov. 2010).

11. www.bestfriends.org/aboutus/ (accessed 9 Nov. 2010).

12. www.code3associates.org/ (accessed 9 Nov. 2010).

13. www.ifaw.org/ifaw_united_states/join_campaigns/emergency_relief/index.php (accessed 9 Nov. 2010).

14. /www.noahswish.org/ (accessed 9 Nov. 2010).

15. www.humanesociety.org/issues/animal_rescue/ (accessed 9 Nov. 2010).

16. www.uan.org/ (accessed 9 Nov. 2010).

17. www.wspa-usa.org/pages/38_disaster_relief.cfm (accessed 9 Nov. 2010).

18. Interview with Tracy Reis (17 Sept. 2010).

19. Interview with Tracy Reis (17 Sept. 2010).

20. Interview with Diane Robinson (19 Sept. 2010).

21. Interview with Diane Robinson (19 Sept. 2010).

22. Interview with Tracy Reis (17 Sept. 2010).

23. Interview with Tracy Reis (17 Sept. 2010).

24. Interview with Diane Robinson (19 Sept. 2010).

25. Interview with Diane Robinson (19 Sept. 2010).

26. Interview with Tracy Reis (17 Sept. 2010).

27. Interview with Diane Robinson (19 Sept. 2010).

28. Interview with Tracy Reis (17 Sept. 2010).

CHAPTER 11

1. Idaho, South Dakota, and North Dakota do not have felony animal cruelty laws as of 2010.

2. Animal Legal Defense Fund www.aldf.org/article.php?id=446 (accessed 10 Nov. 2010).

3. www.aldf.org/userdata_display.php?modin=51 (accessed 10 Nov. 2010).

4. www.aldf.org/article.php?id=277 (accessed 10 Nov. 2010).

5. www.animallawcoalition.com (accessed 10 Nov. 2010).

6. www.amazon.com/Lawyers-Guide-Dangerous-Dog-Issues/dp/1604425520/ref=sr_1_1?ie=UTF8&s=books&qid=1289422858&sr=1-1 (accessed 10 Nov. 2010).

7. www.amazon.com/Litigating-Animal-Law-Disputes-Complete/dp/1604420014/ref=sr_1_4?ie=UTF8&s=books&qid=1289422909&sr=1-4 (accessed 10 Nov. 2010).

8. www.amazon.com/Introduction-Animals-Palgrave-MacMillan-Animal/dp/0230235646/ref=sr_1_3?ie=UTF8&s=books&qid=1289422728&sr=1-3 (accessed 10 Nov. 2010).

9. www.aldf.org (accessed 10 Nov. 2010).

10. Interview with Joan Schaffner (14 Sept. 2010).

11. Interview with Joan Schaffner (14 Sept. 2010).

12. Julie Fershtman, "Considering a Career in (Equine) Law?" www.equinelaw.net.

13. Interview with Julie Fershtman (6 Aug. 2010).

14. Julie Fershtman, "Considering a Career in (Equine) Law?" www.equinelaw.net.

15. Interview with Julie Fershtman (6 Aug. 2010).

16. Interview with Julie Fershtman (6 Aug. 2010).

17. Interview with Julie Fershtman (6 Aug. 2010).

18. Interview with Julie Fershtman (6 Aug. 2010).

19. Interview with Julie Fershtman (6 Aug. 2010).

20. Interview with Julie Fershtman (6 Aug. 2010).

21. Interview with Julie Fershtman (6 Aug. 2010).

22. Interview with Julie Fershtman (6 Aug. 2010).

23. Interview with Julie Fershtman (6 Aug. 2010).

24. Interview with Julie Fershtman (6 Aug. 2010).

25. Interview with Julie Fershtman (6 Aug. 2010).

26. Interview with Julie Fershtman (6 Aug. 2010).

27. Interview with Diane Balkin (21 Oct. 2010).

28. Interview with Diane Balkin (21 Oct. 2010).

29. Interview with Diane Balkin (21 Oct. 2010).

30. Interview with Diane Balkin (21 Oct. 2010).

31. Interview with Diane Balkin (21 Oct. 2010).

32. Interview with Diane Balkin (21 Oct. 2010).

CHAPTER 12

1. Humane Scorecard www.hslf.org/humanescorecard/ (accessed 22 Nov. 2010).

2. Compassion Index http://capwiz.com/compassionindex/dbq/vote_info (accessed 22 Nov. 201).

3. HSUS 2009 Annual Report www.humanesociety.org/assets/pdfs/publications/2009-annual-report/2009_annual_report.pd (accessed 7 Nov. 2010).

4. Interview with Lauren Silverman Simon (15 Oct. 2010).

5. Interview with Lauren Silverman Simon (15 Oct. 2010).

6. Interview with Lauren Silverman Simon (15 Oct. 2010).

7. Interview with Lauren Silverman Simon (15 Oct. 2010).

8. www.voiceless-mi.org/ (accessed 20 Nov. 2010).

9. Interview with Holly Thoms (19 Nov. 2010).

10. Interview with Holly Thoms (19 Nov. 2010).
11. Interview with Holly Thoms (19 Nov. 2010).
12. Interview with Holly Thoms (19 Nov. 2010).
13. Interview with Holly Thoms (19 Nov. 2010).
14. Interview with Holly Thoms (19 Nov. 2010).
15. Interview with Holly Thoms (19 Nov. 2010).
16. Interview with Holly Thoms (19 Nov. 2010).
17. Interview with Holly Thoms (19 Nov. 2010).
18. Interview with Holly Thoms (19 Nov. 2010).
19. Interview with Holly Thoms (19 Nov. 2010).
20. Interview with Holly Thoms (19 Nov. 2010).

CHAPTER 13

1. Discovery Channel Timeline http://corporate.discovery.com/our-company/company-timeline/ (accessed 14 Nov. 2010).
2. www.animalradio.com (accessed 28 Dec. 2010).
3. www.progressiveradionetwork.com/animal-magnet-pet-radio/ (accessed 28 Dec. 2010).
4. For more information about Steve Dale, please visit www.stevedalepetworld.com or his blog, www.chicagonow.com/stevedale (accessed 14 Nov. 2010).
5. Interview with Steve Dale (22 Sept. 2010).
6. Interview with Steve Dale (22 Sept. 2010).
7. Interview with Steve Dale (22 Sept. 2010).
8. Interview with Steve Dale (22 Sept. 2010).
9. Interview with Steve Dale (22 Sept. 2010).
10. Interview with Steve Dale (22 Sept. 2010).
11. Interview with Steve Dale (22 Sept. 2010).
12. For information about Dusty Rainbolt, please visit www.dustyrainbolt.com (accessed 14 Nov. 2010).
13. Interview with Dusty Rainbolt (2 Sept. 2010).
14. Interview with Dusty Rainbolt (2 Sept. 2010).
15. Interview with Dusty Rainbolt (2 Sept. 2010).
16. www.examiner.com/cat-rescue-in-harrisburg/mandy-moore (accessed 14 Nov. 2010).
17. Interview with Mandy Moore (25 Sept. 2010).
18. Interview with Mandy Moore (19 Dec. 2010).
19. Interview with Mandy Moore (19 Dec. 2010).
20. Interview with Mandy Moore (19 Dec. 2010).
21. Interview with Mandy Moore (25 Sept. 2010).

CHAPTER 14

1. Jeffrey Kluger, "Inside the Minds of Animals: Science Is Revealing Just How Smart Other Species Can Be—And Raising New Questions about How We Treat Them," *Time* (August 16, 2010): 38.

2. Virginia Morell, "Minds of their Own: Animals Are Smarter Than You Think," *National Geographic* 213, no. 3 (March 2008): 51.

3. Interview with Christina Montana (28 Sept. 2010).

4. Interview with Christina Montana (28 Sept. 2010).

5. Interview with Christina Montana (28 Sept. 2010).

6. Interview with Christina Montana (28 Sept. 2010).

7. Christina's website can be found at www.animalwhisperer.org or www.bigsky-spirit.com/page/page/425711.htm.

8. Interview with Christina Montana (28 Sept. 2010).

9. Interview with Diane Roadcap (18 Oct. 2010).

10. Diane's website can be found at www.animalstalktoo.com.

11. Interview with Diane Roadcap (18 Oct. 2010).

12. Interview with Diane Roadcap (18 Oct. 2010).

13. Interview with Diane Roadcap (18 Oct. 2010).

14. Interview with Diane Roadcap (18 Oct. 2010).

15. Greater Reiki Center of Washington website, www.reikicenter.info/ (accessed 7 Dec. 2010).

16. www.manifestedharmony.com.

17. Integrated Energy Therapy website, www.learniet.com/ (accessed 7 Dec. 2010).

18. Healing Touch for Animals www.healingtouchforanimals.com/ (accessed 7 Dec. 2010).

19. www.shelteranimalreikiassociation.org/our_mission.html (accessed 9 Oct. 2010).

20. Interview with Kathleen Prasad (27 Sept. 2010).

21. Interview with Kathleen Prasad (27 Sept. 2010).

22. Interview with Kathleen Prasad (27 Sept. 2010).

23. Shelter Animal Reiki Association www.shelteranimalreikiassociation.org/code_of_ethics.html (accessed 7 Dec. 2010).

24. Interview with Kathleen Prasad (27 Sept. 2010).

25. Interview with Kathleen Prasad (27 Sept. 2010).

26. Just Cats, Naturally website, www.justcatsnaturally.com/ (accessed 8 Dec. 2010).

27. Interview with Dr. Andrea Tasi (8 Oct. 2010).

28. Interview with Dr. Andrea Tasi (8 Oct. 2010).

29. Interview with Dr. Andrea Tasi (8 Oct. 2010).

30. Interview with Dr. Andrea Tasi (8 Oct. 2010).

31. Interview with Dr. Andrea Tasi (8 Oct. 2010).

32. Interview with Dr. Andrea Tasi (8 Oct. 2010).

33. Interview with Dr. Andrea Tasi (8 Oct. 2010).

34. American Holistic Veterinary Association, www.holisticvetlist.com/ (accessed 8 Dec. 2010).

35. The Academy of Veterinary Homeopathy, www.theavh.org/ (accessed 8 Dec. 2010).

36. The International Veterinary Acupuncture Society, www.ivas.org/ (accessed 8 Dec. 2010).

37. The American Academy of Veterinary Acupuncture, www.aava.org/ (accessed 8 Dec. 2010).

38. The Chi Institute, www.tcvm.com/ (accessed 8 Dec. 2010).

39. Pet Sage website, www.petsage.com (accessed 8 Dec. 2010).

CHAPTER 15

1. Family violence shelters that house pets on-site with their families can be found at http://alliephillips.com/?page_id=526 (accessed 28 Dec. 2010).

2. Personal e-mail from Suzanne Clark, executive director of Kingman Aid for Abused People (12 Aug. 2010).

3. Personal e-mail from Tracy Black, program coordinator (9 Sept. 2010).

4. Family violence shelters that house pets on-site with their families can be found at http://alliephillips.com/?page_id=526 (accessed 28 Dec. 2010).

5. Dr. Frank Ascione, *Safe Havens for Pets: Guidelines for Programs Sheltering Pets for Women Who Are Battered* (Utah State University, 2000) www.vachss.com/guest _dispatches/ascione_safe_havens.pdf (accessed 29 Oct. 2010).

6. Ahimsa House Safe Haven's director, www.ahimsahouse.org/directory (accessed 29 Oct. 2010).

7. www.animalalliancenyc.org (accessed 10 Aug. 2010).

8. Interview with Jenny Coffey (3 Aug. 2010).

9. Interview with Jenny Coffey (3 Aug. 2010).

10. http://petpeace.blogspot.com/ (accessed 30 Oct. 2010).

11. http://petpeace.blogspot.com/ (accessed 30 Oct. 2010).

12. www.petsofthehomeless.org/what-we-do (accessed 31 Oct. 2010).

13. www.petsofthehomeless.org/ (accessed 30 Oct. 2010).

14. www.petsofthehomeless.org/.

15. www.chai.vcu.edu/.

16. rechai.missouri.edu/.

17. www.vet.purdue.edu/chab/.

18. www.tufts.edu/vet/capp/research_areas/human-animal_interactions.html.

19. www.humananimalconnection.org/edu_hac.htm.

20. www.animalsandsociety.org/.

21. www.apa-ahi.org/.

CHAPTER 16

1. www.facebook.com/pages/You-Can-Do-More-for-Animals/134171893284427?ref=ts.

APPENDIX A

1. www.aphis.usda.gov/animal_welfare/downloads/manuals/dealer/requirements.pdf.

2. www.animalearn.org.

3. Physicians Committee for Responsible Medicine www.pcrm.org.

4. www.usatoday.com/tech/science/2008-02-14-animal-tests_N.htm?POE=click-refer.

5. "Scientific and Humane Issues in the Use of Random Source Dogs and Cats," Institute for Laboratory Animal Research Division on Earth and Life Studies, National Research Council of the National Academies of Science www.nap.edu/catalog/12641.html (The National Academies Press, 29 May 2009).

6. http://grants.nih.gov/grants/olaw/Random_Source_Dog_and_Cat_Report.pdf.

7. USDA 2007 Annual Report, 8, www.aphis.usda.gov/publications/animal_welfare/content/printable_version/2007_AC_Report.pdf.

8. USDA 2007 Annual Report, 9, www.aphis.usda.gov/publications/animal_welfare/content/printable_version/2007_AC_Report.pdf.

9. www.awionline.org/ht/d/sp/i/12974/pid/12974.

10. Personal e-mail with between Allie Phillips and USDA/APHIS, 30 April 2009.

11. www.dealingdogs.com/#axzz10ebg8X5E.

12. National Academies of Science, meeting January 2009, notes taken by author.

13. www.nacanet.org/guidelines.html#pound.

14. www.sheltervet.org/associations/4853/files/Pound%20Seizure.pdf.

15. www.americanhumane.org/assets/docs/about-us/AU-animal-welfare-position-statements.pdf.

16. www.aspca.org/about-us/policy-positions/pound-seizure.html.

17. www.americanhumane.org/assets/docs/advocacy/ADV-pound-seizure-survey-results.pdf.

18. Written statement to the Montcalm (Michigan) County Commissioners, 26 January 2009.

APPENDIX B

1. *See* Christopher Henry, et al., "Myocardial Injury and Long-Term Mortality Following Moderate to Severe Carbon Monoxide Poisoning," *The Journal of the American Medical Association*, vol. 295, no. 4, 2006.006.

2. "Sodium Pentobarbital Is Not Considered a Health Hazard to Staff unless It Is Deliberately Misused or Handled Incorrectly." American Humane Association, *Operational Guide for Animal Care and Control Agencies: Euthanasia by Injection,* p. 19, 2005.

3. American Veterinary Medical Association Guidelines on Euthanasia, pp. 10–11. (2007).

4. American Humane Association, *Euthanasia by Injection—Training Guide*, p. 8 (2008).

5. American Veterinary Medical Association Guidelines on Euthanasia, p. 30 (2007). AVMA Guidelines also "recommend that inhalant agents not be used alone in animals less than 16 weeks old except to induce loss of consciousness, followed by the use of some other method to kill the animal." (p. 10).

6. Grim, Randy. *Miracle Dog: How Quentin Survived the Gas Chamber to Speak for Animals on Death Row* (Alpine Books, 2005, p. 27).

7. *See* Gunning, Mike. *Puppy Survives Euthanasia Attempt, Trip to Dump*, at www.freewebs.com/animalshelternews/index.htm.

8. Doug Fakkema is a trainer and consultant for American Humane with more than thirty-five years' experience in animal protection. He conducts euthanasia workshops around the country. *See* Doug Fakkema, *Comparison of Sodium Pentobarbital and Carbon Monoxide as Euthanasia Agents*. www.crean.com/kindness/ebi-vs-co.html.

9. Mott, Maryann. "Animal Gas Chambers Draw Fire in U.S." *National Geographic News*, April 11, 2005.

10. www.americanhumane.org/assets/docs/protecting-animals/PA-resources-state-euthanasia-09.pdf.

11. Mr. Fakkema states, "I can euthanize a dangerous dog in his/her kennel by feeding sodium pentobarbital—no handling necessary." *See*]www.animalpeoplenews.org/06/10/carbongaschambers106.html.

12. January 2009; Doug Fakkema, consultant to Animal Care & Control, commissioned by American Humane Association. *Study available upon request.*

Resources

Allie Phillips (www.alliephillips.com)
Alley Cat Allies (www.alleycat.org)
American Anti-Vivisection Society (www.aavs.org)
American Humane Association (www.americanhumane.org)
American Society for the Prevention of Cruelty to Animals (www.aspca.org)
Animal Law Coalition (www.animallawcoalition.com)
Animal Legal Defense Fund (www.aldf.org)
Animal Whisperer (www.animalwhisperer.org)
Animals & Society Institute (www.animalsandsociety.org)
Animals Talk, Too (www.animalstalktoo.com/)
Barn Cat, Inc. (www.barncats.org)
Barnwater Cat Rescue (www.barnwatercats.org)
Best Friends Animal Sanctuary (www.bestfriends.org)
Carol's Ferals (www.carolsferals.org)
End Pound Seizure Minnesota (www.endpoundseizuremn.org)
Equine Law (www.equinelaw.net)
Going to the Dogs (www.goingtothedogsrescue.org)
Help Furry Friends (www.helpfurryfriends.com)
Humane Education Advocates Reaching Teachers (HEART) (www.teachhumane.org)
The Humane Society of Midland County (http://www.hsomc.org/)
The Humane Society of the United States (www.hsus.org)
International Fund for Animal Welfare (www.ifaw.org)
Just Cats, Naturally (www.justcatsnaturally.com)
King Street Cats (www.kingstreetcats.org)
Latham Foundation (www.latham.org)
Leaping Bunny (www.leapingbunny.org)
Manifested Harmony (www.manifestedharmony.com)
Mayor's Alliance for New York City Animals (www.animalalliancenyc.org)
National Link Coalition (www.nationallinkcoalition.org)
Nevada Humane Society (www.nevadahumanesociety.org)
No Paws Left Behind (www.nopawsleftbehind.org)

Petfinder (www.petfinder.org)

Pets from Paradise Program (http://www.stcroixawc.org/programs/pets-from-paradise/)

Rolling Dog Ranch Animal Sanctuary (www.rollingdogranch.org)

Rolling Rescue (www.rollingrescue.info and http://pets.groups.yahoo.com/group/rolling
   rescue/)

Roscommon County Animal Center (http://www.roscommonanimalcenter.com/)

San Diego Humane Society and SPCA (www.sdhumane.org)

Shelter Animal Reiki Association (www.shelteranimalreikiassociation.org)

Sheltering Animals & Families Together (SAF-T) (www.alliephillips.com)

St. Croix Animal Welfare Center (www.stcroixawc.org)

Sunshine Foundation (www.sunshinefoundation.org)

United Animal Nations (www.uan.org)

United States Department of Agriculture (Public Records) (http://www.aphis.usda.gov/
   footer_items/foia_reading_room.shtml)

United States House of Representatives (www.house.gov)

United States Senate (www.senate.gov)

Voiceless-MI (www.voiceless-mi.org)

World Society for the Protection of Animals (www.wspa-international.org)

Index

About the Author

Allie Phillips is an author, attorney, and advocate for protecting animals and vulnerable victims and promoting human-animal interactions. She is licensed to practice law in Michigan and Maryland. Allie is nationally-recognized on the co-occurrence between animal abuse and violence to humans, animal advocacy and protection, investigation and prosecution of animal cruelty, banning the practice of shelters providing cats and dogs for experimentation (pound seizure), and helping pets caught in the financial crisis. Allie has conducted more than 150 trainings nationally and has authored more than forty-five publications on these topics. Her first book, *How Shelter Pets are Brokered for Experimentation: Understanding Pound Seizure*, which tackles the concept of pound seizure and shelters that provide homeless, abused, and unwanted cats and dogs for research, was published in August 2010.

Allie has more than eight years of criminal prosecution experience as an assistant prosecuting attorney in Michigan and since 1998 has been training and consulting with prosecutors and criminal justice professionals. Allie has been employed with the National District Attorneys Association as a senior attorney in their National Center for Prosecution of Child Abuse and as director of the National Center for Prosecution of Animal Abuse, which she launched in 2011. She was employed with the American Humane Association as the vice president of public policy and vice president of human-animal strategic initiatives where she spent more than three years overseeing the Public Policy Office in Alexandria, Virginia, and was responsible for lobbying and advocacy on child and animal welfare legislation, including drafting legislation and providing expert testimony to legislatures. She was also in charge of developing and managing national initiatives on human-animal interactions, including the creation of the Pets and Women's Shelters (PAWS)® Program and co-creation of the Therapy Animals Supporting Kids (TASK)™ Program.

Allie is an active animal advocate and volunteer and has helped over a thousand homeless, abused and neglected pets. In 2000, she co-founded Friends of Ingham County Animal Shelter, a nonprofit animal rescue organization in Michigan that advocated to successfully ban Class B dealers from the county animal shelter as well as increased adoptions at the shelter by almost 500 percent. Since 2004 she has been a volunteer, and previously past-president, of King Street Cat Rescue in Alexandria, Virginia, a free-roaming cat orphanage. She assists the St. Croix Animal Welfare Center's Pets from Paradise Program to help relocate shelter cats and dogs to the mainland for purposes of adoption. Since 2003 she has been a council member of the State Bar of Michigan's Animal Law Section, and provides pro bono legal advice to animal welfare organizations. After assisting with the animal relief effort in Mississippi following Hurricane Katrina in 2005, she was nominated to the American Bar Association's Animal Disaster Relief Network. In 2008, she became the volunteer vice president of No Paws Left Behind, a nonprofit formed to address pets abandoned in the foreclosure crisis. She is on the steering committee of the National Link Coalition, a practitioner member of the Shelter Animal Reiki Association, and is a certified Usui Reiki Master-Teacher and Integrated Energy Therapy® Master-Instructor.

Learn more about Ms. Phillips's books and work to help animals at www.alliephillips.com and www.manifestedharmony.com.

OS   9-22-11
AG   12-1-11
PL   2-2-12
FT   4-2-12
WH   6-4-12
AM   8-6-12
FL   10-8-12
SF   12-10-12

ST 12-13-12 KP